THE ANARCHIST MOMENT

THE ANARCHIST MOMENT
Reflections on Culture, Nature and Power

JOHN CLARK

BLACK ROSE BOOKS Montréal

Copyright 1984©
BLACK ROSE BOOKS LTD.

No part of this book may be reproduced or transmitted in any form by means, electronic or mechanical, including photocopying and recording, or by any information storage or retrieval system, without written permission from the author or publisher, except for brief passages quoted by a reviewer in a newspaper or magazine.

Black Rose Books No. M83
Hardcover ISBN: 0-920057-08-X
Paperback ISBN: 0-920057-07-1

Canadian Cataloguing in Publication Data		
Clark, John P.		
The Anarchist moment		
ISBN 0-920057-08-X (bound).	ISBN 0-920057-07-1 (pbk.).	
1. Anarchism and anarchists.	2. Libertarianism.	
I. Title.		
HX833.C54 1984	320.5'7	C84-090172-0

Cover design: John Sims

BLACK ROSE BOOKS
3981 boul. St-Laurent
Montréal, Québec H2W 1Y5

Printed and bound in Québec, Canada

For
Kristin
Brian
and
Jeremy

Table of Contents

Acknowledgements 11
Preface 15
Chapter 1 — **The Politics of Liberation: From Class to Culture** 19
Chapter 2 — **Marx, Bakunin, and Historical Materialism** 33
Chapter 3 — **Marx, Bakunin, and Social Revolution.** 65
Chapter 4 — **Marxism and Technology** 101
Chapter 5 — **What is Anarchism?** 117
Chapter 6 — **Anarchism and the Present World Crisis** 141
Chapter 7 — **Master Lao and the Anarchist Prince.** 165
Chapter 8 — **Ecology, Technology, and Respect for Nature** 191
Chapter 9 — **The Social Ecology of Murray Bookchin.** 201
Chapter 10 — **The Labyrinth of Power and the Hall of Mirrors** 229

Acknowledgements

I want to express my deep gratitude to Murray Bookchin for his invaluable contribution to the development of the ideas presented in these essays. His synthesis of critical and dialectical theory, teleological philosophy, social ecology, and libertarian and utopian thought has carried on the great tradition of philosophy in this anti-philosophical age. It has been a great pleasure and privilege to know him and his work.

There are many others who have also been of assistance to me in numerous ways. Vernon Richards gave me the idea of collecting some of the essays that I've published over the past five years, and Dimitri Roussopoulos and Black Rose Books made it possible to produce a more diverse collection than might otherwise have appeared. Many people helped me through personal discussions, correspondence, comments on manuscripts, publication and translation of texts, and by their friendship and inspiration. Included in one or more of these categories are Roger Ames, Martha Ackelsberg, Graham Baugh, Amedeo Bertolo, Ronald Creagh, Rosella Di Leo, John Ely, Marianne Enckel, Kathy Ferguson, Olivier Guibert, Lucia Kowaluk, Len Krimerman, Les Mazor, Brad Ott, Jacques Perrier, Lydia Voigt, David Wieck, and Michael Zimmerman. I want especially to mention the generosity of my friend and colleague Anthony Waters, who commented carefully and extensively on many of these essays, and whose recent untimely death cut short the promising career of this highly dedicated and capable educator.

I also want to thank Loyola University for granting me a sabbatical leave during the 1979-80 academic year, thus giving me the opportunity to do research on several of the essays included here. Professor Ronald Creagh of l'Université Paul Valéry was of assistance to me in many ways during my stay in Montpellier, France, that year. I am also grateful to the Loyola University Committee on Grants and Leaves for its support for research at the Centre International de Recherches sur l'Anarchisme in Geneva and the International Institute for Social History in Amsterdam. I am especially grateful to Lucia Kowaluk of Black Rose Books for her careful work in editing the manuscript. Her efforts have resulted in greater clarity and conciseness in many passages, and have contributed much to increasing the consistency between somewhat diverse essays written over a number of years.

Finally, I wish to thank the publishers of some of the material in this book for their permission to include it in the collection. "The Politics of Liberation: From Class to Culture" was presented at a conference on "La Problematique Libertaire" at L'Université Paul Valéry on May 8, 1980, and was published in *Freedom*, vol. 41, pp. 9-11, 15-16. Portions of "Marx, Bakunin, and Historical Materialism" and "Marx, Bakunin, and Social Revolution" were presented at the 1977 American Political Science Association Convention, and others were published in *Telos*, no. 42, pp. 80-97. "Marxism and Technology" appeared in *Freedom*, vol. 40, pp. 9-13. "What is Anarchism?" was published in *Anarchism* (*Nomos XIX*) (New York: New York University Press, 1978), pp. 3-28. "Anarchism and the Present World Crisis" was published in *Alternative Futures*, vol. 4, pp. 67-86. "Master Lao and the Anarchist Prince" appeared as "On Taoism and Politics" in *The Journal of Chinese Philosophy*, vol. 10, pp. 65-87. "Respect for Nature" was presented at the Louisiana Conference on Science, Technology, and Human Values at Tulane University, October 22, 1981, and has not previously been published. "The Social Ecology of Murray Bookchin" was published in part in *Telos*, no. 52, pp. 224-30, and in *Our Generation*, vol. 15, no. 2, pp. 52-59. "The Labyrinth of Power and the Hall of Mirrors" was presented in part at a conference entitled "Le Pouvoir et sa Négation," sponsored by the Centro Studi Libertari (Milan) and the Centre International de Recherches sur L'Anarchisme, and held in Saignelégier, Switzerland, July 10, 1983. Portions were also presented at the Social Philosophy Conference, World Congress of Philosophy, Université de Montréal, August 24, 1983, and published in the *Journal of Social Philosophy*, vol. 14, no. 3.

Preface

If Aristotle is correct, "the end of politics" is "the supreme good attainable in our actions."¹ Divested of all ideological trappings, this goal can only mean the pursuit of universal self-realization, the achievement of the greatest possible harmonious good in nature. This end requires, on the one hand, a thorough-going *an-archist* critique—that is, a critique of all forms of domination that block the attainment of this goal. And it demands, on the other hand, a theoretically guided practice that is adequate to realize this project.

The anarchist moment is thus not a point in history, but rather a theoretical moment, a necessary movement of negation constituting an essential element of the theory of liberation. It does, however, find expression in history, or, to speak more accurately, in the interstices of history. To the extent that it has so far been manifested in liberatory social practice, there has existed a counter-history, in which some have attempted to impede or evade the triumphal march of civilization. It has thus been a practice of resistance to "World History"—what Hegel so accurately described as "the slaughter-bench at which the happiness of peoples, the wisdom of States, and the virtues of individuals have been victimized."² There is also another dimension of this expression which precedes history, for in a significant sense "the end of prehistory" marked the beginning of domination. The primitive, being based on structures antithetical to the forms of political and economic power that are central to civilization, constitutes an enduring critique of these institutions of domination. And finally, the anarchist moment has a post-historical aspect in its utopian dimension. If the anarchist critique of domination expresses the ideal of a liberatory society through the medium of critical reason, utopianism expresses it by means of the imagination, the symbolic, and the mythopoeic. These are themselves modes of rationality, though they take on an irrational form to the extent that they are repressed, or separated from a narrowed and impoverished conception of reason.

While the concept of an "anarchist moment" indicates the vital necessity for a theory and practice aimed at the abolition of all forms of domination, it signifies equally that this theory and practice are not completed totalities, but rather that they point beyond themselves. I am not in these essays proposing "Anarchism" as an ideological substitute for Liberalism, Marxism, and other obsolete political ideologies. I am arguing rather that the anarchist moment is essential in the project of transcending the system of domination and the society of separation and fragmentation. Yet this negative moment only finds its completion, and, indeed, its meaning, in an affirmative vision of reality.

My purpose in this work is therefore to present a critique of classical radical theory, and to show that critical social thought requires a new vision of the self, society, and nature. This analysis places in question the materialism, productivism, economism, and humanism of the past, and proposes instead a cultural politics founded on an ecological, organicist world view. In the context of this perspective, I attempt to lay the groundwork for a coherent analysis of systems of power and domination, and to reorient libertarian thought toward a problematic of social and ecological regeneration.

Notes

1. J. A. K. Thomson, trans., *The Ethics of Aristotle* (London: George Allen and Unwin, Ltd., 1953), p. 16.
2. G. W. F. Hegel, *The Philosophy of History* (New York: Dover Publications, 1956), p. 21. Hegel was, of course, stressing that the sacrifice was worth the price, and attacking the "sentimentality" that would question its historical necessity.

Chapter 1

The Politics of Liberation: From Class to Culture

It was not so long ago that to pose the question of the nature of "the libertarian problematic" must have seemed a rather quixotic undertaking. Where could such a "problematic" be situated? In the dreams of survivors of long-dead labour movements? In the fantasies of concocters of utopian visions? True, libertarian practice had never wholly died, but a once historically momentous movement had certainly dwindled to practical insignificance. The once heroic idea that moved masses seemed relegated to the realm of nostalgia, if not that of science fiction. Anarchism had never been abolished, despite even the efforts of those dictatorial regimes that had striven so hard to annihilate it and all its adherents. Yet, ironically, it seemed well on the road to withering away.

Yet dormant historical forces have to slumber somewhere, and it is perhaps appropriate that this one retreated temporarily into the sphere of the imagination. It is no doubt better to have imagination without a movement than a movement without imagination. Perhaps now we can have both. For to the surprise of practically all observers (excepting the small remnant of believers and visionaries) the movement began its return to the historical stage in the late 60's. It now becomes possible to speculate that anarchism is capable of being much more than a noble dream, and, in fact, that its future role in history will make its past appear to be only faltering first steps, a minor episode in its evolution.

What basis is there for such a hope? While it is true that only a generation ago anarchism had been (to use the language of bureaucrats) "taken off the agenda," the time may be coming when it is capable of forcing its way back on the agenda, perhaps rewriting it, and maybe even tearing it up. It seems that we are now at a juncture in history in which the relevant problems begin to pose themselves, the concrete historical project begins to take form, and the problematic therefore begins to situate itself in the real world. The two reigning world ideologies are now definitively revealing their bankruptcy. For the masses, whether they be subjected to capitalist or socialist systems of domination, the old faith is entering a period of deep crisis. The growing mood of these masses is one of cynicism and hopelessness, dangerous dispositions for all ideologies founded on the myth of unlimited progress and worldly messianism. This is not to say that people no longer *accept*; rather they accept with ill-natured resignation and poorly disguised resentment. They are quickly moving to the point at which a new set of options begins to arise: not capitalism or socialism, but rather cynicism or rebellion. Either unprecedented depths of bad faith and self-deception, or the recognition of the brokenness of the old symbolic structures. Either the kind of mindless, spiritless dogmatism which is required to perpetuate a dead religion, or the creative negation of illusions which have been revealed for what they are. Perhaps for the first time, human beings (and not merely theorists) begin to see the essential opposition not as that between one ideology and another, but between ideology and reality. As Nietzsche prophetically saw, the naked power relationships which underlie all ideologies, no matter how "democratic," "humanist," or "socialist," are finally being revealed, and the terrifying prospect of conscious choice lies before us.

In the context of this decay of traditional ideologies, both of the right and of the left, the task of formulating the libertarian problematic takes on increasing urgency. The question is whether the libertarian movement will shake off its own attachment to the remnants of these moribund ideologies, and give some sort of conscious direction to the construction of a new social reality, or whether it will pass up this opportunity for making its contribution to the break with past forms of domination. While we can point to both "objective" and "subjective" factors which constitute the material, social and psychological basis for the developing crisis of the dominant world systems (depletion of resources, ecological stress, economic stagnation, resistance to neocolonialism, internal social disintegration, decline of repressive structures of motivation, weakening of institutional legitimacy), the importance of the emerging struggle cannot be underestimated, since there is no assurance that alternative liberatory possibilities will be developed, except insofar as adequate theoretical and practical agents of social transformation are created. We cannot rely on some inexorable march of history to save us if our own historical self-transformation is a failure. Furthermore, as the prevailing patterns of domination become increasingly threatened by internal disintegration and external challenges, the amount of overt psychological and physical force which will be used to maintain them can only be expanded. For this reason there is growing truth in the old saying that the new society must be created within the shell of the old—both because the old must be transformed as rapidly as possible into a mere shell, which is increasingly perceived as a contrivance, a mechanism, and a barrier to human development; and because this relative unreality must be placed in contrast to the new society's growing fullness and reality.

If this does not occur, we will once again revert to the patterns of the past, although perhaps in even more destructive forms. On the one hand, a critically unconscious and underdeveloped radicalism, which is itself a mere reaction, will generate an entrenched reactionary dogmatism that will secure itself through even greater repression. Or, on the other hand, should such a radicalism succeed in harnessing the energies of fear and frustration, we will see more "revolutions" which themselves turn out to be the most advanced transformations of the old forms of domination. After having observed the history of this century we should not be at all shocked by the idea that underdeveloped and one-sided "revolutionary" activity can be a powerful contributor to the conquest of power by the authoritarian forces of both right and left. In fact, we must recognize that the fetishism of "the Revolution" has itself been one of the most powerful mechanisms of domination.

What, then, is the libertarian response to this historical predicament? It seems to me that there are two lines of development within the libertarian left, or, more specifically, the social anarchist movement, which have deep historical roots, and which are presently re-emerging as distinct currents. On the one hand, there are those who continue to conceive of the project of social emancipation primarily in terms of the mode of production, economic class analysis and class struggle. On the other, there are those whose approach is more multi-dimensional, and might be described as a cultural orientation. Both perspectives find numerous adherents at present within the libertarian political movements of both the United States and Western Europe, although the relative strength of the two factions varies considerably from country to country.

In the United States and Western Canada the libertarian tradition of class-based organization and strategy can be traced back to the European immigrant labour movements of the late 19th century and also to the largely local revolutionary syndicalism of the IWW. The ideas of these movements coincided on many major points with the principles of European anarcho-syndicalist and revolutionary syndicalist movements of the 19th and early 20th centuries. The roots of domination are seen to lie above all in capitalism and the state. The essential project is to organize the working class into a force which can successfully overthrow the state, the effective power behind economic exploitation, the paradigm for, and root cause of, all forms of domination. When the workers succeed in fulfilling their historical mission, either through insurrection ("the Revolution") or economic class action ("the General Strike") a new economic order based on self-management can be established, and with it a society of equality, freedom, and justice. The story is quite familiar, for this faith once exerted powerful force in much of Southern Europe and Latin America, in the days before the labour movements in these areas became dominated by Marxism and reformism, or were crushed by Fascism. The unique North American contribution was the version presented by the Wobblies (Industrial Workers of the World), who sought to develop an even more radically economistic programme based entirely on economic class analysis, and in which the religious and political questions so central to European anarcho-syndicalism were rather unrealistically (yet appropriately for a *North American* movement) relegated to the domain of "private opinion." For the Wobblies, the picture presented of the future society was that of a world organized economically by the workers according to the IWW system of industrial unions. Thus there was no anti-state line—members were free to participate in political activity, to refrain from it, or to oppose it, so long as their political stance did not intrude into the One Big Union.* The IWW thus sought to form a broadly based class alliance, a kind of radical version of American pragmatism, attained at the expense of coherence and comprehensiveness on the levels of both theory and strategy. Yet despite these problems and ambiguities, for a long time it was, and to an extent still is, within the IWW that numerous libertarians chose to work, especially after the possibilities for organizing large and enduring immigrant anarcho-syndicalist movements failed to materialize.

The second current, which I have called "the cultural orientation," has always existed as part of the North American libertarian tradition, and, given the relative weakness of class-based organizations in the United States, it has been disproportionately strong in comparison to its place in the European movements. Thus in the 19th century the communitarian movement was an important sphere of libertarian activity, in which a myriad of problems of everyday life, including many issues related to sexuality, child-raising, and small group decision-making, were confronted. Although the 19th century communities remained peripheral to the mainstream society, they have been a continual source of inspiration for the renewal

---

* The One Big Union remained a concept in the United States. In Canada in 1918 the Western delegates to the Trades and Labour Congress (an affiliate of the AFL) meeting succeeded in formally founding One Big Union with 400,000 members at its height. It was short-lived, however, and was crushed by 1924 by combined tactics of the Canadian government and the traditional labour movement.

of the movement for communalism. In the 20th century, this tradition was carried on by a number of groups which emphasized cooperative production, decentralization, and, often, non-violent patterns of living. Movements like the Catholic Worker and the School of Living were among those that perpetuated such values. But it was in the 1960's, with the emergence of the counterculture, that this tendency became once again a central focus of libertarian creative activity. The explosive growth of communalism was only one area in which libertarian cultural developments began to take place. For strong libertarian impulses underlay much of the activity in the many movements for liberation which then proliferated—the free school and alternative education movement, children's liberation, women's liberation, gay liberation, radical psychiatry, ecology, black liberation, the Native American movement, the antiwar movement, the student movement, the co-op movement, the alternative media, and the development of neighbourhood organization. Although these movements were diverse in makeup, they all contained significant currents emphasizing participation, decentralization, cooperative modes of interaction, and liberation from entrenched patterns of domination. Furthermore, the counterculture itself (which might be seen as a more generalized movement for social recreation, only partially overlapping with these more particularized movements) exhibited a strong cultural dimension, stressing the importance of consciousness, values, and personality structure, and raising questions about the repressive/liberatory implications of forms of language, communication, music, art, and the symbolic dimension in general.

In short, a kind of libertarian proto-culture began to develop, and it was in many ways one of the most advanced foreshadowings of what a future libertarian society may be. Yet it was, unfortunately, merely a foreshadowing—more a revelation of possibilities than an achievement of actualities. Its roots were not deep in American society. It was too much a product of fortuitous events and ephemeral conditions. It embodied a positive vision to a degree, but on the whole it was still shaped by immediate negativity, by a largely unreflective, undeveloped (as it said, "gut") reaction against the dominant culture. It lacked a sense of history to the extent that it failed to grasp even the very forces which created it, or those with which it contended. It failed to comprehend the magnitude of the power of commodification, and the dominance of the code of values of the spectacle. It was therefore an easy prey for absorption into the spectacular system. It was theoretically impoverished and incoherent, which is not surprising given its fragmented, rather than totalistic, nature. It was capable of giving rise to brilliant insights and brave experiments, yet could not reach the needed synthesis that would give it strength and durability. In short, although it developed many of the materials necessary to create a libertarian culture, it could not become such a culture.

The result was the 70's, with its disintegration and recuperation. It is possible to argue that many of the gains of the 60's were preserved, or that some of the values which emerged took root and even developed further during the next decade. And it is true that we cannot judge historical evolution by the content of media coverage. Yet for those who saw intimations of a movement toward a culture founded on libertarian and communal values, the 70's could only be pervaded by a sense of failed possibilities: the period of humanization of work, black mayors (and even black Republican mayors!), women executives, "decriminalization" of marijuana, porno theatres, Gov. Jerry Brown, Quaker Natural Cereal, and Friends of the Earth. In short, the confrontation between the old reality and, as it has been aptly put, "artificial negativity." If we are fortunate enough to fight off the old patterns of domination—nationalism, racism, sexism, heterosexism—which seem to be making a powerful comeback lately, we are confronted with the alternative of a perfected society of commodity consumption—one in which all achieve the equal right to be commodity consumers and to offer themselves as commodities to be consumed.

What is the libertarian response to this dilemma? Is it a revival of class politics, a new attempt at a cultural transformation, or some synthesis of the two?

First, it should be understood that the traditional politics of class struggle had in its own way a cultural dimension, and, even more, that it embodied an implicit view of humanity and nature. From its perspective, the person is above all a worker, a producer. The great tragedy of history is therefore seen to lie in the fact that workers, who produce all the goods necessary for life and well-being, and on whose activity the future progress of society depends, are robbed of the benefits of their production. Work is the essential means toward social progress: the liberation of humanity from want, from bondage to nature. Being a worker is therefore a virtue, while being a non-worker is a vice, inseparable from exploitation. The problem is to transform all people into workers, and to gain for these workers control over production—to establish universal self-management. When this is attained the utopia of production will be achieved. As the IWW put it, "all the good things in life"—meaning products and services, the "goods"—will no longer be monopolized by the capitalists, but will be shared by all.

This ideology, while encompassing a bitter attack on capitalism and those who benefit from its system of exploitation, is, in spite of itself, a particular formulation of the productivist ideology of developing capitalism—the version formulated from the perspective of the working class (and it should be remembered that the proletariat, like the bourgeoisie, is an eminently *capitalist* class). On almost all key points it is identical with the early capitalist project of salvation through material production. In a sense it is the Protestant version of the religion of production—the hierarchy is to be overthrown, yet the faith remains firmly embedded in the consciousness, the conscience, and even the unconscious of each believer.

This faith still lives on; yet the irony is that it is an ideology that capitalism is itself in the process of transcending. It should therefore be no surprise that its proletarian version is increasingly confronted with reactions ranging from unclass-conscious yawns to class-collaborationist sneers on the part of the toiling masses. For late capitalist society has increasingly passed further into the realm of the values of consumption, and into the sphere of domination by the commodity. The cult of the working class and salvation through labour appears increasingly less appealing in a society in which work becomes more and more fragmented and abstract, in which class membership becomes less clearly defined and less central to social identity, and in which privatized consumption becomes the ultimate refuge for a desocialized individual.

In a society in which the will to power is increasingly channeled in the direction of commodity consumption, not only the old class politics but even the most seemingly radical social theories have quickly revealed their impotence. For example, Wilhelm Reich was able to confront capitalism with the explosive issue of instinctual repression, bringing into question not only the reigning economic system, but also the state and patriarchy. Yet, capital has shown itself to be quite capable of moving beyond the stage of instinctual repression, at least on its own terms, and achieving what Marcuse called "repressive desublimation," as has become especially clear in the 70's. So it can sponsor its own versions of sexual revolution, not to mention its own varieties of women's liberation and minority rights. Liberation comes to mean rebellion against all the obsolete social forms which restrain the process of commodification. In its most radical forms it demands equality—the right to consume and be consumed without discrimination.

The prevailing system of domination seems to have almost infinite capacity to recuperate critical thought and practice. Should we therefore fall into the mood of despair and resignation that seems to be so fashionable lately? Should we seek to profit from the current market value of the kind of chastened idealism that can even masquerade as a new "philosophy"? I believe that before we succumb to disillusionment or begin to market our lost illusions, we should consider the possibility that our critique has often been less than critical, and that our practice has been left lamentably underdeveloped. For the mainstream of the left, while it challenged the system of domination in many ways, still defined its problematic in terms of the politics of class struggle, and therefore still accepted many of the presuppositions of the society of domination. Thus, even in its best historical moments it remained largely uncritical of the industrial system of technology and the project of human domination of nature.

The libertarian problematic today is, of course, to develop a coherent, systematic and thoroughly critical view of reality, and a practice adequate to transform reality in accord with this vision. If we are successfully to challenge the system of domination, we must achieve an understanding of reality as a whole, including the total symbolic universe by which we interpret and indeed construct reality. Consequently we must confront a multitude of questions of ontology, of social and cultural theory, and of psychology. Fortunately, libertarian thought has been moving slowly but consistently in the direction of such an all-embracing vision in recent years, especially as it has come to see the ecological perspective as the macrocosmic correlate (indeed, the philosophy of nature) of the libertarian conception of a cooperative, voluntarily organized society. It has been moving toward a fully developed, organic theory of reality, a theory which proposes a distinct view of nature, of human society, of the group, and of the self or person. Further, it points toward a coherent practice which can successfully found a new libertarian culture which challenges the social, political, economic and psychological dominance of the official culture, with its values of atomistic individualism, egoistic consumption, and the will to power. In the place of this view of the world as a collection of fragmented, antagonistic parts (whose metaphysics, ethics, and social philosophy are epitomized in deterrence theory), the organic, ecological world view delineates a reality in which the whole is a unity-in-diversity, in which the development and fulfillment of the part can only proceed from its complex interrelationship and unfolding within the larger whole. The universe is seen not as a lifeless mechanism but rather as an organic whole, a dynamic totality consisting of non-discrete, interpenetrating processes. Society must become, like nature itself, an organic, integrated community. Human beings can only realize their personhood, their individuality in the fullest sense, through non-dominating interaction, or as Martin Buber put it, in a society which is a community of communities. The existence of such a society depends on the growth of a multitude of small personalistic groups which are the organic fabric of the organic society. These groups must be founded on human social instincts and needs, on the one hand, and offer a framework for the development of creative desire and social imagination on the other. And underlying all must be a new vision of the self—a self which is itself organic, having the nature of a process. It must be a self which is not objectified, or divided against itself, but rather is a harmonious synthesis of passion, rationality, and imagination. Such a self is a social creation, an embodiment of our common human nature in its process of historical development, yet also the most individualized and unique self-expression of reality, and therefore the most ultimately creative process.

What does this imply on the level of concrete practice? It means that the libertarian problematic in the field of action and organization is above all a problematic of social regeneration. Confronted with the final truths of Western civilization—disintegration, atomization, egoism, and domination—the libertarian movement must place the highest priority on creating libertarian (and even more, *communitarian*) patterns of interaction at the most basic level, the affinity group. This means that organizations like anarcho-syndicalist unions and anarchist federations will, at best, remain incapable of social transformation, and, at worst, become frameworks for reproducing the system of domination, unless they are rooted in a firmly established libertarian culture, in libertarian human relationships, and in a libertarian perception of reality.

The problem is thus in a sense to again take up the task of the counterculture of the 60's, but this time within the context of a self-conscious libertarian cultural movement. None of the concerns of the 60's have lost their relevance. Therefore, the movement must not only be firmly rooted in the affinity group, and concern itself with the development of libertarian primary relationships, but it must also strive toward building a larger cultural and organizational structure. While discarding the fatal illusion that any mere organizational form can lead to liberatory social transformation, it must regenerate the impulse toward the establishment of cooperatives, collectives and communes as necessary elements in the evolution of a libertarian culture. It will continue the development and application of decentralist, liberatory technology. It will once more grasp the centrality of libertarian education, an area of the most advanced libertarian practice from the time of Tolstoi to the most mature and historically conscious experiments of the 60's. And it will never forget the importance of the aesthetic dimension, continuing the rich tradition of libertarian self-expression, for anarchism is as much as anything the synthesis of art and life, and as Murray Bookchin has said, the conception of the community as a work of art.

In this confrontation between the values of egoism, commodification, and domination and those of libertarian communalism the struggle is no longer a struggle of classes in the traditional sense. It is rather a struggle of the community against *class society*, the society of division, the society of domination. It is therefore not the struggle of socialist *worker* to succeed the bourgeois *individual* as the subject of history. Rather it is the emergence of the *person*, the organic social self, who must through social, communal self-realization combat those forces and ideologies which reduce this self to asociality (individualism, privatism) or being a producer (productivism).

Whatever the impression may be that I have given so far, it should be understood that none of the foregoing means that class analysis and class struggle in the broadest sense of these terms have lost their meaning. In fact, one of the key elements of the libertarian problematic is the development of a more adequate analysis of the class structures of both contemporary and past societies. Libertarian theory has already begun to show great promise for considerable contributions in this area. Not being tied to the fetishism of the working class, it can show the creative role which peasant societies and tribal cultures have played in history and even prehistory, and their amply manifested potential for the development of libertarian and communitarian social forms. Furthermore, it can continue to document the fact that the working class itself has been most revolutionary, most libertarian, most critical, and most socially creative in its transitional stages, rather than at the points at which it has been most classically "proletarian" and "industrial." This is exemplified in the past by those groups which were torn out of traditional, communal society, and were only beginning to be socialized into the industrial system, and can be expected to recur in the future only insofar as the classic working class continues to disintegrate and a growing number of its members come under the influence of, or begin to participate in, a developing libertarian communalist post-industrial culture. Furthermore, recognizing the irreducible reality of political power, libertarian theory can more fully delineate the role of the developing techno-bureaucratic class in state capitalist and corporate capitalist society. Substituting the more adequate concept of the *system of domination* in the place of obsolete reductionist, economistic conceptions, it can contribute to understanding the interaction between such forms of domination as patriarchy, political power, technological domination, racism and economic exploitation, thereby showing the interplay—both the contradictions and the mutual reinforcement—within the total system between economic class, sex class, political class and ethnic class. Such a formulation turns out to be especially fruitful in linking the structure of domination in classical capitalist society to that existing in pre-capitalist, late capitalist and post-capitalist societies. Corresponding to this expanded conception of class analysis, there will also be an amplified practice of class struggle, though certainly not in the traditional sense of finding the most suitable present-day strategies for the messianic working class. Rather, the task of the libertarian movement will be to combat the material and ideological power of all dominating classes, whether economic, political, racial, religious, or sexual, with a multi-dimensional practice of liberation. Such a practice will integrate within the framework of this many-sided fight against domination a variety of sorts of activity. It will certainly include *economic* actions, like strikes, boycotts, job actions, occupations, organization of direct action groups and federations of libertarian workers' groups, and development of workers' assemblies, collectives and cooperatives. It will also entail *political* activity, including not only anti-electoral activity, but in some cases strategic voting, especially in referenda and local elections. In addition, there will be active interference with implementation of repressive governmental policies, like pursuance of imperialistic war policies or dangerous assaults on the biosphere; non-compliance and resistance against regimentation and bureaucratization of society, including technological surveillance and control of the population, and participation in movements for increasing direct participation in decision-making and local control. There must also be *cultural* struggle, including the development of arts, media and symbolic structures which expose the forces of domination and counterpose to them a system of values based on freedom and community. And in all cases there must be a practice of *psychosocial* transformation, in which all groups functioning to combat domination self-consciously seek to maintain their basis in personalistic human relationships, direct participation, non-hierarchical internal structure, and respect for the integrity and individuality of each member. One lesson of the 60's is the futility of any attempts to submerge the libertarian presence in basically non-libertarian mass organizations or vague ecumenical "movements." If the libertarian movement is to experience organic growth it must fiercely defend the libertarian character of primary groups, and realize the fundamental nature of all libertarian organization, not as mere forms of mobilization for struggle against any or even all kinds of domination, but above all as elements in the more comprehensive process of cultural recreation.

The libertarian problematic is indeed a problematic which entails negation—the negation of all forms of domination, alienation, and social disintegration. Yet a movement which degenerates into pure negativity—into mere collective resentment on the part of the alienated—is condemned to impotence and lack of creative energy. The revolutionary subject was once described as a class with radical chains, one which says "I am nothing. I should be everything." Yet the attempt to move from total nothingness to a fullness of being is something that might be accomplished by the Absolute Idea, and perhaps even by the proletariat, but it is beyond the capacities of mere mortals. Our need is therefore not merely a *class* with radical chains, but a *culture* with radical freedom.

The most radical bonds are not those of class oppression but those of free community.

Chapter 2

Marx, Bakunin, and Historical Materialism

In their debates of the 1860's and 1870's, Marx and Bakunin presented to the revolutionary movement of their day two distinct interpretations of the process of social change, the nature of domination, and the conditions for human liberation. Although their opposition was founded on differences concerning fundamental theoretical issues of radical theory over the past century, the dispute has for many years been of interest primarily to historians, rather than political theorists. And, indeed, whatever one's assessment of the merits of the contending viewpoints, the debate has had undeniable historical importance. First, its effects were reflected in the power struggles which led ultimately to the dissolution of the First International. Later, it left its mark on the ensuing conflict between two increasingly polarized segments of the international labour movement. While on the one hand both parliamentary socialism and revolutionary Communism looked to Marx for theoretical and practical guidance, the anarcho-syndicalist movement, which then showed great strength in Southern Europe, Latin America and other areas, carried on the tradition of Bakunin. Yet, by the end of the 1930's, anarcho-syndicalism appeared to be moribund. The syndicalist unions had all lost their mass bases, either from defections to Communism, largely inspired by the Bolsheviks' successful rise to power, or because of repression by authoritarian regimes of both right and left. To the extent that practical success is seen as the criterion by which to judge the significance of a movement's political analysis, history had decided for Marx and against Bakunin, relegating their dispute to past history.

For political theorists, on the other hand, the debate has never aroused much interest, primarily because Bakunin failed to attain intellectual respectability, except within the anarchist movement. Always considered primarily a political activist, he has perhaps been admired by some as a romantic revolutionary, but he has certainly not been recognized as a political theorist of any merit. Sabine represents the mainstream of political theory well by failing to mention him even once in his lengthy history of Western political thought.[1] To take a more recent example, as late as the early 70's, Lichtheim, in a discussion of a familiar work on Marx and his contemporaries, comments that "it is a relief not to have [Bakunin] served up as a 'thinker'."[2]

The consensus has been, then, that the dispute between Marx and Bakunin is of interest largely as *past* history, and that, because of Bakunin's intellectual mediocrity, his contributions to the debate deserve little serious attention. It is my contention that, quite to the contrary, the controversy in question is still of great historical and theoretical significance, and that Bakunin is indeed a "thinker" with ideas worthy of consideration by political theorists. Furthermore, as issues like worker self-management and the rights and liberties of the individual create stirrings within officially Marxist parties and societies, as disillusionment with the evolution of state socialism continues to grow, and as the same arguments once made by Bakunin reappear even within the context of contemporary Marxist theory, the relevance of the debates of the 1860's and 70's becomes increasingly apparent.

Although there is obviously much more to Marx's thought than the aspects on which this discussion will focus, this chapter will deal only with those which are of particular relevance to his disputes with Bakunin. In fact, those elements of Marx's thought which are taken here to be his most valuable contributions to social theory—his method of dialectical analysis and his critique of ideology—are not seen at all to be *issues* in this dispute. Rather, they are seen as the foundation for much of Bakunin's most incisive criticism of Marx. As we will see, Bakunin's critique is directed precisely at those aspects of Marx's thought in which he fails to follow his own dialectical method, and in which he is less than consistent in pursuing a thorough-going critique of ideology. In this sense, Bakunin, though Marx's historical opponent, is in some ways the heir to the most revolutionary aspects of Marx's thought.

The disagreements between Bakunin and Marx over questions such as revolutionary strategy and the means of creating a liberatory society have their basis in further, and more fundamental, disputes: questions like the nature and dynamics of economic classes, the process of development of social forms, and, ultimately, the status of various determining factors in social change. In order to understand the important divergence in outlook between the two thinkers, we have to show the connection between their answers to basic questions and the answers they give to the derivative ones. This requires an analysis which begins with an issue which, while appearing to be merely speculative and not connected to practical political proposals, in fact sets the two thinkers in opposition to each other in a way which underlies all their social and political theory. This issue concerns the meaning and validity of historical materialism.

Bakunin's view of reality, developed in part through the influence of Marx, is deterministic and materialist.[3] Contrary to the impression that many have of his standpoint, he consistently put forth a deterministic interpretation of reality, and attributed absolutely no significance in history or human action to "free will," which he looked upon as a religious or metaphysical illusion. Thus, the dispute between Marx and Bakunin depended in no way on an opposition between causal and noncausal explanations of history. Similarly, the conflict should not be traced to the issue of materialism versus idealism. Both theorists accepted the natural, material world as a sufficient basis for explaining reality, and posited no transcendent realm. The area of dispute is situated, rather, within a common materialist, deterministic world view, and centres around the question of the degree to which economic factors, and especially the forces and relations of production, determine the nature of other phenomena.

Bakunin appears at times to accept a position on this issue which is very close to the one for which he attacks Marx. In *God and the State* he asserts that "the whole history of humanity, intellectual and moral, political and social, is but a reflection of its economic history."[4] In "The Political Theology of Mazzini" he similarly claims that "the development of economic forces has always been and still continues to be the determinant of all religious, philosophical, political and social developments."[5] He concludes that on the basis of this outlook socialism proclaims "that the economic subjection of the man of labour to the monopolizer of the means of labour... lies at the bottom of servitude in all its forms," and that therefore "the economic emancipation of the working classes is the great end to which every political movement ought to be subordinate as a simple means."[6] This, he says, is the position of the International "in all its simplicity."[7]

This position certainly has the virtue of simplicity, not to mention that it was the perfect complement to the economistic outlook of the bourgeoisie, and thus entirely in the spirit of the times. Yet the problem was to cope with reality in all its complexity, and to transcend the narrowly economic interpretation of reality that the workers' movement inherited from bourgeois society. Fortunately, Bakunin showed the beginnings of such a break, as he came to realize that certain bourgeois economistic categories embedded in the presuppositions of the Marxist wing of the movement threatened to reproduce the forms of domination that the entire movement purported to combat.

In an important section of *The Knouto-Germanic Empire and the Social Revolution*, Bakunin argues for the necessity of a resolutely critical standpoint toward historical development. Determinists and materialists, while accepting necessity in history, must judge historical development in light of the ideal immanent in the struggles of humanity throughout history—the development of non-dominating human community, or, as he phrases it, "the most complete conquest and establishment of personal freedom—material and moral—for every individual, through the absolutely unrestricted and spontaneous organization of economic solidarity."[8] While all humanity's creations hold seeds of such freedom, including (surprisingly, coming from a 19th century European revolutionary) "all the religious symbols of all epochs,"[9] both the liberatory and reactionary aspects of each epoch, including the one in process of development, must be critically assessed. It is this assessment which leads Bakunin to question Marx's analysis of the liberatory implications of the development of capitalist production.

More important to note at this point is that Bakunin questions that element of Marx's thought (and thus his own) which claims economic causes as the basis for all historical development.[10] In this connection, he presents one of his most important insights: that if humanity is to achieve liberation, this liberation cannot come from any activity (whether economic or political) to which people are *driven* through exploitation and misery; rather, it must come from an active process of struggle for liberation, and from the reflective knowledge which people attain as a result of this struggle. "How can the working masses acquire any knowledge of their rights? Only through their great historical experience, through this great tradition, unfolded over the centuries and transmitted from generation to generation, continually augmented and enriched by new sufferings and new injustices, finally permeating and enlightening the great proletarian masses."[11] This accumulated knowledge must also find expression in the development of consciously libertarian forms of organization and interpersonal relationships. Without such consciousness, and the liberatory culture in which it is embodied, the masses cannot become creatively active in history (they will act out of reflex rather than reflection, as inert masses), and they therefore become victims of renewed domination. Bakunin contends that Marx overlooks this problem in his discussion of historical change and class struggle determined by changes in economic conditions.

Does Marx, the economic determinist, who is the object of Bakunin's attack, really exist? In a recent article on "Lenin and the Problem of the Transition," the authors, libertarian Marxists, attempt to divorce Marx from the position that historical development is the result of contradictions between productive forces and other social institutions. Their method is to attribute to Lenin the view that "the central axis of economic transformation" is "the increase in the productivity of labor, the development of the productive forces...."[12] This position can then be conveniently distinguished from "the Marxism bequeathed to us by Marx and Engels."[13] While the authors all too typically take this distinction for granted, there are noteworthy recent attempts to defend it. An example is presented by Harrington's *Twilight of Capitalism*[14]. In confronting the question of economic determinism head-on, he is forced to admit that ample passages in Marx point to his adherence to such a position. The embarrassment is aggravated by the fact that the vast majority of Marxists have attributed great importance to these passages. Harrington's solution to the problem is the discovery of an "unknown Marx," who has none of the undesirable qualities of the "known" Marx, an "underground Marx" far more appealing than the "above ground" Marx, and, we presume, a *real* Marx far superior to the *actual* one that history has unfortunately given to us. Yet what do such distinctions contribute to our understanding of Marx's theoretical strengths and weaknesses? We can learn most from Marx if we do not protect him from his own limitations and self-contradictions. While recognizing the brilliance of his contributions to social theory, we can at the same time admit the centrality to his thought of those aspects of his theory which are the objects of Bakunin's criticism, and which have had such fateful historical consequences.

The *locus classicus* which determines the nature of Marx's historical materialism is, of course, the preface to his *A Contribution to the Critique of Political Economy*, widely used as a proof text both for those Marxists who wish to use his authority to support economic determinism, and for those critics of Marx who wish to attack him for holding such a view. In the preface he asserts that the relations of production correspond to "a given stage in the development of [humanity's] material forms of production,"[15] and that the economic structure of society is "the real foundation, on which arises a legal and political superstructure and to which correspond definite forms of social consciousness."[16] "Social being" is distinguished from "consciousness" and the former is identified as the determinant of the latter. Furthermore, changes in the all-important relations of production (or "property relations") are traced back to changes in "material productive forces."[17] The contradictions which sometimes occur between these forces and relations of production Marx credits with giving rise to periods of social revolution. As the "contradictions" in the economic sphere are resolved, this will "lead sooner or later to the transformation of the whole immense superstructure."[18] The constituents of the superstructure, "legal, political, religious, artistic or philosophic," are reduced to mere ideological forms (as they certainly are *to a large degree* in bourgeois society) and the realm of consciousness embodied in these forms is reduced to an expression of "the contradictions of material life."[19] Finally, having established productive forces as the foundation of all social transformation, and having reduced consciousness to a reflection of material conditions, what is left is only to make explicit the connection between the development of productive forces and social progress. The social revolution which takes place in order to resolve the contradiction between forces and relations of production, Marx's argument continues, can only occur when the existing mode of production has fully developed its forces of production to their limit. To that point it plays a progressive role in history. What is impossible is that "superior relations of production" can be established before "all the productive forces" of the lower stage have developed.[20] The assumptions are thus that capitalism has been a progressive mode of production, that previous modes of production have been "lower," and that what will be established when capitalism has completed its beneficial tasks is some "higher" system of social relationships. Bakunin questions all these contentions. But before resuming the discussion of Bakunin, it is important to investigate further the degree to which Marx adheres to this disputed position, and the ways in which he develops its details.

The standpoint of the "preface" to *A Contribution to the Critique of Political Economy* is a continuous strand in Marx's thought, from *The German Ideology* to *Capital*. All the theses found in the "preface" can be found in *The German Ideology*. The productive forces are considered fundamental in determining all social forms, including their evolution. The "multitude of productive forces" (defined at this point as encompassing the relations of production) "determine the nature of society."[21] Furthermore, "the material production of life" and "the form of life connected with this and created by this" are seen as "the basis of all history."[22] From these, the state and the "whole mass of different theoretical products and forms of consciousness"[23] can be explained.[24] Social evolution is explained as the development of productive forces: "all collisions in history have their origin... in the contradiction between the productive forces and the form of intercourse."[25] Corresponding to this productivist view of history is the reduction of thought to a reflection of material reality. "The phantoms formed in the human brain are... sublimates of their material life-process, which is empirically verifiable [and thus more real from the positivistic viewpoint that Marx sometimes adopts] and bound to material premises."[26] Individuals are incapable of moving the process of critical analysis beyond the limitations imposed by technical-economic development, because, according to Marx, "morality, religion, metaphysics" depend on changes in "material intercourse" for their evolution.[27] "Life is not determined by consciousness, but consciousness by life,"[28] according to Marx's celebrated formulation. Idealism is thus avoided. On the other hand, Marx's project of investigating reciprocal relationships is itself abandoned when it leads him into the realm of consciousness.[29] His tendency toward an objectivistic conception of materialism creates a barrier to the achievement of a fully materialist and fully dialectical view.

Similar conceptualizations are found in later works of the 1840's. *The Poverty of Philosophy* restates the view that the mode of production corresponds to the development of productive forces, whose progress requires the overturn of obsolete forms in order to assure their continued development.[30] Proudhon is attacked, moreover, for suggesting that the political realm could determine the nature of economic institutions, whereas in fact "legislation... does nothing more than proclaim, express in words, the will of economic relations."[31] In a letter of 1846 to Annenkov, Marx reiterates the view that given a "particular state of development in the productive forces of man... you will get a particular form of commerce and consumption," which in turn produces a corresponding set of other social institutions.[32] In addition, he again defines social revolution as the resolution of the contradiction between forces and relations of production. As is well known, Marx applies these principles in the *Communist Manifesto* in explaining the transition from feudal to capitalist production.[33] However, the absence of some of the sweeping generalizations present in the early works might indicate that he was in the process of moderating his position into showing that economic and technical factors are the ultimate determining factors for only one specific social form—bourgeois society. Consciousness and culture could then be promoted from their merely derivative status.

An examination of Marx's greatest later works—the *Grundrisse* and *Capital*—shows that the old position continues to occupy a central place in his thought, and that the comments in *A Contribution to the Critique of Political Economy* are far from an isolated aberration. Although he cautions in the *Grundrisse* against seeing bourgeois relations in all societies, he holds that the *categories* developed to explain bourgeois society also suffice to explain previous societies. "The bourgeois economy thus supplies the key to the ancient, etc."[34] He also applies this principle to tribal society. "In the last analysis, their community, as well as the property based on it, resolves itself into a specific stage in the development of the productive forces of working subjects—to which correspond their specific relations amongst one another and towards nature."[35] In the *Grundrisse* we find a brilliant analysis of the interconnection between the pre-capitalist development of the productive forces, the formation of monetary wealth, and the availability of free labour. In this analysis, the productive forces are again discovered to be the determining factor in the rise of the new mode of production.[36] Once again, the account of the genesis and developement of bourgeois society is taken as a paradigm, not only for understanding precapitalist forms, but, as will be discussed further, for anticipating the nature of the conditions necessary for the dissolution of capitalism, and the rise of a higher social formation.

Similar views are found in *Capital*. The best known example is from the afterword to the second German edition, where Marx favourably cites the following interpretation, which was presented by a Russian reviewer of the book: "Marx treats the social movement as a process of natural history, governed by laws not only independent of human will, consciousness and intelligence, but rather, on the contrary, determining that will, consciousness and intelligence..."[37] This statement can be interpreted as meaning simply that the process of determination of both material reality and consciousness can, in principle, be explained (a view which Bakunin also held), and that consciousness can in no way act independently of such determination. But it is clear that this is not what Marx is saying here. Rather, he is claiming that there are *laws* accounting for the development of material reality, and that the development of consciousness only dependently follows this material evolution. "With me... the ideal is nothing else than the material world reflected by the human mind, and translated into forms of thought."[38] In the chapter on commodities, Marx shows that he still holds the view that the mode of production determines the nature of other social institutions, and that the base-superstructure division has not disappeared from his thought. In that chapter he considers objections to his "view that each special mode of production and the social relations corresponding to it, in short, that the economic structure of society, is the real basis on which the juridical and political superstructure is raised, and to which definite social forms of thought correspond; that the mode of production determines the character of the social, political, and intellectual life generally..."[39]

How then can he explain periods in history when the political system or religion seemed to play an essential role in determining the nature of society? His answer is to make a distinction between the apparent history and the "secret history" of the various epochs. Marx is correct in assuming that he will get little argument against his contention that "the middle ages could not live on Catholicism, nor the ancient world on politics."[40] Yet this is hardly enough to convince us, as he wishes to, that "it is the mode in which they gained a livelihood that explains why here politics, and there Catholicism, played the chief part."[41] Even less does it convince us that in tribal societies the variation between matriarchal and patriarchal institutions, or between libertarian and repressive social norms, is merely an expression of the "secret economic history" of the societies.

The productivist element in Marx's thought appears to have had a profound effect on his conception of human nature.

Partisans of the humanistic Marx have quite understandably emphasized those aspects of his thought which depict humanity as creative, active, and self-transcending. They stress Marx's vision of people as social beings, pursuing their common destiny through the creation of culture and the transformation of the social and material environment through collective activity. There is certainly much to be gained through the study of this side of Marx. Yet there is another side also—one which is very close to the first, but which ultimately leads in a different direction. If the essence of humanity is to *create*, it is also to *produce*. Of course, if "production" is taken in the broadest sense, everything human beings do is a form of production, since all action produces some effect. Yet Marx often takes "production" in a more significant, narrower, sense of the transformation of the material world according to some design. He sees this kind of production as the key to understanding human nature. In *The German Ideology* he contends that although there are many criteria by which to distinguish humans from lower animals, "they begin to distinguish themselves from animals as soon as they begin to *produce* their means of subsistence..."[42] He thus chooses a characteristic which humans share with many animals (unless "social" species are to be classed as human, and hunting and gathering societies are to be classed as animal societies, to mention obvious difficulties), rather than a uniquely human activity, such as the creation and utilization of systems of symbolic forms. For Marx, what human beings are "coincides with their production, both with *what* they produce and with *how* they produce. The nature of human beings thus depends on the material conditions determining their production."[43] He wisely admits later in the same work that the "essence of man" is in fact the result not only of productive forces, but also of "the social forms of intercourse,"[44] although these are still taken as determined ultimately by productive forces. This raises the question of the degree to which culture, which can be distinguished from the process of material transformation, is essential to understanding the human essence. Yet the productivist tendency continues.

Although, as has often been noted, the more speculative philosophical element in Marx's thought becomes less evident in his later works, there is still much such discussion in the

Grundrisse. There too is found evidence of the productivist view of humanity. This is the case not only in Marx's discussion of humanity under capitalist production, but also in his treatment of pre- and post-capitalist society. In discussing primitive society, Marx deals with myth, one of the most complex and richly developed symbolic forms created by human beings. He sees myth as a primitive attempt to dominate nature, an imaginary domination which arises from humanity's temporary inability to achieve actual domination through production. "All mythology overcomes and dominates and shapes the forces of nature in the imagination and by the imagination; it therefore vanishes with the advent of real mastery."[45] Myth is thus absorbed into the sphere of instrumental activity and associated with the impulse for using nature simply as a means. Mythological consciousness thus becomes technique—albeit an idealist, ineffectual technique—to be transcended by the more effective and therefore "higher" technique of material transformation.

Such an interpretation ignores evidence that myth often expresses symbolically the perception of some cultures that the relation between humanity and nature can be one of reciprocity and non-dominating interaction. Dorothy Lee discusses such mythology in her description of the Wintu Indians: "An examination of the myths of the Wintu shows that the individual was conceived as having a limited agentive role, shaping, using, intervening, actualizing and temporalizing the given, but never creating."[46] Wintu mythology reflects a culture with a truly ecological consciousness. While "our attitude toward nature is colored by a desire to control and exploit [as is our symbolism, which depicts nature as a "resource," and domination of nature as "development" and "progress"], the Wintu relationship to nature is one of intimacy and mutual courtesy."[47] The mythology of such cultures has been destroyed in many cases not by the *domination of nature* by humanity, but rather by the *domination of traditional societies* by more technologically developed ones, a process which Marx sees as progressive.

The productivist viewpoint also underlies Marx's notion of the economy of time, as discussed in the *Grundrisse*, in which he argues that the essential economic question is the productive use of time. For society, as for the individual, "the multiplicity of its development, its enjoyment and its activity depends on economization of time."[48] The significant point is what is to be gained through this process. If the time required for necessary production (subsistence in a broad sense) is reduced, there will be more time "for other production, material or mental."[49] This illustates Marx's propensity, as pointed out by such diverse critics as Habermas and Baudrillard,[50] to reduce the problem of emancipation to questions of production, at the expense of factors like interaction and communication.

Perhaps the most incisive critique of Marx on this point has been presented by Sahlins. Central to human existence is a cultural reason which, according to Sahlins, cannot be conflated with pragmatic or instrumental rationality, no matter how firmly the latter may be grounded in a social conception of human development. "The species to which Marx's 'species-being' belongs is *Homo Economicus*," whose programme for human liberation exhibits "a spiritualized 'market mentality,' combining human needs (of self-realization), natural scarcities (of objective means), and man's progressive liberation from this dismal condition by purposive action...."[51] The vision of the project of emancipation through production is founded in large part in Marx's epistemology, in which meaning is merely the act of naming, and cultural creation is reduced to a reflection of material practice. But this reduction ignores the central meaning of the symbolic process. "The unity of the cultural order is constituted by... meaning. And it is this meaningful system that defines all functionality; that is, according to the particular structure and finalities of the cultural order."[52] This analysis shows clearly how the Marxian position ignores the fact that all values, including use values, can only be ordered by (and in fact are in large part *constituted* by) a system of meanings which cannot be reduced to an idealized expression of biological needs, or even of higher needs generated by advances in the process of material transformation. Because Marx's productivist view of human activity ignores this, he is unable to see how relative are the assumptions of bourgeois society and of civilization itself concerning practice, instrumental action, and technique. What is more, this productivist view, by restricting Marx's critique, in turn restricts his view of the parameters

45

within which the project of human emancipation is to take place.

This entire aspect of Marx's thought—his tendency toward economic determinism and a productivist view of human nature—underlies the dispute between Bakunin and Marx over the historical significance of capitalist production. It is Bakunin's claim that Marx uncritically accepts the necessity of many elements of bourgeois society and capitalist production as a stage toward the liberation of humanity. The implication is (and it was only partially developed by Bakunin himself) that Marx and a large segment of the workers' movement were still unable to look critically at many of the presuppositions of the age, and that a thorough analysis of how the categories of bourgeois ideology dominate political discourse, and a radical break with this ideology, were necessary.

Bakunin accepts the validity of materialism and determinism, and attributes great importance to the influence of economic factors in history. Yet he criticizes Marx for considering the economic factor as *ultimate*, and linking all historical progress to economic development. As Bakunin explains, "we recognize, indeed, the necessary and inevitable character of all events that occur but we no longer bow before them indifferently, and above all we are careful about praising them when, by their nature, they show themselves in flagrant contradiction to the supreme end of history,"[53] which he sees as the development of non-dominating community. Specifically, the subject of dispute is the historical significance of bourgeois society. According to Bakunin, Marx sees the development of capitalism as the advance toward social revolution emerging to free society. The latter holds that (as Bakunin formulates it) if "countries are more backward from the viewpoint of capitalist production they are necessarily equally backward from that of social revolution."

This interpretation of historical progress, a strong current in Marx's thought, is rooted in his conception of human social development as analogous to the stages of individual human maturation. Ancient society and all primitive societies thus represent the childhood of the human race. Typically 19th century in his thought, Marx has a condescending, paternalistic view of children (not to mention women). Myth, a primitive attempt to dominate nature, an infantile fantasy of the race, disappears when "real mastery"—note the reality principle rooted in power—intervenes. Similarly, classical art is a product of the childhood of humanity, and is thus "charming," like the naïve products of childhood. "Why should not the historic childhood of humanity, its most beautiful unfolding, as a stage never to return, exercise an eternal charm?"[54] When Marx deals with non-Western societies, he sees them as equally childish, but somehow less charming. The bourgeoisie, in making "the country dependent on the towns... the barbarian and semi-barbarian countries dependent on the civilized ones, nations of peasants on nations of bourgeois, the East on the West," performs the service of rescuing increasing numbers of people "from the idiocy of rural life."[55]

In an important passage in the *Grundrisse*, Marx discusses the "civilizing influence of capital," which consists of the creation of "general industriousness" and "a system of general exploitation of the natural and human qualities, a system of general utility,"[56] that encompasses all of reality. Capitalism thus has the historic mission of instituting an instrumental view of reality, which dissolves all the traditional prejudices that create barriers to the domination of nature. The reverence for nature embodied in the mythology and consciousness of primitive people must be destroyed, for the sake of "the development of the forces of production." As Marx states it:

> Hence the great civilizing influence of capital; its production of a stage of society in comparison to which all earlier ones appear as mere *local developments* of humanity and as *nature-idolatry*. For the first time, nature becomes purely an object for humankind, purely a matter of utility; ceases to be recognized as a power for itself; and the theoretical discovery of its autonomous laws appears merely as a ruse so as to subjugate it under human needs, whether as an object of consumption or as a means of production. In accord with this tendency, capital drives beyond national barriers and prejudices as much as beyond nature worship, as well as all traditional, confined, complacent, encrusted satisfactions of present needs, and reproductions of old ways of life. It is destructive towards all of this, and constantly revolutionizes it, tearing down all the barriers

which hem in the development of the forces of production, and expansion of needs, the all-sided development of the forces of production, and the exploitation and exchange of natural and mental forces.[57]

Marx gives a concrete example of this process in his discussion of the means by which the British brought "civilization" to India. He argues that though the British rule may have been destructive of culture and even of people's happiness, it still performed the constructive task of undermining Oriental Despotism, which had its basis in traditional Indian village life. Imperialism opens the possibility of progress beyond the ignorance, superstition, and stagnation that he saw as the essence of Indian society. England has, he says, "a double mission in India... the annihilation of old Asiatic society, and the laying of the material foundations of Western society in Asia."[58] The British carried out this mission through a process of centralization and industrial development. It unified political rule, developed a system of communication and transportation, created a disciplined army, instituted a "free press" (albeit controlled by an élite), developed a governing class ("endowed with the requirements for government and imbued with European science"[59]—thus constituting a *bureaucratic* and *technical* stratum), and, not least of all, introduced high technology, in the form of steam energy. In short, it created the basis for the entire centralist, Westernized course of development that the Gandhian movement (with its ideal of village cooperative production) has been valiantly but ineffectually combatting for the past several generations. But what these Indian advocates of non-domination and organic development have not seen is that, as Marx states it:

> The bourgeois period of history has to create the material basis of the new world—on the one hand the universal intercourse founded on the mutual dependency of mankind, and the means of that intercourse; on the other hand the development of the productive powers of man and the transformation of material production into a scientific domination of natural agencies.[60]

In Bakunin's view, factors other than technical and economic development must be given more consideration than Marx allows, if any society's potential for liberation is to be accurately assessed. Marx, he says, overlooks "the individual temperament and character of all races and peoples, which are themselves the product of a host of ethnographic, climatological and economic, as well as historical, causes but which, once established, exert a considerable influence over the destinies and even the development of a country's economic forces, outside and independent of its economic forces, outside and independent of its economic conditions."[61] Bakunin here presents a position as inadequate in many ways as the one he attacks Marx for holding, since, while attempting to avoid the "superstructural" interpretation of non-economic factors, he tries to explain away the reciprocal interaction between these and the economic. Yet his criticism has value in that it points out the importance of cultural factors which have never convincingly been reduced to mere mediating terms between ultimate economic causes and other social realities. He argues for the importance of a sense of community and of the existence of what he calls "the instinct of rebellion."[62] He sees in many more traditional societies a greater capacity for social revolution than the more "advanced" or "civilized" societies that Marx saw as progressive. For example, Bakunin perceived certain libertarian and communal feelings of Latin cultures to be an advantage over the authoritarian and hierarchical outlook of the Germans, whom Marx often saw as the advance guard of the coming revolution.[63] Bakunin cautions us to beware of those who wish to "civilize" the less economically developed societies and groups within society.[64] He believes this desire to be reactionary for two reasons: both because it will require oppressive means in order to reach its goal; and, even more important, because it will result in the destruction of cultural conditions with libertarian potential in order to replace them with conditions that open even greater opportunities for domination.[65]

But what, precisely, is Marx's view of the "civilizing" nature of bourgeois production? One finds in his works a ringing endorsement of the revolutionary achievements of capitalism. His remarks on imperialism in India, cited above, are an indication. The progressive function of capital is, above all, to develop the productive forces to the limits of their capacity and to create conditions which will prepare the way for the social revolution and will in turn make possible their vastly greater expansion. Capitalism, he argues, has performed a necessary centralizing function in history. The bourgeoisie, he says in the *Communist Manifesto*, "has agglomerated population, centralized means of production, and has concentrated property in a few hands. The necessary consequence of this was political centralization,"[66] which has allowed the bourgeoisie to develop the productive forces far beyond the dreams of previous societies (or at least those that had such dreams, since most didn't). This development has required not only centralization and the attendant destruction of traditional culture ("ancient and venerable prejudices and opinions"[67]), but also the imposition of a rigid and hierarchical system of organization. "As privates of the industrial army [the workers] are placed under the command of a perfect hierarchy of officers and sergeants. Not only are they slaves of the bourgeois class, and of the bourgeois State; they are daily and hourly enslaved by the machine, by the over-looker, and, above all, by the individual bourgeois manufacturer himself."[68]

What then should be the standpoint of the workers toward these dehumanizing techniques? Their immediate reaction to what Mumford has called "paleotechnics"—the hierarchical, centralizing forms of mechanization of the industrial revolution—was rebellion. They smashed the machines that were destroying their creativity, lowering the quality of their products, and making possible more effective exploitation of their labour. But according to Marx this was a utopian approach, for in such actions "they direct their attacks not against the bourgeois conditions of production, but against the instruments of production themselves..."[69] The techniques which, as Marx himself holds, form much of the basis (indeed, are at times seen as the ultimate basis) of the bourgeois mode of production, are distinguished from "the bourgeois conditions of production." Thus given a kind of neutral existence as mere means to be used, they are available, without fundamental transformation, as the foundation for progressive social development.[70]

Marx's position on technology and the development of capitalist production is extensively elaborated in the *Grundrisse*, where he continues certain themes which go back in his works to the *Paris Manuscripts*. In mechanized production, work does not appear as the self-activity of the worker. Machinery becomes a system, "a moving power that moves itself,"[71] while the worker's activity becomes "a mere abstraction of activity... determined and regulated on all sides by the movement of the machinery, and not the opposite."[72] Fixed capital is domination through "alien labour merely appropriated by capital."[73] Objectified labour has come to rule living labour, transforming living labour "into a mere accessory of this machinery."[74] Furthermore, the alienation of the product from the producer is completed as mass production "destroys every connection of the product with the direct need of the producer, and hence with direct use value."[75] All the creative qualities which labour once developed in the process of production are progressively alienated by the machine. Through the machine the capitalist robs labour "of all independence and attractive character."[76] Ultimately, the "accumulation of knowledge and skill, of the general productive forces of the social brain, is thus absorbed into capital, as opposed to labour, and hence appears as an attribute of capital...."[77] In these and other passages of the *Grundrisse*, Marx presents his most clearly and concretely developed presentation of the processes of alienation and dehumanization under capitalist production and mechanization. What is surprising, especially in view of the usual Marxist humanist discussion of these issues, which relies heavily on the *Paris Manuscripts* (with all their richness of ambiguity), is that these views are expressed in the context of a defence of the *liberatory* nature of capitalist productive forces.

Anarchist social theory has always questioned the validity of the view that large-scale, centralized, highly mechanized industry can be the means toward a humane society. Classical anarchism, from Proudhon to Kropotkin, proposed instead humanly-scaled, decentralized, labour-intensive production, which was seen as compatible with social and political institutions based on individual freedom, democracy, and self-management.[78] One of the strongest arguments put forth for such technology is that it makes possible the synthesis of manual and mental labour, and thus helps prevent the emergence of technocratic and bureaucratic élites which appropriate the responsibility for decision-making and social creation. While these anarchist principles only came to fruition in the classical period in the works of Kropotkin,[79] they are echoed in Bakunin's emphasis on small-scale productive and communal groups as fundamental, his abhorrence for centralized plans and the élites that administer them, and his advocacy of "integral education," which would seek immediately to develop in each individual the ability to comprehend social processes and to participate knowledgeably in decision-making.[80]

In the context of these principles, capitalist production is seen by Bakunin as a force which, far from engendering the conditions for a liberatory society, creates a lack of power and understanding which places increasingly more formidable barriers in the way of social emancipation. However, Marx assessed the situation in a quite different way. Early in the chapter of the *Grundrisse* on capital, he explains the function of capitalist production:

> The great historic quality of capital is to *create* this *surplus labour*, superfluous labour from the standpoint of mere use value, mere subsistence; and its historic destiny is fulfilled as soon as, on one side, there has been such a development of needs that surplus labour above and beyond necessity has itself become a general need arising out of individual needs themselves—-and, on the other side, when the severe discipline of capital, acting on succeeding generations, has developed general industriousness as a general property of the new species—and, finally, when the development of the productive powers of labour, which capital incessantly whips onward with its unlimited mania for wealth, and of the sole conditions in which this mania can be realized, have flourished to the stage where the possession and preservation of general wealth require a lesser time of society as a whole, and where the labouring society relates scientifically to the process of its progressive reproduction, its reproduction in a constantly greater abundance; hence where labour in which a human being does what a thing can do has ceased.[81]

The regimentation and dehumanization of capitalist production are necessary because only through such means can the productive forces be developed sufficiently so that (after the revolution and their even further development) toil will not dominate people's lives. Contrary to the anarchist tradition, the Marxists cannot conceive of liberation within the realm of necessary labour. Work and play, necessity and freedom, cannot possibly be reconciled. Instead, automated machinery must be looked to as a force which will reduce labour so that freedom can be pursued in the realm of free time. The same mechanization which robbed the worker of all individuality becomes the condition for the most highly developed individuality:

> Capital's ceaseless striving towards the general form of wealth drives labour beyond the limits of its natural paltriness, and thus creates the material elements for the development of the rich individuality which is as all-sided in its production as in its consumption, and whose labour also appears no longer as labour, but as the full development of activity itself, in which natural necessity in its direct form has disappeared; because a historically created need has taken the place of a natural one. This is why *capital is productive; i.e., an essential relation for the development of the social productive forces*. It ceases to exist as such only where the development of these productive forces themselves encounters its barrier in capital itself.[82]

Again, development of productive forces is seen as central to social progress. Human needs develop and become more sophisticated, more civilized, as production increases. Production itself creates needs for that which is produced (and, as is also mentioned, for consumption, for the materials of production, for distribution) so that the development of production means development (in the sense of enrichment) of needs. Yet several problems arise. One is the possibility that as the expanded system of production produces ever greater needs for objects (whether these objects be capitalist commodities or not), such needs may come to occupy the central place in our value system, displacing needs that Bakunin identified as ultimate (freedom and community). Bakunin has little to say about this possibility, although the distinction is implicit in his thought. Recent thinkers very much in the tradition of Bakunin have said a great deal about it, as we come to see that a "rich individuality" based on high levels of consumption can be quite compatible with social impoverishment. Both critical theory and situationism have developed this line of analysis. But another related possibility is of more immediate concern, since it was elaborated by Bakunin in some detail. This is the possibility that the system of technology which is proposed as a means toward liberation may create new potential for class domination.

The analysis of both these possibilities requires further consideration of Marx's discussion of technology in the *Grundrisse*, where he describes in great detail the process by which mechanization reduces the amount of necessary labour, which will in turn "redound to the benefit of emancipated labour, and is the condition of its emancipation."[83] He explains that with the development of the productive forces "the creation of real wealth" loses its proportional relationship to human labour (a point ignored in many discussions of Marx), and comes to depend "rather on the general state of science and on the progress of technology, or the application of this science to production."[84] On the one hand, as a result of this development, humans are reduced to functionaries whose activity is determined by the nature of the technological system which makes possible abundant production. "Labour no longer appears so much to be included within the production process; rather, the human being comes to relate more as a watchman and regulator to the production process itself."[85] The worker "steps to the side of the production process instead of being its chief actor."[86] But, on the other hand, at the same time quite antithetical developments are taking place as the social process of production creates the social individual who is its regulator and the social knowledge which is embodied in its realization. The inevitable movement is toward social regulation of the process by this social individual. As this takes place, production becomes the servant of humanity rather than the means for its enslavement, and the repression which has thus far been necessary to produce the conditions for emancipation can be abolished. The result is the "free development of individualities, and hence not the reduction of necessary labour time so as to posit surplus labour, but rather the reduction of necessary labour of society to a minimum, which then corresponds to the artistic, scientific, etc., development of the individuals in the time set free, and with the means created, for all of them."[87]

This idea is expressed in the more famous statement in Volume Three of *Capital*, where the realm of freedom is defined as lying beyond the realm of necessary production:

> The realm of freedom actually begins only where labour which is determined by necessity and mundane considerations ceases; thus in the very nature of things it lies beyond the sphere of actual material production. Just as the savage must wrestle with Nature to satisfy his wants, to maintain and reproduce life, so must civilized man, and he must do so in all social formations and under all possible modes of production. With his development this realm of physical necessity expands as a result of his wants; but, at the same time, the forces of production which satisfy these wants also increase. Freedom in this field can only consist in socialized man, the associated producers, rationally regulating their interchange with Nature, bringing it under their common control, instead of being ruled by it as by the blind forces of Nature; and achieving this with the least expenditure of energy and under conditions most favourable to, and worthy of, their human nature. But it nonetheless still remains a realm of necessity. Beyond it begins that development of human energy which is an end in itself, the true realm of freedom, which, however, can blossom forth only with the realm of necessity as its basis.[88]

This view of liberation through productive development poses serious problems for Marx in relation to his discussion of human need. There is no doubt that Marx's work contains a critical theory of needs. This is most obvious when he either explicitly or implicitly treats as real human needs those which can be deduced from the character of humanity as species being. Thus, in the *Paris Manuscripts* he asserts that "the rich human being is simultaneously the human being *in need* of a totality of human manifestations of life...."[89] Consequently, he is able to introduce the critical concept of a distinction between "crude need" and "human need."[90]

Yet Marx's productivism creates barriers to the consistent development of this critical theory of need. The very existence of such a theory is obscured at times by his tendency to use language that appears to equate needs with conscious desires, so that under capitalism a "sophistication of needs" for some is contrasted with "complete, crude, abstract simplicity of needs" for others.[91] Nevertheless, this difficulty can be overcome through interpretive principles which distinguish carefully among Marx's varying uses of language.[92] The existence of subjectively felt needs generated by ones placed in a system of social relations can then be seen to conflict in no way with the existence of needs which may or may not be experienced subjectively, but which are grounded in the human potentiality for development as social being.

The question being posed is thus not that of the existence of a critical theory of needs in Marx, but rather that of the problematical relation between this theory and his vision of liberation through development of production. In *The Poverty of Philosophy* Marx discusses the generation of human needs by the system of production. In a discussion dealing with various kinds of needs (from potatoes to lace and lawyers) he states that "most often, needs arise directly from production or from a state of affairs based on production."[93] Furthermore, in the "Introduction" to *A Contribution to the Critique of Political Economy*, he develops his dialectical account of the relation between production and needs, explaining how production produces needs, rather than merely arising in response to them.[94] In the context of such a conception of the generation of need, the passage cited from *Capital* takes on an ominous significance. For is not the expansion of conscious needs also an expansion of the realm of necessity, and thus a continually growing threat to the realization of the realm of freedom? After all, in Marx's view we no more choose the state of the development of the productive forces than we choose the character of our biological makeup. "Are men free to choose this or that form of society for themselves? By no means."[95] For "at each stage there is found a material result; a sum of productive forces... which, indeed, is modified by the new generation on the one hand, but also gives it a definite development, a special character."[96] We can thus envision the subordination of human creative activity to an ever-expanding system of needs imposed on humanity by the process of technological development.

In Marx's view, social transformation depends on the existence of a contradiction between the developed forces of production and the relations of production. The "forces of production and social relations... appear to capital as mere means for it to produce on its limited foundation," while in reality they are "the material conditions to blow this foundation sky-high."[97] But does such an irreconcilable contradiction exist, or can increased production, and even socialized, centralized management be absorbed into the system of domination? This is the question which the anarchist critique poses (and, anarchists would argue, history has answered). For Marx, "the development of fixed capital indicates to what degree general social knowledge has become a *direct force of production* and to what degree, hence, the conditions of the process of social life itself have come under the control of the general intellect and have been transformed in accordance with it."[98] But in the absence of an already self-conscious populace who understand social processes: in the absence of what Bakunin (and many of his successors in the anarcho-syndicalist movement, like Pelloutier) saw as the "integral education" of the workers, will such knowledge really become "general," leading to management of society by the general intellect? In Bakunin's opinion, vast technical development can occur while both knowledge and control remain the possession of only a *part* of society. Thus, the system of domination contains within itself the means by which to reconcile contradictions that Marx thought would lend to a necessary process of transcendence.

Notes

1. George Sabine, *A History of Political Theory* (New York: Holt, Rinehart and Winston, 1937).
2. George Lichtheim, *From Marx to Hegel* (New York: Seabury Press, 1974), p. 50.
3. Ironically, the best analysis along lines suggested by Bakunin is being done by theorists who have come out of the Marxist tradition, but have broken with it to varying degrees. See the following: Cornelius Castoriadis, *La Société Bureaucratique* (Paris: 10/18, 1973), *L'Expérience du Mouvement Ouvrier* (Paris: 10/18, 1974), *Les Carrefours du Labyrinthe* (Paris: Éditions du Seuil, 1978), and *L'Institution Imaginaire de la Société* (Paris: Éditions du Seuil, 1975); Claude Lefort, *Les Formes de l'Histoire* (Paris: Gallimard, 1978) and *Éléments d'une Critique de la Bureaucratie* (Paris: Droz, 1971); Murray Bookchin, *Post-Scarcity Anarchism* (Montréal: Black Rose Books, 1977), *Toward an Ecological Society* (Montréal: Black Rose Books, 1980) and *The Ecology of Freedom* (Palo Alto: Cheshire Books, 1982); Jean Baudrillard, *The Mirror of Production* (St. Louis: Telos Press, 1975) and *For a Critique of the Political Economy of the Sign* (St. Louis: Telos Press, 1981); Albrecht Wellmer, *Critical Theory of Society* (New York: Seabury, 1974); Kostas Axelos, *Alienation, Praxis, and Techné in the Thought of Karl Marx* (Austin: University of Texas Press, 1976); and Daniel Guérin, *Anarchism: From Theory to Practice* (New York: Monthly Review Press, 1970).
4. Michael Bakunin, *God and the State* (New York: Dover Publications, 1970), p. 9.
5. Arthur Lehning, ed., *Michael Bakunin: Selected Writings* (New York: Grove Press, 1974), p. 224.
6. *Ibid.*, pp. 224-25.
7. *Ibid.*, p. 225.
8. Sam Dolgoff, ed., *Bakunin on Anarchism* (Montréal: Black Rose Books, 1980), pp. 310-11.
9. *Ibid.*, p. 310. Cf. Habermas's discussion of Bloch's analysis of the religious impulse: "Certainly, the transparency of a better world is refracted by hidden interests, even in those aspects which point beyond the existing state; but still, the hopes which it awakens, the longings which it satisfies, contain energies that at the same time, once instructed about themselves, become critical impulses." *Theory and Practice* (Boston: Beacon Press, 1974), p. 239. See also Gustav Landauer, *For Socialism* (St. Louis: Telos Press, 1978), pp. 100-102, on the coinciding decline

of both superstition and illusion on the one hand and symbolic unity and community on the other.
10. Dolgoff, *op. cit.*, p. 310.
11. *Ibid.*, pp. 209-10.
12. Ulysses Santamaria and Alain Manville, "Lenin and the Problem of the Transition," *Telos* 27: 90.
13. *Ibid.*, p. 79.
14. Michael Harrington, *The Twilight of Capitalism* (New York: Simon and Schuster, 1976). Harrington's defense is limited to Marx, and does not encompass Engels. The book is a very strong defense of the dialectical quality of much of Marx's analysis. See, for example, pp. 94-95, on how Marx's specific analysis departs from technological determinism. Harrington's assessment is in some ways similar to that of Habermas, but for some reason (probably not theoretical) turns into a quest for a new Marxist orthodoxy.
15. Karl Marx, *A Contribution to the Critique of Political Economy* (New York: International Publishers, 1970), p. 20.
16. *Ibid.*
17. *Ibid.*, p. 21.
18. *Ibid.*
19. *Ibid.*
20. *Ibid.*
21. Karl Marx and Frederick Engels, *The German Ideology* (New York: International Publishers, 1947), p. 18.
22. *Ibid.*, p. 28.
23. *Ibid.*
24. Significantly, Marx states at this point that he wishes to analyze the superstructure as a totality and to show the reciprocal action of the various elements. If the totality is taken as the whole of society, rather than the superstructure, and if the reciprocity is extended to encompass all relations, including the economic ones, then this presents a model for a dialectical social theory in the full sense, which would avoid many of the criticisms made by Bakunin and his successors. It is this model which is adopted by later critical Marxists.
25. *Ibid.*, p. 73.
26. *Ibid.*
27. *Ibid*, p. 14.
28. *Ibid.*, p. 15. As if such a uni-directional determination could hold for such inseparable phenomena!
29. Marx confronts the dilemma of explaining or explaining away advanced social theory (like his own), which is also the product

of the material conditions of society, and thus subject to condemnation as ideology. Social evolution proceeds at different rates of speed in relation to different groups and institutions in society, he explains. Advanced consciousness can be the product of the newly developing material conditions, while an obsolete "form of intercourse" is still in control of society and is expressed through the dominant ideology. Thus, the progressive nature of radical social theory is vindicated—if all bets are placed on the progressive nature of historical development.

30. Karl Marx, *The Poverty of Philosophy* (Moscow: Progress Publishers, 1955), p. 107.
31. *Ibid.*, p. 36.
32. *Ibid.*, p. 156.
33. Robert Tucker, ed., *The Marx-Engels Reader* (New York: Norton, 1972), pp. 339-40.
34. Karl Marx, *Grundrisse* (New York: Vintage Books, 1973), p. 105.
35. *Ibid.*, p. 495.
36. *Ibid.*, pp. 506-509.
37. Karl Marx, *Capital* (New York: International Publishers, 1967), 1:18.
38. *Ibid.*, 1:19.
39. *Ibid.*, 1:82.
40. *Ibid.*
41. *Ibid.* As Marshall Sahlins points out concerning survival needs as opposed to others, "there are other 'needs' as compelling as eating—and not merely sex but, for instance, the necessity of classification..." *Culture and Practical Reason* (Chicago: University of Chicago Press, 1976), p. 146. Yet he notes that even this reply is not a sufficient criticism of Marx's standpoint, since it is still compatible with a "functionalist framework" which fails to consider the context in which such needs exist—an all-embracing cultural logic which generates the symbols and meanings pervading human experience, and which is essential to our ordering of *all* needs.
42. Marx and Engels, *German Ideology, op. cit.*, p. 7.
43. *Ibid.*
44. *Ibid.*, p. 29.
45. Marx, *Grundrisse, op. cit.*, p. 110.
46. Dorothy Lee, *Freedom and Culture* (Englewood Cliffs: Prentice-Hall, 1959), p. 172. Lee presents similar analyses of the Hopi, Navaho, Tikopia, and other cultures.
47. *Ibid.*, p. 129.

48. Marx, *Grundrisse, op. cit.*, pp. 172-73.
49. *Ibid.*, p. 172.
50. See Jürgen Habermas, "The Idea of the Theory of Knowledge as Social Theory" in *Knowledge and Human Interests* (Boston: Beacon Press, 1971), and Baudrillard, *The Mirror of Production, op. cit.*, footnote 3.
51. Sahlins, *op. cit.*, p. 161.
52. Lehning, *op. cit.*, p. 244.
53. Dolgoff, *op. cit.*, p. 310.
54. Marx, *Grundrisse, op. cit.*, p. 111.
55. Tucker, *op. cit.*, p. 339.
56. Marx, *Grundrisse, op. cit.*, p. 409.
57. *Ibid.*, p. 410.
58. Tucker, *op. cit.*, p. 583.
59. *Ibid.*
60. *Ibid.*, pp. 587-88. In view of such a strong affirmation of the productivist position it is not surprising that a later exponent of orthodox Marxism like Trotsky can proclaim that "Marxism sets out from the development of technique as the fundamental spring of progress, and constructs the communist program upon the dynamic of the productive forces." *The Revolution Betrayed* (Garden City: Doubleday, Doran and Co., 1937), p. 45. This work is an enlightening example of the productivist side of Marx, and the domination of productivist ideology in orthodox Marxism, especially in view of the fact that it is formulated as a "critique" of the authoritarianism and "bureaucratism" of Stalin.
61. Lehning, *op. cit.*, p. 256.
62. *Ibid.* One of Bakunin's serious errors is his overemphasis on rebellious *instincts*, which at times obscures his analysis of the importance of conscious, reflective social transformation.
63. Lehning, *op. cit.*, p. 257.
64. Dolgoff, *op. cit.*, p. 203.
65. Although Bakunin himself was unable to pose the question, his comments on culture point toward the significance of the opposition on the one hand between the primitive and the civilized, and, on the other, between culture and the state. Consideration of the relation between these two oppositions points to the necessity of a movement from the critique of the state to a critique of civilization itself. Recent work by Pierre Clastres suggests what some implications of such a critique might be. According to Clastres, the lesson of primitive society is that "it is the political break [coupure] that is decisive, and

not the economic transformation." *Society Against the State* (New York: Mole Editions, Urizen Books, 1977), p. 171. Primitive society, he says, saw "the great affinity of power and nature, as the twofold limitation of the domain of culture" (p. 35). Primitive society is a society of abundance, as Sahlins has convincingly shown in his work *Stone Age Economics* (Chicago: Aldine-Atherton, 1972). Following this analysis, Clastres holds that it is "an essentially egalitarian society" in which "men control their activity, control the circulation of products of that activity" (p. 167). History presents us with only two qualitatively different forms of society—primitive society with its cultural scheme of organization, and statist or politically organized society. Clastres' empirical study of Amerindian societies leads him to the conclusion that although diverse systems of production can exist and even succeed one another without corresponding variations in other cultural institutions, the transition to statist forms inevitably produces revolutionary changes in the entire social structure, changes which result in "hierarchical authority, the power relation, the subjugation of men" (p. 171). He suggests that would we wish to preserve the Marxist concepts of infrastructure and superstructure, it might be necessary to label the former as political and the latter as economic. Yet Clastres himself does not fall into this non-dialectical trap (a kind of vulgar anarchism encountered frequently enough), nor does he accept the alternative of a simplistic demographic determinism. While there is abundant evidence of the importance of population growth as a key factor in the rise of the state (pp. 180-81, and see also Robert Carneiro, "A Theory of the Origin of the State" in *Science* 169: 733-38) attention must also be devoted to any given culture's struggle to reverse the tendencies which lead to the emergence of political society (pp. 182-86). In Clastres' study we find dramatic evidence of the profound significance of that struggle between culture and the state to which Bakunin merely alludes.
66. Tucker, *op. cit.*, p. 339.
67. *Ibid.*, p. 338.
68. *Ibid.*, p. 341.
69. *Ibid.*, p. 343.
70. In *Theories of Surplus Value* Marx praises Ricardo, who "rightly for his time, regards the capitalist mode of production as the most advantageous for production in general..." (Moscow: Progress Publishers, 1968, Part II, p. 117). Ricardo's position is seen as historically progressive, because "production for its

own sake means nothing but the development of human productive forces, in other words the *development of the richness of human nature as an end in itself*" (pp. 117-18). Marx goes on to defend an evolutionary doctrine in which the suffering and "sacrifice" of the individual is justified by the ultimate advance of the species (p. 118).
71. Marx, *Grundrisse, op. cit.*, p. 692.
72. *Ibid.*, p. 693.
73. *Ibid.*, p. 705.
74. *Ibid.*
75. *Ibid.*, p. 694.
76. *Ibid.*, p. 701.
77. *Ibid.*, p. 694.
78. This view is even stronger in contemporary anarchism, which is more ecologically conscious and more communalist.
79. See Kropotkin, *Fields, Factories and Workshops Tomorrow* (London: George Allen and Unwin, 1974).
80. See G.P. Maximoff, ed., *The Political Philosophy of Bakunin* (New York: Free Press, 1953), pp. 411-12.
81. Marx, *Grundrisse, op. cit.*, p. 325.
82. *Ibid.*
83. *Ibid.*, p. 701.
84. *Ibid.*, p. 704-05.
85. *Ibid.*, p. 705.
86. *Ibid.*
87. Ibid., p. 706.
88. Tucker, *op. cit.*, p. 320.
89. Karl Marx,*Economic and Philosophic Manuscripts of 1844* (Moscow: Progress Publishers, 1974), p. 98.
90. *Ibid.*, p. 101.
91. *Ibid.*, p. 102. Thus "even the need for fresh air ceases to be a need for the worker."
92. See Zillah Eisenstein, "Species Being, Needs, and the Theory of Alienation," unpublished manuscript kindly made available by the author.
93. Marx, *Poverty of Philosophy, op. cit.*, p. 36. The need for lawyers is a result of the existence of civil law, "which is but the expression of a certain development of property..."
94. Marx, *Grundrisse, op. cit.*, p. 92. Production produces consumption in several ways, including "by creating the products, initially posited by it as objects, in the form of a need felt by the consumer."
95. Marx, *Poverty of Philosophy, op. cit.*, p. 156.
96. Marx, *German Ideology, op. cit.*, p. 29.

97. Marx, *Grundrisse, op. cit.*, p. 706.
98. *Ibid.*

Chapter 3

Marx, Bakunin, and Social Revolution

Marx's conception of social revolution is an integral part of his historical materialist theoretical framework. Accordingly, in his major works he consistently depicts the class struggle as the manifestation of underlying contradictions between the forces and relations of production, and denies that social revolution can successfully be achieved without the requisite development of the material preconditions. The proletariat, far from appearing as a self-conscious revolutionary subject, is often presented as the *object* whose destiny is determined by conflicting forces which move inexorably toward a resolution, without requiring the kind of reflective, historically developed knowledge, embodied in a self-conscious social movement, that Bakunin (at least in his better moments) saw as essential.

Marx's early works bear witness to this interpretation. In *The Holy Family* he states that "private property drives itself in its economic movement towards its own dissolution, but only through a development which... is unconscious."[1] This development, he emphasizes, is manifested in class consciousness. The proletariat, conscious of its spiritual and material poverty, has gained a "theoretical knowledge" of its loss of humanity.[2] But consciousness is limited to this negative moment:

consciousness of misery and deprivation. Creative, self-directing consciousness seems at this stage to be unnecessary, since "history" will take care of the future. Thus, when we get to the matter of activity, of historical movement, "it is not a question of what this or that proletarian, or even the whole proletariat, at the moment *regards* as its aim. It is a question of *what the proletariat is*, and what, in accordance with this *being*, it will historically be compelled to do."[3] In *The German Ideology* "all collisions in history" are also seen as a result of "the contradiction between productive forces and the form of intercourse."[4] According to this view, theory can only come into conflict with the established order as a result of these contradictions.[5] Consciousness must wait for productive powers to prepare the way. Without a great increase in these powers, social revolution would at best achieve an equal distribution of scarcity. Since low productivity is seen as being inseparable from struggle with nature and struggle between human beings, "all the old filthy business"[6] would be destined to reappear. In *The Poverty of Philosophy* the problem is stated perhaps most clearly, and certainly most dismally from the perspective of the present. "For the oppressed class to be able to emancipate itself it is necessary that the productive powers already acquired and the existing social relations should no longer be capable of existing side by side."[7] Unless this passage is interpreted tautologically, it makes the prospects for revolution look rather dim at this stage in history, as productive powers strain toward what is perhaps their historic limit, while relations of domination appear to have adapted rather successfully to their supposed technological barriers.

The *Communist Manifesto* presents a similar view of the nature of social revolution. The present era is said to be revolutionary because it is the stage at which productive forces begin their revolt against the relations of production. "The conditions of bourgeois society are too narrow to comprise the wealth created by them."[8] The bourgeoisie, much like the proletariat, is incapable of dealing creatively with the problems of its historical predicament. It looks for new markets and more effectively exploits old ones, only driving the system to new crises and pushing the proletariat into even more revolutionary depths of misery. The workers are only conceded what is necessary for subsistence.⁹ (Of course, as much of his specific analysis testifies, Marx often recognizes that this is not true, but he presents it as fact in his more polemical, and historically most influential, works.) The bourgeoisie thus produces its own gravediggers by involuntarily creating associations of labourers—"their revolutionary combination."[10] This association must be revolutionary because its activity is a manifestation of the contradictions within the capitalist mode of production. As Marx states in the *Grundrisse*, the tendency of capital is

> always, on the one side, *to create disposable time, on the other, to convert it into surplus labour*. If it succeeds too well at the first, then it suffers from surplus production, and then necessary labour is interrupted, because *no surplus labour can be realized by capital*. The more this contradiction develops, the more does it become evident that the growth of the forces of production can no longer be bound up with the appropriation of alien labour, but that the mass of workers must themselves appropriate their own surplus labour.[11]

The bourgeoisie can, however, discover, by analyzing its own historical experience, that if disposable time is created and the surplus is divided with the worker (as Marx states sometimes happens), exploitation can be institutionalized and gain legitimacy, even among the exploited. If capital can supply a continuous stream of commodities, and through "free time" domesticate the members of the "revolutionary combinations" (who, after all, are merely "combined" through the relations of production, rather than "combiners" through the conscious aim of social creation) as consumers of their segment of the surplus, the contradiction does not appear to be irresolvable within the bounds of capitalist production. So much less does it appear so if, as Bakunin suggests, the bourgeoisie can creatively reconstitute itself as the leadership of the "revolutionary combinations" of workers. This possibility is one of the central issues in the opposition between Marx and Bakunin over the nature and goals of the revolutionary movement. This aspect of their dispute must now be analyzed.

Much of Bakunin's critique of Marx deals with the problem of ends and means. It has sometimes been proposed (by Bakunin himself, for example) that Marxists and anarchists agree about their goals but not about their means. This is only partly true. While their means certainly differ markedly, it would be an over-simplification to identify their final goals. While both foresee the disappearance of the state, the achievement of social management of the economy, the end of class rule, and the attainment of human equality, to mention a few common goals, significant differences in ends still remain. Marxist thought has inherited a vision which looks to high development of technology with a corresponding degree of centralization of social institutions which will continue even after the coming of the social revolution. It also presents a model of human nature which sees people as producers, and sees productive activity as the primary achievement of the future communist human being. Finally, there is a view of the future in which the individual and society are reconciled, and in which individual activity becomes thoroughly social. However, this view devotes little attention to those institutions which permit close personal interaction, an area given great importance by anarchists.

The anarchist vision sees the human scale as essential, both in the techniques which are used for production, and for the institutions which arise from the new modes of association. Human nature is seen less as directed toward artisanship or productivity (although this is still an important theme), and more toward cultural interaction, and the person's enjoyment of free social activity. For anarchists, the goal of society is one in which many small-scale groups will form the basis for a larger social unity. As Martin Buber put it, the good society is a community of communes.[12] In addition, the anarchist ideal has a strong hedonistic element which has seen Germanic socialism as ascetic and Puritanical. While Bakunin also succumbed to revolutionary asceticism at times, he still asserts that "the socialist... takes his stand on his positive right to life and all its pleasures, both intellectual, moral and physical. He loves life, and intends to enjoy it to the full."[13] Such a person is distinguished by "*his frank and human selfishness*, living candidly and unsentientously for himself, and knowing that by doing so *in accordance with justice* he serves the whole of society."[14] The anarchist ideal of community proclaims the collective realization of individual desire.[15] In spite of the often repeated clichés about the two ideals being one, there are in fact significant differences in emphasis.

Based on this, then, the differences between the two views of the relation between means and ends become more striking. Anarchism takes as one of its cardinal principles the proposition that only libertarian means can be used (not merely "should be used") to successfully create a libertarian social order: or to quote Bakunin (seen as incomprehensible nonsense by some of his opponents), "liberty can only be created by liberty."[16] Accordingly, the revolutionary movement must itself be a microcosm of the new society, which is thus being "created within the shell of the old." Humanity cannot work toward a non-dominating community if it is regimented by a revolutionary élite which holds the knowledge of historical movement, or if the structures of the revolutionary organizations are modelled after bourgeois hierarchical structures. The revolutionary structures must instead be those which develop self-consciousness, responsibility, and free activity. Humanity develops not through a new seizure of power, but rather through the creation of new forms of human interaction.

Bakunin, for all his suggestiveness, left much of the task of analyzing the various forms of domination to future anarchists and other anti-authoritarians (although for a 19th century European he was unusually perceptive concerning patriarchal domination and imperialism by "developed" societies). However, on the matter of the nature of the state and bureaucratic domination his thought is especially fertile. One of the most extensively developed themes in his works is the idea that the state, as a tool of domination, cannot be used as a means toward liberation, no matter who controls it, and in whose name they act.

Bakunin, like anarchists in general, opposes the state for both moral and political reasons. In *God and the State* he maintains that "the liberty of man consists solely in this: that he obeys natural laws because he has *himself* recognized them as such, and not because they have been externally imposed upon him by any extrinsic will whatever, divine or human, collective or individual."[17] He is, of course, incorrect when he rhetorically claims that this exhausts the question of freedom, for it is obviously a much more complex matter; yet he is pointing

69

out an essential element in the anarchist conception of freedom, the contention that social freedom in the fullest sense cannot be achieved until the members of society have come, through voluntary choice, to participate cooperatively in a harmonious system of the human community and the community of nature. The state, because it imposes the will of some on others, hinders the development of that organic unity which comes from within each individual and thus creates the strongest bonds uniting all. With this important principle, anarchists oppose coercive, statist organization with the idea of federation, or voluntary association. The anarchist goal is to replace, to the greatest practical degree, all governmental institutions with voluntary ones. Most anarchists have recognized that because this will be a gradual process, some degree of political organization is necessary for the present. Consequently, they propose severely limited political control, situated in small-scale communal and productive groups, which will federate for their larger purposes. But the state, with its centralization of authority and concentration of power, must be eliminated immediately.

The anarchist critique of the state goes far beyond this, however. If state action could help the appearance of a free society, anarchists would be forced to recognize it as a necessary, though temporary, evil. (The essence of anarchism is, after all, not the theoretical opposition to the state, but the practical and theoretical struggle against domination.) The anarchist analysis has led, however, to quite the opposite conclusion, and much of anarchist theory explains why that institution inhibits the establishment of free human community. Bakunin's logic demands the immediate abolition of the state and the powerful, large-scale, centralized institutions which are inseparable from it (bureaucracy, standing armies, state police, etc.).[18] The state, he says, implies minority rule, the government of the vast majority by the few, whether these few gain power through election, heredity, or seizure of power. The rulers (even those who are openly despotic) always act in the name of "the people" (the common interest, the public good, the general will). But the "will" and "interest" of "the people" are fiction (ideological concepts) that disguise the wills and interests of particular groups of people within society.[19] The further we get from primary groups, in which all participate actively in decision-making, and in which all voluntarily associate, the more the "people's will" becomes an abstraction legitimated by ideologies like the social contract, or representative mass democracy as "the consent of the governed." The state, as Marx recognized, must always represent the interest of some specific group which controls it. The hope of statists (including those who are theoretical critics of the state) is that those who rule will act on behalf of the interest, or perhaps even the needs, of all, with their actions directed toward making their own authority unnecessary. This aspiration, Bakunin replies, is based on a misunderstanding of human nature and of the effects of power, and is ridiculously optimistic (even "utopian," in the pejorative sense of that term) about the capacities of human beings for benevolent, non-egoistic action. In fact, history has shown that those in power invariably constitute themselves as a class, and seek to institutionalize and perpetuate the power at their disposal. Even a "revolutionary" seizure of state power will result in a hierarchical system of social organization. The resulting power and social status will be socially perceived as good, as individual and class privilege, even if economic equality is accepted as a social norm. Economic inequality will itself reappear and grow, once hierarchical political organization is securely established as "the will of the people" and the path toward freedom.

Bakunin's rejection of the state as a means of liberation implies a rejection of electoral politics as a revolutionary strategy as well. He and the Alliance for Social Democracy "rejected all collaboration with bourgeois politics, in however radical and socialist a disguise."[20] If the revolutionary movement involves the majority of the population, consciously working toward a new libertarian society, then the only serious strategy is direct action as the people move to replace centralized authoritarian institutions with decentralized, federalist, participatory, libertarian ones. Electoral politics would not only be ineffective, but even counter-revolutionary, reinforcing the legitimacy of forms of domination which are ripe for destruction. If, on the other hand, the revolutionary movement involves only a minority, electoral politics could not possibly improve its position, and would only divert its energies from more effective struggles, and would even work to create a new élite of working class leaders. The only groups that stand to gain are the liberal bourgeois leaders who benefit from the coalitions which are formed, and the new proletarian leaders, who advance to a similar privileged position.[21]

Bakunin proposes that both electoral and extraparliamentary party politics be rejected, and that instead a non-authoritarian, decentralist revolutionary movement, a model for the new libertarian society, be formed. This movement "will create its revolutionary organization from the bottom upwards and from the circumference inwards, in accordance with the principle of liberty, and not from the top downwards and the centre outwards, as is the way of all authority."[22] The nature of such a movement can be inferred from his discussion of certain practical problems in the International. He deplores the growth of bureaucratic tendencies accompanied by the abdication of responsibility by some groups of workers. He argues that to combat this trend no salaries be given to officials of labour organizations.[23] Decisions should be made by the members of the sections with no authority surrendered to committees elected to represent the workers. Responsibility must lie with the groups of workers themselves. There must be active workers' assemblies, in which the participants have a good grasp of the problems they face, and in which they shape the strategies that will be used.[24] Finally, he cautions the workers against the dangers of the rise of leaders within their own ranks, and of the tendency to subordinate the judgement of all to the decision-making of the few.[25] Principles like these have helped give direction to the anarcho-syndicalist movement, which developed the principles far beyond the suggestions made by Bakunin, especially by applying his federalist principles for building mass-based industrial unions. The best measure of the strengths and limitations of these principles is the successes and failures of the Spanish anarchist movement, the anarchist labour movement with the widest popular support, which was able to use many of Bakunin's proposals in its prerevolutionary organizing, in the constructive achievements of the collectives during the revolution, and in its recent reorganization.[26]

While historical developments such as these have been the richest historical legacy of Bakunin, there is another side to his idea of social change: his belief in the importance of secret associations and small groups of advanced militants. It is clear that there is a strong vanguardist undercurrent in Bakunin's thought, though it is neither so central to his outlook as his opponents allege, nor so trivial and innocuous as some of his defenders claim.

In the "Programme and Purpose of the Revolutionary Organization of International Brothers" Bakunin proposes a secret association of revolutionaries who are to assist in developing the revolutionary movement, and giving events a libertarian direction when a revolutionary situation arises. With no official positions and no coercive power at the members' disposal, their authority is to be entirely moral and intellectual. The association "rules out any idea of dictatorship and custodial control."[27] Clearly, according to Bakunin, revolutionary change cannot come through the action of small numbers of individuals, or of secret societies and conspiracies, but through the populace prepared by a long history of struggle and of consciousness as to the task of creating libertarian institutions. Social revolution must be the autonomous action of those who create the new society; it cannot be accomplished through the directives of leaders. Those who have greater abilities in particular areas, like organizing, speaking, writing, will perform those functions according to their abilities, without gaining institutionalized power or superior status.

It might seem, then, that Bakunin's proposals in this area are in accord with his anti-authoritarian position. Unfortunately, this is not at all the case. Although he warns against the power of leaders, his own description of the secret association disguises the dangers which are inherent in the influence of those with greater abilities. Camouflaging the superior *power* of these individuals under the illusion of a difference in *function* or task creates a barrier to the effective limitation of this power by those who have ultimate responsibility for decision-making. In spite of his rejection of the idea of dictatorship, Bakunin contradicts himself and goes so far as (in a letter to Albert Richard) to describe the association as an "invisible dictatorship," albeit one "without insignia, titles or official rights."[28] He may have used the term to contrast his position on leadership to the open dictatorship with concentrated power that he sees implicit in Marx's proposals, but it still betrays a contradictory, authoritarian tendency in his own thought. For as he notes, such a "dictatorship" is "all the stronger for having none of the paraphernalia of power."[29] It becomes, he says, a kind of "general staff" of the revolutionary movement,[30] a strange metaphor for someone who usually stresses the danger of excessive reliance on leaders.

Bakunin sometimes appears to see the inconsistency between his general position and such proposals. In his repudiation of Nechaev's conspiratorial methods, he attacks the idea that the organization should in any way impose its ideas on the people. It must only "express" those "popular instincts that have been worked out in history."[31] Its function is "to help people towards self-determination on the lines of the most complete equality and the fullest freedom in every direction, without the least interference from any sort of domination, even if it be temporary or transitional, that is, without any sort of government control."[32] This hardly goes far enough, for what is really needed is an anarchist theory which carefully delineates the problem of reconciling the need for the "authority of competence" with mechanisms to avoid the dangers of domination inherent even in such necessary authority. Yet it shows that Bakunin had developed some awareness of the seeds of authoritarianism which still remain even in a decentralist, libertarian political movement.[33]

Another central issue in the debate between Bakunin and Marx concerns the role of classes in social change. Bakunin has often been depicted as the defender of the revolutionary role of the lumpenproletariat, a class whose counter-revolutionary tendencies are strongly emphasized by Marx. Bakunin presumably saw the revolution being created by rampaging hordes of criminals and vagabonds, whose ranks would no doubt be swelled by the spread of inflammatory anarchist propaganda. In fact, Bakunin saw revolutionary potential in several classes, including the lumpenproletariat; however, the classes he considered the primary revolutionary forces were the industrial workers and the peasants. His disagreement with Marx concerning the revolutionary potential of classes was most significantly, therefore, a dispute over the place of peasants in history. Bakunin believed that in the most industrialized Western countries the proletariat is the most revolutionary class, but that in less developed countries, like Russia in his time, the peasants could play a more revolutionary role.[34] He criticized the Marxist view that the defeat of the peasants, with the consequent growth of state power and capitalist economic relations, had been a progressive development in the more "advanced" countries, and that it should be followed in others.[35] He believed that the peasants in many countries were capable of moving directly from their existing state of oppression into a form of libertarian socialism. He maintained that they will support such a transformation largely out of self-interest. Because they do not wish to continue to be exploited by landowners, taxed by the state, or conscripted into standing armies, the alternative of communal management of production, abolition of the centralized state, and reliance on popular militias for self-defence, he argued, will appeal to them.[36]

Significantly, in Spain, the country in which there has been the largest movement based on principles close to Bakunin's, when the time came to put the ideas into practice, the results more than verified his predictions. While the urban proletariat was highly successful in establishing the first stages of libertarian socialism, in the form of worker self-management, the peasants went much further and began to institute libertarian communism. They proved much more prepared for advances like communal management, the abolition of money, and distribution according to need.[37] Furthermore, most of the important revolutions since Bakunin's time have taken place in primarily peasant societies, and have depended on the discontent and rebellion of the peasants for whatever success they achieved. Bakunin would argue that their failure (in the form of the institution of a new class domination) has largely been due to the absence of a self-conscious and organized libertarian movement among these peasants, who almost inevitably have had the correct libertarian "instincts."[38]

What, then, is the constructive programme of such a conscious libertarian movement? It has often been alleged that anarchist revolutionaries, and especially those in the tradition of Bakunin, have an entirely negative viewpoint, that they are set on universal destruction, and that they offer nothing to take the place of what they attack. Thus, one of the few books in English on Bakunin's political thought labels his position "pan-destructionism."[39] As everyone knows, Bakunin said that "the passion for destruction is a creative passion."[40] Yet, as is obvious by now, he had some very significant positive proposals for a libertarian social movement that would lead to a transformed society. He describes the organizational basis for this transformation as "the reorganization of each region, taking as its basis and starting point the absolute freedom of individual, productive association, and commune."[41] Free association of productive and (especially) communal groups is the foundation of the new society.[42] It is this "free organization of the working masses from below upwards" that Marx specifically dismissed as "nonsense" in his commentary on Bakunin's *Statism and Anarchy*,[43] and it is the central practical issue in their dispute.

For Bakunin, the new society and the movement which creates it must be based on voluntarism and federalism. Each primary productive and communal group must be formed voluntarily by its members, and each higher level of association—local, regional, national, and international—must be voluntarily formed federations. Direct democracy must be practised in the primary groups with higher levels being as democratic as possible. Bakunin vacillated in his theory of higher-level democracy between seeing federations as controlled by the constituent groups, and controlled by direct election of delegates by all the individuals who are members of groups in the federation.[44] Furthermore, he proposed regional (and higher) legislative, executive, and judicial institutions with certain delegated powers over federating groups so long as the latter remained in the federation.

Many later anarchists would question these proposals as presenting dangers to the autonomy of primary groups, as these groups became dependent on the benefits gained through federation. Most anarchist thought has been even more radically decentralist than is Bakunin. Yet he adheres to the basic anarchist principle that secession is an essential right if the dangers always present in large-scale organization are to be avoided. Each individual must have the right to secede from any communal or productive group that he or she joins, and each group within a federation must have the right of secession without any penalty beyond the loss of whatever benefits accrue from cooperative endeavour (as, for example, the mutual aid programmes, instituted by drawing on the diverse resources of large federated groups). Even if an individual should have penalties imposed on him or her because of antisocial acts, that individual should have the right to leave the group (or federation of which the group is a part), while forfeiting in the process all rights within, and protected by, the group. "The right of free union and equally free secession comes first and foremost among all political rights; without it, confederation would be nothing but centralization in disguise."[45] Furthermore, the commitment to libertarian principles at all levels of the federation is essential, for Bakunin is not proposing that a mere organizational *structure* will assure freedom and non-domination. None can do this. An anarchist federation can only be formed by people with a commitment to socialism, equality, freedom of association, free speech and expression, and acceptance of diverse patterns of life.[46] If society is not pervaded by these values, no organizational structure can "liberate" humanity.

Clearly, Marx and Bakunin have fundamental disagreements about the processes of transition between forms of social organization, about the structure and content of the revolutionary movement, and about the character of the society that is to be established. Bakunin advocates a decentralist, federalist, antiauthoritarian movement which will develop relationships and structures similar to those which are to prevail in the libertarian society toward which it advances. Marx, on the other hand, advocates a centralized, disciplined movement which seeks to capture state power in order to vastly increase that power, which is supposedly the only means through which the dominance of obsolete relations of production, the effects of which so thoroughly pervade the entire social fabric, can be broken, allowing the new revolutionary state to fulfill its task of developing the productive forces and ushering in the resulting realm of freedom. These questions concerning the organizational forms of the revolutionary movement are inseparable from another question: the class content of the movement, that is, the identity of those groups which will play a central role in social transformation (i.e., the identity of the "revolutionary subject").

According to Marx, "the proletariat alone is a really revolutionary class."[47] All other classes fight to maintain bourgeois privileges, even when they subjectively fight the bourgeoisie. The proletariat, on the other hand, stripped of all possessions belonging to previous classes—property, traditional family ties, "national character"[48]—have no hope of advancing their interest through the existing property relations; they have "nothing to lose but their chains." Revolution is therefore the only course open to them. Furthermore, this abstract proletariat, divested of all its qualities save its function in production, constitutes the "immense majority" of society (even when "the lower middle class, the small manufacturer, the shopkeeper, the artisan, and the peasant" are excluded from it).[49] For this reason, the proletariat can do what no previous class could do: it can act on behalf of society as a whole.

Marx gives the proletariat several options concerning the method of struggle, depending on the nature of prevailing social conditions. Although in all cases a workers' party should be formed, this party will at some times function through legal, electoral methods, while in other cases illegal tactics will be necessary. The workers' party will present candidates for office, whether or not there are chances for success.[50] Marx entertained the possibility of electoral success in some countries, like England, the United States, and Holland.[51] But, on the other hand, even when the workers' delegates are a minority and can be expected to remain so, they are essential for expressing the proletarian view more effectively and for advancing the revolutionary programme by supporting progressive legislation. Prerevolutionary measures that centralize state power and reform legislation like the Ten Hours Bill are judged to be real advances for the working class that deserve parliamentary support.[52] But even if election is impossible, political action will perform the essential function of placing the proletarian programme before the people.[53] In any case, electoral strategies do not preclude illegal activity, should conditions change, or even simultaneous non-electoral activity. In order to prepare for the violent confrontation which will be likely under most conditions, the workers must form "revolutionary workers' governments, whether in the form of municipal committees and municipal councils or in the form of workers' clubs or workers' committees." They must arm themselves, and select "commanders" and a "general staff."[54]

What kind of experience would the workers gain from participation in a revolutionary movement? Bakunin's answer is that in a libertarian socialist movement the workers learn about non-dominating forms of association through creating and experimenting with forms such as libertarian labour organizations, which put into practice, through the struggle against exploitation, principles of equality and free association. Workers' cooperatives and mutual aid associations, though in themselves incapable of thoroughly transforming society, give the workers invaluable experience in self-management.[55] Marx's answer seems to be that the workers gain experience in political organization. The most valuable product of the class struggle is the growing "organization of the proletarians into a class, and consequently into a political party."[56] As the workers' party gains strength, promoting the necessary centralization of power, it will "compel the democrats... to concentrate the utmost possible productive forces, means of transport, factories, railways, etc., in the hands of the state..."[57] This will prepare the way for the development of productive forces which will occur when the "immediate aim of the Communists," the "conquest of political power by the proletariat," is achieved.[58]

In advocating this "conquest of power," Marx and his followers place themselves in direct opposition to Bakunin and the federalist faction of the workers' movement. In his "Address to the Communist League," he asserts that the workers "must strive... for the most determined centralization of power in the hands of the state authority,"[59] and that it "is the task of the really revolutionary party to carry through the strictest centralization."[60] The programme of the *Communist Manifesto* shows just such a programme of centralization, aimed at the rapid development of production. The proletariat will "centralize all instruments of production in the hands of the State, i.e., of the proletariat organized as the ruling class; and... increase the total of productive forces as rapidly as possible."[61] In "the most advanced countries" the state will assume such exclusive functions as rentier, sole creditor, controller of transportation and communication, owner of factories and means of production (though not all of them at this stage), organizer of "industrial armies, especially for agriculture," and educator through a system of public schools.⁶²

In the "Address to the Communist League" Marx returns to the subject of agricultural production. When feudal property is confiscated, the workers must demand that it "remain state property and be converted into workers' colonies cultivated by the associated rural proletariat with all the advantages of large-scale agriculture."⁶³ The anarchist objection to this programme is that instituting centralized control prevents the peasants from developing a system of free collectivization. Marx replies that the workers "must not allow themselves to be misguided by the democratic talk of freedom for the communities, of self-government, etc.,"⁶⁴ which will be used by the bourgeois democrats for reactionary purposes. Instead, in countries with remnants of feudalism, "it must under no circumstances be permitted that every village, every town and every province should put a new obstacle in the path of revolutionary activity, which can proceed with full force only from the centre."⁶⁵

Marx not only wishes to prevent the peasants from creating obstacles to the revolutionary activity of other, more advanced groups, but also to prevent them from interfering with their own liberation. He discusses this issue in his commentary on *Statism and Anarchy*, advocating a more conservative approach for societies in which the peasants are really small landowners and have a petit bourgeois outlook. Rather than abolishing inheritance or property, the state should try to "win the peasant over" by "improving his position."⁶⁶ But although Bakunin's hopes for such groups were exaggerated, it was among the severely oppressed peasants of southern and eastern Europe that he saw the greatest hope for a libertarian revolution. For these groups Marx prescribes immediate abolition of property and inheritance. The peasants should not be allowed to confiscate the property of landowners and stand in the way of the necessary centralization process.⁶⁷ In either case, according to Marx—whether the peasants are to be gradually "won over" or immediately made employees of the state—this is a matter to be decided not by the agricultural workers themselves, but by the workers' state on their behalf.

Marx argues that such statist, centralist policies do not in fact create a new domination. For as we are informed in the *Communist Manifesto*, "when, in the course of development, class distinctions have disappeared, and all production has been concentrated in the hands of a vast association of the whole nation, the public power will lose its political character."[68] When the proletariat becomes the ruling class, political power will no longer exist, for all will be (or will be in the process of becoming?) proletarians. Since "political power, properly so-called, is merely the organized power of one class for oppressing another,"[69] its existence is impossible in a one class society. The same explanation of the abolition of "political power properly so-called" is presented in *The Poverty of Philosophy*.[70]

Marx was, of course, aware of the contrast between the free, communist society that he saw as the final goal, and the kind of society that he proposes as a transition stage. He begins to develop the concept of transitional society as early as the *Paris Manuscripts* where he refers to an early stage of communism in which abundance has not yet been achieved, the productive forces are in a process of accelerated development, and the conditions stemming from the capitalist mode of production have not yet been superseded. "The community is only a community of *labour* and of equality of *wages* paid out by the communal capital—by the *community* as the universal capitalist."[71] In more concrete detail in the *Critique of the Gotha Program*, Marx discusses the first stages in the emergence of communist society, that is, communist society "not as it has *developed* on its own foundations, but, on the contrary, just as it *emerges* from capitalist society; which is thus in every respect, economically, morally and intellectually, still stamped with the birth marks of the old society from whose womb it emerges."[72] In such a society production is not controlled by individual capitalists and based on exchange regulated by the law of value. Instead, "the same amount of labour" which each worker "has given to society in one form he receives back in another,"[73] with the retention by "society" of deductions for necessary social services. The mechanism for this exchange is a system of labour certificates, in which the certificates are distributed according to hours of labour contributed, again subtracting labour for necessary social purposes. Marx recognizes that although such a system does not establish true equality, since the bourgeois principle of exchange of equivalents is still present, "principle and practice are no longer at loggerheads."[74] Marx runs through the usual, and quite valid, socialist criticisms of such abstract right, showing that it constitutes an illusory equality when the unequal needs and capacities of individuals are considered. Yet he is resigned to the fact that we cannot leap beyond "the economic structure of society and the cultural development conditioned thereby."[75] Only after "the productive forces have also increased with the all-round development of the individual, and the springs of cooperative wealth flow more abundantly"[76] can we reach the higher stages of communist society, when the principles of contribution according to ability and distribution according to need are established, and the realm of freedom finally emerges.

According to Bakunin, however, Marx's proposals lead in an entirely different direction, since Marx misunderstands the nature of political power, and his analysis of class is inadequate. Bakunin holds that those in control of concentrated political power are profoundly affected by their exercise of that power, and that as a group they take on the characteristics of a distinct social class. This will happen even when the rulers have "democratic sentiments or intentions."[77] Social change is not accomplished through mere good intentions, as Marx himself recognizes. Whatever intentions the rulers may have, they are subject to the pervasive effects of their concrete social circumstances. Bakunin argues that we must not forget such "powerful motivating forces" as "institutional positions and their attendant privileges."[78] The goal of social evolution is the abolition of *all* forms of domination, not just economic exploitation. He warns that "political power means domination,"[79] one form of domination can be substituted for another, and if the newest form masquerades as "socialism" and "revolution" it may prove to be even more difficult to displace than were its predecessors.

Bakunin predicts that the application of Marx's proposals will lead to a new stage of capitalist development. While there may be no contradiction between highly developed productive forces and capitalist relations of production, there *is* a contradiction between capitalist relations of production and a working class which is organized and prepared to destroy these relations by means of a social transformation. A revolutionary movement based on a programme of state capitalism can save the day for capitalism. "This new statist system, basing itself on the alleged *sovereignty* of the so-called *will of the people*... incorporates the two necessary conditions for the progress of capitalism: state centralization, and the actual submission of the sovereign people to the intellectual governing minority, who, while claiming to represent the people, unfailingly exploits them."[80] Such a regime will retain hierarchy, since political power will be distributed unequally. Even if formal economic equality were established (which Bakunin doubts will happen, since he expects those with political power to claim economic privileges), economic power would still be unequal, since the control of surplus production would be in the hands of the leaders of the centralized state. The plight of the workers would remain in many ways the same. They would still labour under a regimented, mechanized, hierarchical system of production, without direct control over the product of their labour. The forces controlling society would still seem remote and alien. Workers' powerlessness would only grow as the rulers solidified their class position and as high technology, under centralized control, made the decision-making and production processes increasingly incomprehensible and mystifying.

At this point Bakunin's analysis (whether he realized it or not) is one with that of Marx, insofar as the latter remains true to his critical project. Bakunin, using Marx's critique of bourgeois ideology as the theoretical construct which both legitimates and veils the power relations of capitalist society, extends this critique to Marxism itself which has become the ideology of a developing social class, a new class whose power is rooted in the growth of centralized planning and specialized technique. On the one hand, this technobureaucratic class absorbs and expands the functions of previous bureaucracies, and utilizes statist ideology, which prevents political domination as necessary for social order, to legitimate its existence. But, on the other hand, this class incorporates the new hierarchy and domination created by high technology and legitimated by the ideology of productivity and economic growth. The result is a highly integrated system of planning and control, which can bypass the long process of achieving the level of order and stability found in societies in which technobureaucratic functions continue to be distributed among competing systems of power and authority. Bakunin's originality is in his recognition, at a very early stage, of both the political-bureaucratic aspects and the scientific-technical side of such a structure, and in his perception of the nature of its legitimating underpinnings.

"The State," Bakunin asserts, "has always been the patrimony of some privileged class: a priestly class, an aristocratic class, a bourgeois class. And finally, when all the other classes have exhausted themselves, the State then becomes the patrimony of the bureaucratic class and then falls—or, if you will, rises—to the position of a machine."[81] The revolutionary movement will supply an abundance of aspiring political leaders, bureaucrats, and technocrats. If the movement is itself hierarchical, it will both *attract* individuals who find the career of a revolutionary political leader appealing to their desire for status and position (especially if their ideological commitments or other factors close traditional avenues to power), and it will also *produce* an attachment to power, prestige, and privilege among those who occupy high positions in the movement. When the goal of seizure of state power and further centralization of social institutions is achieved, the revolutionary élite can then take their positions in the expanded hierarchy and recruit new members for the remaining positions.

According to Bakunin, the thing that these aspiring leaders of the toiling masses fear most is revolution itself. For it often happens that a revolutionary upheaval creates participatory, self-managing forms of social organization, forms which threaten all hierarchical power. Bakunin could point to the sections of the French Revolution and the movement toward decentralization and self-management in the Paris Commune. He could now point to the soviets and communes of the Russian Revolution (including the Ukrainian Revolution and the Kronstadt rebellion), the collectives and communes of the Spanish Revolution, the emergence of self-management in the Algerian Revolution, the worker councils of the Hungarian Revolution, and so forth. He could also point to the countries in which libertarian institutions were crushed by the revolutionary leaders, who were able to attain power and consolidate their control. These revolutions failed, not due to "bad" leaders who "betray" the revolutions, but due to the dynamics of centralist, hierarchical movements themselves. He concluded that:

> We are the natural enemies of those revolutionaries—future dictators, regimenters, and custodians of revolution—who, even before today's monarchic, aristocratic and bourgeois States are destroyed, are already longing to create new revolutionary States just as centralist and despotic as those we already know—who are so habituated to the order created from above by authority and so horrified by what they see as disorder (which is in fact nothing but the frank and natural expression of popular life) that even before revolution has produced some good healthy disorder they are already wondering how to halt and muzzle it, by the intervention of some authority which would be revolutionary in name only, but in practice would be nothing more than a new reaction whose effect would be once again to condemn the popular masses to rule by decree and to obedience, stagnation and death, in other words to enslavement and exploitation at the hands of a new quasi-revolutionary aristocracy.[82]

Bakunin makes similar criticisms of authoritarian political movements that seek control through the ballot box. In his view, as the workers begin to send representatives to parliament, "the new worker deputies, transported into a bourgeois environment, living and soaking up all the bourgeois ideas and acquiring their habits, will cease being workers and statesmen and become converted into bourgeois, even more bourgeois-like than the bourgeois themselves."[83] Whether the workers' deputies are a minority in a bourgeois system, or succeed in gaining a majority and capturing power makes no difference. Even if the political rulers were selected from the workers (and this is assuming a lot, considering all the bourgeois defectors who have found their calling as proletarian leaders), they would be "*former* workers, who would stop being workers the moment they became rulers or representatives, and would then come to regard the whole blue-collared world from governmental heights, and would not represent the people but themselves and their pretensions in the government of the people."[84]

The preceding quotation from *Statism and Anarchy* is of particular interest because it elicited a specific reply from Marx in the latter's commentary on Bakunin's book. First, Marx denies that he claims that the representatives of the workers should be workers themselves, but then he argues that if they are workers, they would not lose their proletarian qualities by gaining political position any "more than does a manufacturer today cease to be a capitalist on becoming a town councillor."[85] In other words, if the capitalist, who holds economic power, can assume political power without a fundamental change in outlook, then so can a worker who starts with no power retain his outlook once he gains access to such power. According to Marx, "if Mr Bakunin understood at least the position of a manager in a cooperative factory, all his illusions about domination would go to the devil."[86] But this misses the point of Bakunin's entire analysis. The difference in scale between a factory and a nation-state is immense, and the responsibility held by functionaries is an entirely different question at each level. But even beyond this, one must wonder how much Marx reflected on the problem of decision-making in a cooperative factory. Bakunin's discussion points to dangers which exist even at that level, if the members of the group allow managers and committees to exercise a degree of authority that removes initiative and creative action from the collective. This is a problem that has recently received a great deal of attention in the movement for workers' self-management.[87]

Had Bakunin limited his attack on Marx to a discussion of the dangers of centralization and hierarchical movements for social change, he would have made a significant contribution to the critique of forms of domination. However, his analysis gains further relevance when he deals with the topic of science and technology in relation to the development of state capitalism and the new élite. This analysis helps us uncover the implications of the convergence of two aspects of Marx's thought: his defence of society's need to develop productive forces, and his advocacy of political centralization.

In *God and the State* Bakunin discusses the dangers inherent in a system which unites political power with technical-scientific expertise. He fears that the spontaneity of life will be crushed by the imposition of plans developed "from above" by experts. Having considerable faith in the creative capacities of freely associated individuals, he asserts that life is "an infinitely greater thing than science."[88] He argues that whatever the merits of the centralized plan, it removes creativity and responsibility from each person. In spite of its promises of future liberation, it obstructs the general development of those qualities that are specifically human; it creates "a society, not of men, but of brutes."[89] Furthermore, while he begins his argument by accepting the hypothesis that the plans will be motivated by benevolence ("inspired by the purest love of truth"[90]), he contends that this will not in fact occur. An additional motive, the maintenance of the power and privilege of the planners, will come into play.

These criticisms are in some ways an extension of those made against more traditional forms of bureaucratic domination. However, in the case of technical-scientific control, additional problems arise. One of the most important of these is the mystification of social processes engendered by the vastly increased specialization which takes place under large-scale, high technology. Offering to society the integral education that Bakunin and many other anarchists have advocated, becomes increasingly "impractical." The resulting maldistribution of knowledge, expertise, and control will result in an unprecedented form of domination by the new dominant class of technobureaucrats:

> So there will be no more class, but a government, and please note, an extremely complicated government which, not content with governing and administering the masses politically, like all other governments of today, will also administer them economically, by taking over the production and *fair* sharing of wealth, agriculture, the establishment and development of factories, the organization and control of trade, and lastly the injection of capital into production by a single banker, the State. All this will require vast knowledge and a lot of heads brimful of brains [a reference to a description of Marx by one of his supporters at the Hague Congress]. It will be the reign of the *scientific mind*, the most aristocratic, despotic, arrogant

and contemptuous of all regimes. There will be a new class, a new hierarchy of real or bogus learning, and the world will be divided into a dominant, science-based minority and a vast, ignorant majority. And then let the ignorant masses beware![91]

Just as Bakunin could now point to the undermining of revolutionary developments by centralist, hierarchical tendencies within revolutionary movements, he could also note the emergence of technobureaucratic domination in societies in which the programme of authoritarian socialism has prevailed. The historical importance of Bakunin's critique lies in the fact that while numerous disillusioned Marxists, desperate to hold on to at least some of their illusions, have blamed this monstrous development (reduced to a "deformation") on the betrayal of various individual leaders (guilty of revisionism, right and left "deviations," but never a fundamentally faulty theoretical framework), or on premature action (a securely circular analysis), Bakunin long ago showed that its origins lie, at least in large part, in elements of Marx's own theory: his centralism and his faith in bourgeois technology, the technique of domination.

A recent study of the Soviet political system which sheds light on the interaction between Marxian productivist ideology and the development of the bureaucratic centralist or state capitalist system is Kendall E. Bailes' *Technology and Society under Lenin and Stalin*.[92] Bailes focuses his attention on the position of the "technical intelligentsia" and a smaller "technical élite" within this stratum, both of which are distinguished from groups defined primarily by the exercise of managerial or bureaucratic techniques.[93] Interestingly, he notes that both the party bureaucracy and the technical élite were able to maintain their alliance and legitimate their control through elements of the productivist ideology, including "the belief that mankind could consciously increase the forces of production and manipulate nature to improve the material standard of life."[94] There developed between the two groups a symbiotic relationship in which "the Communist party supplied the machinery of organization—the combination of force with material and moral incentives—to realize more rapidly much of what the technical intelligentsia had only dreamed before the revolution."[95] Similar analyses could be applied to Marxist ideology in other state capitalist societies, as, for example, China, where we see a conflict between the political-bureaucratic and the "pragmatic"-technocratic factions of the technobureaucracy now that the stabilizing factor of the charismatic leader has been removed.[96] Interestingly, the technocratic "Right" can legitimately claim to be restoring an important element of orthodox Marxism, since Maoism, for all its political centralism, bureaucracy, and hierarchy, still retained some elements of decentralism, communalism, and restraints on technical development (mostly in the form of ideological mystifications, but to some degree realized in practice). In analyzing the evolution of state socialist technocracy and bureaucracy we can see not only how orthodox Marxism serves as the ideology of contemporary ruling classes, but even how various components of Marxist ideology serve as ideological tools of opposing factions within these larger groups. Bakunin's critique of Marx (as rudimentary as it may have been in some ways) therefore takes on increasing relevance in the age of bureaucratic state capitalism.

As was pointed out at the beginning of this discussion, the primary concern here is that part of Marx's thought which is most relevant to his dispute with Bakunin, and which has been the aspect that has exerted the greatest influence on history. This is certainly not to deny that there is another side to Marx, a side that one might well wish to have been of more historical importance. Much of his analysis follows his intention of pursuing a dialectical approach, and does not impose on the phenomena a preconceived scheme of economic determination. An excellent example is an unpublished letter to a Russian journal in Geneva, wherein he rejects the attempt to transform his "historical sketch of the genesis of capitalism in Western Europe into an historico-philosophic theory of the general path of development prescribed by fate to all nations, whatever the historical circumstances in which they find themselves...."[97] There are also well-known discussions in which he treats revolutionary activity as much more than a mere product of the development of the productive forces, as in his affirmation of the irreducibility of praxis and critique in the "Theses on Feuerbach."

Furthermore, a definite anti-bureaucratic and anti-statist tendency runs through Marx's thought. In the *Critique of Hegel's Philosophy of Right*, for example, he attacks bureaucracy for its formalism, its secrecy, its authoritarianism, and its promotion of careerism.[98] In *The Eighteenth Brumaire* Marx very perceptively analyzes the dialectical interaction between bourgeois property relations and the rise of bureaucracy, showing how the reciprocal relationship moves society toward atomization, simplification, and the growth of state power: "By its very nature, small-holding property forms a suitable basis for an all-powerful and innumerable bureaucracy. It creates a uniform level of relationships and persons over the whole surface of the land. Hence it also permits uniform action from a supreme centre on all points of this uniform mass. It annihilates the aristocratic intermediate grades between the mass of the people and the state power. On all sides, therefore, it calls forth the direct interference of this state power and the imposition of its immediate organs."[99] It appears, then, that there is ample material in Marx's work to develop a theory of bureaucratic class interest, and of the central role played by bureaucracy in the evolution of the modern authoritarian state.

There is also much evidence of Marx's hostility to the state itself. In the *Critique of the Gotha Program* he attacks LaSalle's "servile belief in the state,"[100] and he advocates independence of schools from state domination. What is more, his opposition to the state is clear not only in his ultimate goal of a stateless society, but also in his approach to the historical events of the Paris Commune. In *The Civil War in France* Marx favours the Commune and its decentralist, anti-hierarchical programmes, including the abolition of the standing army, destruction of bureaucracy, direct democracy, recall of officials, and municipal liberty. The state is left with only a few functions, while the question of whether the various communes to be established throughout France should be forced to join in regional and national unions is judiciously avoided (federalism was, after all, a strong current among the Communards).[101] For many readers, the overall impression of the work has been that Marx was presenting a strongly anti-authoritarian position.

Clearly, Marx's thought presents a powerful critique of the state and bureaucracy, and possesses certain decentralist elements. But also, clearly, if the totality of his thought (with all the presuppositions, categories and problematics that are inadequately synthesized therein) is considered, Marx was attached to centralist and authoritarian structures which are inseparable from statist and bureaucratic forms of domination. To have rejected that attachment, Marx would have also had to reject the logic of productivism which gives a structural framework to his programme for social transformation. It is true that Marx could argue that if this logic is valid, then the state, bureaucracy and the entire framework of domination would soon come crashing down. The development of productive forces under the restraints of the capitalist mode of production would lead to a growing consciousness of exploitation. This consciousness of exploitation would lead to the growth of organization of the proletariat. This development of political organization would lead to the seizure of state power and the establishment of a proletarian state. The proletarian state would facilitate the unleashing of further productive powers. The further development of the productive forces would create abundance, the abolition of toil, and the dissolution of the age-old repressive mechanisms under which humanity has laboured and agonized. Thus we would reach the realm of freedom.

But this scheme reveals the enormous leap of faith that Marx proposes. With his almost unbounded faith in the liberating potentialities inherent in material progress, Marx was able to dismiss the spectre of renewed domination conjured up by critics like Bakunin. As he contends in the 1852 edition of *The Eighteenth Brumaire*, centralization only produces domination so long as it plays a part in the development of bourgeois society. In a revolutionary society centralization will not lead to the growth of bureaucracy, nor will bureaucratization be necessary to achieve centralization. "The demolition of the state machine will not endanger centralization. Bureaucracy is only the low and brutal form of centralization that is still afflicted with its opposite, with feudalism."[102] The possibility that even greater centralization and technological development could generate a new bureaucratism having little or nothing to do with feudal remnants is too great a threat to Marx's assumptions about historical progress to receive serious attention. Faced with such a possibility Marx is forced to resort to the most blatant ideological blocking, shown by the abuse and ridicule he heaps on Bakunin in place of a confrontation with the content of the latter's arguments. With the victory of the proletariat, centralization *cannot* lead to bureaucratic despotism. One who thinks so can only be "a charlatan and an ignoramus!"

Similar "utopianism" shows in Marx's anti-statism. Marx notes that at times the state is capable of developing a "relative autonomy"—opening the way to interpret political domination as part of a larger system of domination, as a totality within a greater totality, displaying immanent processes of development, yet interacting with the other parts of a larger system. Yet Marx refuses to allow this aspect of his theory of the state to develop. As Miliband points out in regard to both Marx and Engels, "despite the refinements and qualifications they occasionally introduced in their discussion of the state—notably to account for a certain degree of independence which they believed the state could enjoy in 'exceptional circumstances'—they never departed from the view that in capitalist society the state was above all the coercive instrument of a ruling class, itself defined in terms of its ownership of the means of production."[103] The decision for this model of the state avoids the challenge posed by the alternative one to both the productivist conception of liberation and to the strategy of centralist politics. The dangers of statism can then be limited to the prerevolutionary era of economic class conflict, and the troubling spectre of domination of the masses under socialism can be exorcised. As a result, the concentration of economic and political power in the centralized state can be reconciled with the most thorough-going "anti-statism."

This utopian rather than practical nature of Marx's anti-bureaucratism and anti-statism explains his apparent libertarianism in regard to the Paris Commune. In view of the enormous working-class sympathy for the Commune, it was politically expedient for Marx to ally himself strongly with it, in spite of his irreconcilable differences with the Blanquist and mutualist elements found in its most active factions. Furthermore, he could not fail to be moved by its working class character, its heroism, and its tragic end. Yet he hedged a bit from the beginning. Its "true secret," that it was a working class government[104] rather than a libertarian project, was seen as the basis for its great historical importance. In the first outline of his analysis Marx notes that the Commune was necessary because "the centralized and organized governmental power" was "the master instead of the servant of society."[105] The validity of centralized government *per se* is, of course, not questioned. Ten years later, in a letter to Domela-Nieuwenhuis, he concludes that "this was merely the rising of a city under exceptional conditions, the majority of the Commune was in no wise socialist, nor could it be."[106] The best strategy, he says, would have been a compromise with Versailles.[107] In view of such statements, and more importantly, in the context of Marx's consistent advocacy of centralist programmes, and the part these programmes play in his theory of social development, the attempt to construct a *libertarian* Marxism by citing Marx's own proposals for social change would seem to present insuperable difficulties.

Still, Marx's method of dialectical analysis and critique of ideology united with a political programme which finds inspiration in favourable judgements on the Paris Commune (or what some would like to think Marx approved of in the Commune) holds great appeal. Whether the result is really Marxism or not, the position seems in many ways more in the spirit of Bakunin than of Marx. While it is quite possible to construct a Marxism which derives its essential presuppositions and proposals for organization from the work of Marx himself, ignoring the implications of his critical and dialectical methodology, it may very well be impossible to pursue the anarchist project—the critique and transcendence of all forms of domination—without adopting this aspect of Marx's position. Whatever the limitations of Bakunin's viewpoint, this is, in fact, what he was doing when he argued for a more dialectical approach to the dynamics of political power and technological development, and for extending the critique of ideology to the emergence of technobureaucracy.

Notes

1. Karl Marx, *The Holy Family* (Moscow: Progress Publishers, 1956), p. 44.
2. *Ibid.*
3. *Ibid.*, pp. 44-45.
4. Marx and Engels, *German Ideology, op. cit.*, Chapter 2, p. 73.
5. *Ibid.*, p. 20.
6. *Ibid.*, p. 24.
7. Marx, *Poverty of Philosophy, op. cit.*, Chapter 2, p. 151.
8. Tucker, *op. cit.*, Chapter 2, p. 340.
9. *Ibid.*, p. 347.
10. *Ibid.*, p. 345.
11. Marx, *Grundrisse, op. cit.*, Chapter 2, p. 708.
12. See *Paths in Utopia* (New York: Scribner, 1958). Anarchist theory has been greatly enriched by the development of the communal anarchist tradition. To appreciate this development as reflected in anarchist theory, one should begin by tracing its elaboration in the works of Charles Fourier, Peter Kropotkin, Gustav Landauer, Martin Buber, and Murray Bookchin.
13. Lehning, *op. cit.*, Chapter 2, p. 101. Bakunin is, of course, using the term "socialist" to mean "libertarian socialist."
14. *Ibid.*, p. 102. Bakunin's view thus aims at a synthesis of the general and particular interests. It has nothing in common with the self-contradictory egoist "anarchism" of Stirner. For a detailed critique of Stirner and egoist "anarchism" see my book *Max Stirner's Egoism* (London: Freedom Press, 1976).
15. As Axelos notes, Marx moves toward, but does not develop, the idea that human activity must enter into the dimension of play, a conclusion which would have been difficult to reconcile with his instrumentalist model of human action (Axelos, pp. 257-58). Yet this is exactly the direction in which anarchist thought has been tending, although it is a long path from Bakunin's confused amalgam of creative joy and revolutionary renunciation to Bookchin's call for the transformation of "labor into play and need into desire." *Post-Scarcity Anarchism* (Montréal: Black Rose Books, 1977), p. 41. For another contemporary anarchist discussion, see Paul Goodman's analysis of artistic activity and play as related to the concept of organismic self-regulation in F. Perls, R. Hefferline and P. Goodman, *Gestalt Therapy* (New York: Dell Publishing Co., 1951), Vol. II.
16. Lehning, *op. cit.*, p. 270.
17. Bakunin, *God and the State, op. cit.*, Chapter 2, p. 106.

18. Lehning, *op. cit.*, p. 66.
19. Dolgoff, *Bakunin on Anarchism, op. cit.*, Chapter 2, p. 319.
20. *Ibid.*, p. 289.
21. Lehning, *op. cit.*, pp. 254-55.
22. *Ibid.*, p. 170. Bakunin here uses the word "authority" to signify "externally imposed authority." He often uses the word loosely for rhetorical purposes, but in his more thoughtful discussions he distinguishes more carefully between valid and invalid authority.
23. *Ibid.*, p. 246. This point is especially important in relation to later discussion of workers' councils. Bakunin is pointing out difficulties which can arise even within this system of economic organization. However, he would certainly see the councilist movement as a major advance in socialist development.
24. *Ibid.*, p. 247.
25. *Ibid.*, pp. 247-48.
26. See, for example, Gaston Leval, *Collectives in the Spanish Revolution* (London: Freedom Press, 1975). It has been argued that the greatest failing of the CNT, the Spanish anarcho-syndicalist labour movement (which should be distinguished from the collectives), was its departure during the Spanish Civil War from some of the principles set forth by Bakunin (among others) and adopted early in the movement's history. Thus, it failed to combat bureaucratic and élitist tendencies adequately, and to keep power firmly rooted in the direct democratic assemblies of the workers. As a result it allowed "influential militants" to enter into a coalition government "temporarily," so that the war could be won. See Vernon Richards, *Lessons of the Spanish Revolution* (London: Freedom Press, 1972), for a devastating critique of this "anarchist" strategy from an anarchist perspective.
27. Lehning, *op. cit.*, p. 172.
28. *Ibid.*, p. 180.
29. *Ibid.*
30. *Ibid.*, p. 172.
31. *Ibid.*, p. 190.
32. *Ibid.*, p. 191.
33. Bakunin's vanguardism has been repudiated by almost all of the historical anarchist movement. Yet this tendency has occasionally reappeared, as, for example, in the "Soviet anarchists" (a minority of Russian anarchists who participated in the "temporary" Bolshevik dictatorship), to a degree in the "Organizational Platform of the Libertarian Communists," and, perhaps

most significantly, in the vanguardist faction of the CNT, to mention the most important examples.
34. Maximoff, *op. cit.*, p. 280.
35. Dolgoff, *Bakunin on Anarchism*, *op. cit.*, p. 310.
36. Maximoff, *op. cit.*, pp. 404-05. Whatever the merits of Bakunin's arguments in other areas, he seemed greatly over-optimistic in his attempts to apply these ideas to the French peasantry. Marx's analysis in the *Eighteenth Brumaire* (footnote 99) seems much more convincing.
37. See Sam Dolgoff, ed., *The Anarchist Collectives* (Montréal: Black Rose Books, 1974); Leval's *Collectives in the Spanish Revolution*, and Augustine Souchy's works in German, French, and Spanish on collectivization.
38. For an example of such an analysis of the Russian Revolution, see Voline, *The Unknown Revolution* (Montréal: Black Rose Books, 1975).
39. Eugene Pyzuir, *The Doctrine of Anarchism of Michael A. Bakunin* (Chicago: Gateway Editions, 1955).
40. Lehning, *op. cit.*, p. 58. It is seldom mentioned that he was not yet an anarchist when he said it in a remarkable essay of 1842, "The Reaction in Germany."
41. *Ibid.*, p. 67.
42. Although Bakunin's collectivism and syndicalism are often contrasted with the communism of Kropotkin and later anarchists, Bakunin also saw the ultimate goal as a free federation of *communes*.
43. Karl Marx, Frederick Engels, and V.I. Lenin, *Anarchism and Anarcho-syndicalism* (New York: International Publishers, 1972), p. 152.
44. Lehning, *op. cit.*, pp. 71-72.
45. *Ibid.*, p. 96.
46. *Ibid.*, p. 67.
47. Tucker, *op. cit.*, p. 344.
48. *Ibid.*
49. *Ibid.*
50. *Ibid.*, p. 370.
51. Marx, Engels and Lenin, *Anarchism and Anarcho-syndicalism*, *op. cit.*, p. 84.
52. Tucker, *op. cit.*, p. 379.
53. *Ibid.*, p. 370.
54. *Ibid.*, p. 369.
55. In this emphasis on the interrelationship between prerevolutionary experience, the development of consciousness, and rev-

olutionary self-activity, Bakunin and anarchist theory exhibit their grasp of the significance of the question of whether, as Lukács aptly formulates it, the revolutionary movement "experiences the crisis as object or subject of decision." *History and Class Consciousness* (Cambridge: M.I.T. Press, 1971), p. 244.
56. Tucker, *op. cit.*, p. 343.
57. *Ibid.*, p. 372.
58. *Ibid.*, p. 346.
59. *Ibid.*, p. 371.
60. *Ibid.*, pp. 371-72.
61. *Ibid.*, p. 352.
62. *Ibid.*
63. *Ibid.*, p. 371.
64. *Ibid.*
65. *Ibid.*
66. Marx, Engels and Lenin, *Anarchism and Anarcho-syndicalism, op. cit.*, p. 148.
67. *Ibid.*
68. Tucker, *op. cit.*, p. 352.
69. *Ibid.*
70. Marx, *Poverty of Philosophy, op. cit.*, Chapter 2, p. 151.
71. Marx, *Economic and Philosophical Manuscripts of 1844, op. cit.*, Chapter 2, footnote 89, p. 89.
72. Tucker, *op. cit.*, p. 386.
73. *Ibid.*, p. 387.
74. *Ibid.*
75. *Ibid.*, p. 388.
76. *Ibid.*
77. Dolgoff., *Bakunin on Anarchism, op. cit.*, p. 221.
78. *Ibid.*, p. 388.
79. *Ibid.*
80. Dolgoff, *Bakunin on Anarchism, op. cit.*, pp. 336-37.
81. *Ibid.*, p. 318. Bakunin's analysis is thus consistent with the emergence of a technobureaucratic class, not only as established through authoritarian socialist movements, but also as such a class grows within bourgeois society and challenges the hegemony of the traditional bourgeoisie itself. An important discussion of this development and its peculiar means of ideological legitimation is presented by Clauss Offe in "Political Authority and Class Structures—An Analysis of Late Capitalist Societies," in *International Journal of Sociology* II: 73-105.
82. Lehning, *op. cit.*, p. 169.
83. Dolgoff, *Bakunin on Anarchism, op. cit.*, p. 172.

84. Lehning, *op. cit.*, p. 269.
85. Marx, Engels and Lenin, *Anarchism and Anarcho-syndicalism, op. cit.*, p. 151.
86. *Ibid.*
87. For example, it is a criticism made against some aspects of the Yugoslav system. For an incisive critique of Yugoslav "self-management," including an analysis of the growth of inequality, hierarchy, and technocracy, see Antonio Carlo, "Capitalist Restoration and Social Crisis in Yugoslavia" in *Telos* 36: 81-110. Unfortunately, the article concludes with a reaffirmation of the administrative mentality, which seeks a reconciliation of "binding macro-economic policies and micro-economic autonomy" (p. 109). We are to look for evidence of the possibility of such a reconciliation in the "Chinese case," which, we are told, " is founded on strong central guidance and on a remarkable autonomy at the peripheral level" (*Ibid.*). Even if we did not have increasing evidence of the centralist and bureaucratic nature of the Chinese system, the illusory quality of such a "solution" is disclosed in the beautifully ironic conception of "an autonomous periphery."
88. Bakunin, *God and the State, op. cit.*, p. 30.
89. *Ibid.*, p. 31.
90. *Ibid.*, p. 30.
91. Lehning, *op. cit.*, p. 266.
92. (Princeton: Princeton University Press, 1978).
93. *Ibid.*, pp. 3-4.
94. *Ibid.*, p. 409.
95. *Ibid.*, p. 417.
96. See Lee Yu See and Wu Che, "Some Thoughts on the Chinese Revolution" in The 70s, ed., *China: The Revolution is Dead-Long Live the Revolution* (Montréal: Black Rose Books, 1977), pp. 242-47.
97. Marx and Engels, *Selected Correspondence* (Moscow: Progress Publishers, 1975), p. 293. Unfortunately, even this affirmation of the "theory of discontinuous social formations," as exemplified by Marx's treatment of the fate of the ancient Roman economy (p. 294), while it implies a rejection of the most simplistic versions of technological and economic determinism, does not constitute a denial of more sophisticated, yet still inadequate, base-superstructure models. Neither does it conflict with the affirmation of the project of liberation through productive development.

98. Karl Marx, *Critique of Hegel's 'Philosophy of Right'* (Cambridge: Cambridge University Press, 1971).
99. Karl Marx, *The Eighteenth Brumaire of Louis Bonapart* (New York: International Publishers, 1963), pp. 128-29.
100. Tucker, *op. cit.*, p. 397.
101. Marx and Engels, *On the Paris Commune* (Moscow: Progress Publishers, 1971), pp. 72-4.
102. Marx, *Eighteenth Brumaire, op. cit.*, p. 148.
103. Ralph Miliband, *The State in Capitalist Society* (New York: Basic Books, 1969), p. 5. See *The German Ideology*, pp. 59-60, for a clear statement of the position.
104. Marx and Engels, *On the Paris Commune, op. cit.*, p. 75.
105. *Ibid.*, p. 153.
106. *Ibid.*, p. 293.
107. *Ibid.* Furthermore, as Murray Bookchin notes, even when Marx made statements in support of the Commune, what he supported is not as libertarian as is sometimes supposed. In praising the synthesis of the executive and the legislative under the Commune, Marx advocated a structure which "simply identified the process of policy-making, a function that rightly should belong to the people in assembly, with the technical execution of these policies, a function that could be left to strictly administrative bodies subject to rotation, recall, limitations of tenure, and, whenever possible, selection by sortition" (*Telos* 36: 6).

Chapter 4

Marxism and Technology

> The atom contains within itself a mighty hidden energy, and the greatest task of physics consists of pumping out this energy, pulling out the cork so that this hidden energy may burst out in a fountain. Then the possibility will be opened up of replacing coal and oil by atomic energy, which will also become the basic motive power. This is not at all a hopeless task. And what prospects it opens before us! This alone gives us the right to declare that scientific and technical thought is approaching a great turning point, that the revolutionary epoch in the development of human society will be accompanied by a revolutionary epoch in the sphere of the cognition of matter and the mastering of it... Unbounded technical possibilities will open out before liberated mankind.[1]
>
> <div align="right">Leon Trotsky, <i>Radio, Science, Technique and Society</i></div>

Today we are coming to a new understanding of the problem of technology. Of course, we have for generations recognized a problem of technology: that is, the problem of how best to develop the predominating technical forms of Western society, and thus to assure the continued march of "progress." But today our assumptions about progress through industrialization, mechanization and technical growth are losing their self-evident character. For we are beginning to see that the unrestrained growth of production, the increased development of high technology, and the intensified exploitation of nature are inexorably leading us toward disaster. It becomes even more obvious that the kind of technological development on which Western society has long depended, and in which it has had so much faith, is resulting in unprecedented degradation of both the natural and social environments. Accordingly, we have seen in the past decade the rapid growth of a movement to combat these tendencies, and to offer to humanity an alternative view of nature, humanity and the future.

In fact there have always been movements of protest against the reigning technological ideology. Early in the Industrial Revolution the Luddites—some of the first radical workers—chose to smash the dehumanizing machinery being imposed on them, rather than submit to domination and degradation in the name of technical progress. Writers like Charles Fourier and William Morris—so called "utopians"—presented visions of a society based on enjoyment, aesthetic values and free association, while condemning the evils of industrialization. Numerous intentional communities were formed in order to seek ways of putting this vision into practice. It is the communal anarchist tradition that perhaps best developed this critique of industrialism, proposing the replacement of the capitalist state and the industrial system by self-managed, decentralized communites, technology of human scale, and non-alienating forms of labour. Yet it is only with the growth and evolution of the ecology movement of recent years that it has been possible to formulate an adequate critique of industrialism, based on a comprehensive vision of organic interrelationships and non-domination.

In presenting this critique, the ecology movement represents a departure from the mainstream of theory and historical practice in Western society. The reigning ideology has identified the growth of high technology and quantitative productivity with progress. What is necessary, according to orthodox Western view, is the amassing of greater *knowledge* of the laws of nature, which can then be used for greater *control* over nature and *exploitation* of its resources. The relationship between humanity and nature is seen as one of struggle and antagonism. We must subjugate nature first, in order to assure our very survival, and then to go on to the production of an abundance of material goods, which is judged necessary for the attainment of human welfare. As knowledge and technique develop, we come ever closer to the goal of conquest (or defeat) of nature, and conversely, the victory of humanity. The achievements of past epochs are seen as inept and futile strivings toward this goal, for it is only the massive, powerful technology of the Industrial Revolution which has brought within view the era of the final subjugation of nature, and the possibility of a developed world society. But this is not yet achieved, and our future success will depend on the degree to which we fully perfect the methods of scientific control, and fully develop the potential for productive growth which are the hallmarks of the present age.

This conception of salvation through technique and productivity has, of course, been one of the central ideological supports for capitalism. While capitalism has in reality produced such effects as the degradation of labour, the replacement of human relationships by commodity relationships, the dissolution of communal ties, the atomization of society, the bureaucratization of life, and the growing destruction of the natural environment, all this has been hidden and justified by a consistently higher level of material productivity which has been interpreted ideologically as "improvement of the standard of living." In spite of occasional protests by "romantics," "utopians," anarchists and assorted schizophrenics, this ideology of technological progress has dominated political discourse in the modern period, and has entered deeply into the popular consciousness (or rather, the mass unconsciousness). So thorough has been this ideological domination that even movements of apparent opposition to the prevailing economic and social systems have failed to make a break with it. As the following discussion will show, "even" Marxism, which claims to be a revolutionary theory (in fact the final revolutionary theory), shares with capitalism a deep commitment to the technological values of industrialism. An examination of the presuppositions of Marxism will show the limitations of this pseudo-revolutionary view of technology, and point to the need for a truly revolutionary critique based on ecological principles.

Marx

A technological utopianism lies at the heart of Marx's theory of human liberation. As we have seen in detail in the preceding chapters, he presents a view of history in which social transformation is seen as the result of contradictions which arise between the forces and relations of production. The social revolution that takes place in order to resolve these contradictions can take place only when the existing mode of production has developed its forces of production to the limit of its capacity to do so. Up to that point the prevailing mode of production plays a progressive role in history. The conclusion follows that capitalism has been a progressive mode of production, that all previous modes of production have been "lower," and that a "higher" system of social relationships can be established only when all the "beneficial" tasks of capitalism have been carried out.

Of course it is no less true that Marx, in his examination of the capitalist mode of production, goes to great lengths to show the evils which it entails. He does this eloquently and brilliantly in his discussion in the *Paris Manuscripts* of the forms of alienation produced by capital, demonstrating that under the capitalist mode of production the worker is alienated from him/herself, from the species, and from nature. The creation of the human essence through labour is subordinated to the demands of capital accumulation, to the enslavement of all by reified commodities, and for the most degraded of the workers, to the mere struggle for survival. No less eloquently does he show in *Capital* the true immiseration of the proletariat by the destructive power of capital, whether this be through the literal driving of the workers to misery and material deprivation in the classical period of capital accumulation that he observed first-hand, or the enduring domination of the commodity and exchange value over human values and human needs. Yet what must be remembered in reading Marx is that this entire disgusting history of exploitation and domination is presented as a *necessary* and *progressive* stage in the development of the productive forces. For all its evils, capitalism and the system of dehumanizing high technology to which it gave birth are a necessary means toward human liberation. Far from condemning the system of technology which capitalism developed, Marx contends that it must be *even further expanded*. The failing of capitalism does not lie in the inherent destructiveness and inhumanity of its technology, but in its incapacity to develop further *this form of technology*. Marx has nothing but disdain for those "utopians" and unscientific socialists who call for the immediate replacement of this technology with less dehumanizing, less manipulative and less hierarchical forms. For they make the error of confusing an emancipating technology with the enslaving economic system which prevents its full development.

According to this view, the socialist revolution will willingly inherit capitalist technology and remove the economic and political barriers to the growth of productive powers (i.e., production for capitalist profit and the necessary support for capitalist production—the bourgeois state). Under such a system, humans are reduced to functionaries whose activity is determined by the nature of the technological system which makes possible expanded production, and creative activity is replaced by attending to the functioning of technology in which "the human being comes to relate more as a watchman and regulator of the production process itself."[2] What Marx hopes is that such a system, for all its evils, will allow such a wealth of production that labour time will be reduced to a minimum, and human freedom can be achieved in the realm of free time.

In view of this boundless faith in high technology Marx logically sees the expansion of this development through imperialism as another progressive aspect of capitalism. No country can be ready for socialism if it is not first endowed with the benefits of capitalist production. It has been shown how he applies this analysis to the Westernization of India by the British, and he wishes the same fate on the other non-Westernized societies of the world. For it is one of the historic missions of capitalism to save these societies from what he condescendingly sees as the "idiocy of rural life." This attitude extends even to the most libertarian and communalist of primitive societies. Far from seeing any enduring value in the cultures of non-Western peoples, in the reverence for nature, the cultural richness, the aesthetic achievements, the non-authoritarian family and social structures that so many exhibit, he sees only one thing—backwardness in social and technological development. Marx's goal can be summarized as follows: to continue the path of technological development initiated by capitalism, while removing the fetters placed on technological growth by the capitalist mode of production.

The result of Marx's proposals is quite clear, and he makes no attempt to hide the result. What he advocates is a system of *state capitalism* based on a programme of development of capitalist technology. As he explains in the *Critique of the Gotha Program*, the state must in the transition period become the owner of the means of production and pay all according to the amount of labour they perform, with deductions for social consumption organized by the state. Since Marx was blind to the possibility that concentration of economic, political and technological power in the state would lead to new forms of bureaucratic and technocratic domination, he ignores the possibility that the surplus production taken from the producers by the state will be used to institute new forms of entrenched hierarchical power. According to his utopian productivist outlook, the only barrier to liberation is economic exploitation by private capitalists, and once this form of exploitation is eliminated, the only problem is to develop production under the proletarian dictatorship.

Unfortunately for Marx, we can now see the bankruptcy of his entire productivist centralist programme. We know that the supposed inability of capitalism to further develop the productive forces is entirely illusory, and that it is in fact capable of increasing production to the extent of exhausting many of the resources it extracts from nature, even to the point of inundating the biosphere with the waste products of this production. The idea of a "socialism" that would unshackle such a technology for even greater exploitation of nature now becomes ludicrous, not to mention grotesque and terrifying. Furthermore, we have come to see that development in capitalist production does not necessarily lead to greater consciousness of exploitation, but often rather to a greater legitimacy for capitalism and the bourgeois state, as long as the ideology of consumption and material progress reigns over society. Where Marx was wrong was in his mythology of technological liberation, but where he was certainly correct was in his analysis of the ideological domination achieved by subordinating all values to those of commodity consumption. A valid development of Marx's critique of ideology extends it to domination through technological and statist ideology also. Such a critique points to the need for a revolutionary movement based on a rejection of capitalist technology and authoritarian political power, and demands the immediate institution of forms of social interaction and organization which replace hierarchy, manipulation and regimentation with cooperation, mutual aid and non-dominating relationships. This is, of course, the precise development foreseen by anarchism, and is the political correlate of the ecology movement.

It is not surprising that Marxism has moved in a quite different direction, and has in fact only intensified the productivist, centralist and authoritarian tendencies of Marx himself, while diluting or eliminating the most critical and dialectical aspects of his thought. The best evidence of this conclusion is the history of this century, in which we have seen so-called socialist states invariably develop systems of bureaucratic and technological control, and institute policies aimed at the development of high technology and centralized planning. In every case, although ideology has denied the truth of this concrete historical development, the reality has been clear. Whatever doubt remains now should be dispelled as the Maoist myth crumbles and the illusion of "decentralism" and "communalism" under state capitalism and bureaucratic centralist administration reveals itself for what it is: blatant ideological mystification.

Some Marxist-Leninists would like to disassociate themselves from the technocratic and bureaucratic excesses of the various "workers' states," and certainly those who wish to justify their precarious position within the ecology movement must attempt to do so. Otherwise it might appear to some understandably sceptical observers that they in fact have nothing in common with the aspirations of the ecologically minded and that their vocal and conspicuous presence in the movement is motivated by blatant opportunism. (If your efforts at creating your own mass movement have been pathetic failures, find someone else's movement and try to lead *it*.) Although this view has, I believe, more than a particle of truth in it, it is not an adequate explanation of the presence of Marxist-Leninists within the anti-nuclear struggle, the present focus of activism within the ecology movement. For there are consistent reasons for Marxist-Leninists to oppose nuclear power, just as there are for liberal capitalists to do so. A liberal capitalist can specifically reject the human costs of nuclear energy while remaining oblivious to the enormous human costs entailed in the entire capitalist system with its exploitative and destructive system of technology. Similarly, a good Marxist-Leninist can be appalled by the dangers of nuclear power, which, after all, is produced for the sake of capitalist profit and in order to support capitalism's legitimating process of increased commodity consumption. Yet this same person might fully support capitalist technology when used by a "true" worker's state, and might, in fact, judge the costs of nuclear energy itself quite differently if it were at the service of socialist development.

In short, the anti-nuclear movement is not a fully ecologically conscious movement, but rather a coalition of diverse elements, many of which are far from accepting the ecological view of reality, and are, in many respects, positively antagonistic to it. The latter is the case with orthodox Marxist-Leninists. Since many Leninist sectarians wish to disassociate themselves from the ruthless industrialization, bureaucracy and technocracy of the varieties of Stalinism, I would like to continue with a discussion of the technological theories of two supposedly less degenerated figures in the Marxist-Leninist pantheon, Lenin himself and Trotsky.

Lenin

Lenin is the key figure in tracing the transformation of Marxist productivist practice. Under his guidance, the Bolshevik party, the vanguard of the technobureaucracy, understood the development of the Soviet economy according to the principles formulated by Marx. (This is not, of course, to say that Marxist ideology was the *cause* of the historical development, but rather that the ideology performed a legitimating function in the rise of the technobureaucracy and was one important factor in the determination of the precise form of historical development taking place.) Lenin fully accepts Marx's position concerning the centrality of economics to social transformation. More specifically, he adheres to the view that a contradiction between the forces and relations of production underlies revolutionary change, and that the productive forces of a given epoch must be fully developed to the capacities of a given mode of production before humanity can move on to a higher level of development. Lenin noted that if the productive forces had not been developed to their limit in advanced capitalist countries, they were in a positively primitive state of development in Russia, a peasant society which had not even gone through a period of bourgeois revolution and liberal capitalism, as in Western Europe. For this reason drastic measures were seen as necessary.

Lenin's solution to the problem of backwardness was to institute a form of state capitalism in which capitalist industrialization was to be accomplished by the centralized actions of the "workers' state" rather than by a multitude of capitalists, as in the liberal capitalist era. Thus, in *The Tax in Kind* Lenin explains that the "working class" must learn "to organize large-scale production along state capitalist lines."[3] Like all orthodox Marxists, Lenin rejected forms of communism which existed in tribal societies, or those proposed by anarchists and libertarian socialists, for these are based on such "utopian" conceptions as decentralization, diversity, smaller scale technology, communal and workplace self-management, and a rejection of regimented patterns of work—all of which are alien to Lenin's productivist mentality. "Socialism," he says, "is inconceivable without large-scale capitalist engineering based on the latest discoveries of modern science. It is inconceivable without planned state organization which keeps tens of millions of people to the strictest observance of a unified standard in production and distribution. We Marxists have always spoken of this, and it is not worthwhile wasting two seconds talking to people who do not understand even this (anarchists and a good half of the Left Socialist Revolutionaries)."[4] So much less would he spend a second listening to them!

One of Lenin's primary goals was to make certain that the Soviet economy would be firmly based on such a system of high technology with centralized planning. Accordingly, he argues that the "chief content" and the "chief condition" for the success of his state capitalist revolution is "the new and higher organization of production and distribution on the basis of large-scale machine [labour] production"[5] (*Six Theses on the Immediate Tasks of the Soviet Government*). To achieve this, "the transformation of the whole of the state economic mechanism into a single huge machine" so as "to enable hundreds of millions of people to be guided by a single plan" is essential[6] (*Extraordinary 7th Congress of the R.C.P. (B.)*). Identifying industrialization and mechanization with progress, Lenin finds German state capitalism a worthy model. All that is needed is the German industrial system combined with a state of different class composition. Germany is "the last word" in modern large-scale capitalist engineering and planned organization, *subordinated to Junker-bourgeois imperialism.*" Cross out the last phrase, Lenin remarks, and substitute "a proletarian state, and you will have the *sum total* of the conditions necessary for socialism."[7] Ironically, this exercise in Bolshevik simple-mindedness comes from an essay on what Lenin calls "Left-wing Childishness," a paradigm of non-dialectical analysis put forth by an alleged champion of "dialectics."

The ideologist of high technology has to make an apology in favour of the hierarchical and manipulative character of such a system of production as he argues that his followers should accept the temporary necessity of administration by bourgeois experts. In *The Immediate Tasks of the Soviet Government* he explains the need for higher wages temporarily paid to these experts. Yet "the sooner we ourselves, workers and peasants, learn the best labour discipline and the most modern technique of labour, using the bourgeois experts to teach us, the sooner we shall liberate ourselves from any tribute to these specialists."[8] What Lenin fails to mention is that under a hierarchical system of production, tribute must continue to be paid to some class of "experts" or "specialists" and long after the "bourgeois" variety are in their graves, power will be in the hands of a new class of technocrats who will hide their power not only under the guise of "science" but also under that of "the proletariat."

Lenin's commitment to mechanization and high technology is not limited to introducing heavy machinery and large-scale production units. In addition, he praises the technology of control of human activity, which goes under the name of "scientific management" or Taylorism. In this typically Marxist view, the major fault of Taylorism is its use for capitalist ends, not in its destruction of creativity, autonomy and human relationships. These later short-comings are, of course, recognized, but are justified by "historical necessity." So, says Lenin, in *The Immediate Tasks of the Soviet Government*, "we must raise the question of piece-work and apply and test it in practice; we must raise the question of applying much of what is scientific and progressive in the Taylor system..."[9] This "progressive" side means progressive from the standpoint of maximizing "socialist" productivity through such measures as "analyzing mechanical motions during work, the elimination of superfluous and awkward motions, the elaboration of correct methods of work, the introduction of the best system of accounting and control, etc."[10]

Nothing is more obvious from Lenin's view of planning, industry and technology than that in him we find the supreme embodiment of the administrative mentality. He has found the key to historical development, the science of revolution, and it is his task and the task of his party to remake society *from above*, to act *upon* society in a way that the "masses" beneath them are utterly incapable of doing for themselves. Liberation can be achieved only through domination: domination of the masses in order to compel them to fulfill their historical destiny, domination of nature in order to reduce it to a resource for expanded production. Not surprisingly, the masses have continued to rebel against this domination, even in Lenin's own "workers' state," sometimes quietly (through sabotage and non-cooperation), sometimes violently (as in the Kronstadt rebellion and the Ukrainian Revolution). Lenin, like the capitalists, knew the definition of a good worker: "Obedience, and unquestioning obedience at that, during work to the one-man decisions of Soviet directors, of the dictators elected or appointed by Soviet institutions, vested with dictatorial powers..."[11] Lenin regrets the fact that his ideal of the perfectly submissive worker has not yet been achieved. And why? "This is the effect of petty-bourgeois anarchy..."

Anarchy: the resistance to domination, manipulation and arbitrary authority; a disease soon to be eliminated from the "revolutionary workers' state" as it triumphantly moves toward "communism."

Trotsky

In some ways, it is hardly worthwhile to examine the technological views of Leon Trotsky, since they are merely a development of themes found in Marx and Lenin, and contain little in the way of new departures or original insights. Yet from another perspective, it is especially important to mention Trotsky. Because of his attacks on Stalinist authoritarianism and bureaucratism, Trotsky has received in some circles a reputation for *anti*-authoritarianism and *anti*-bureaucratism. Yet this reputation is based on a failure to see through the process of ideological mystification, and an examination of Trotsky's views on technology reveals one of the many ways in which he accepts the logic of domination. Furthermore, Trotsky's thought is especially enlightening concerning some aspects of Marxist productivism, since he states in its most blatant form that to which many of his predecessors wisely only alluded. In Trotsky we find vulgar productivism at its most vulgar.

In *The Revolution Betrayed* Trotsky makes the theoretical framework quite clear: "Marxism sets out from the development of technique as the fundamental spring of progress, and constructs the communist programme upon the dynamic of the productive forces."[12] Not being one for understatement, he observes that "Marxism is saturated with the optimism of progress"[13]—not, of course, the "utopian" progress of growing communal consciousness and practice, but rather progress rooted in the concrete development of productive forces. "Socialism has demonstrated its right to victory... not in the language of dialectics [which always remains to him a *foreign* language] but in the language of steel, cement and electricity."[14]

112

Since socialism must justify itself through productive development, there must be practical programmes for the achievement of this development. Here Trotsky reiterates themes developed by Lenin. In *Terrorism and Communism* he goes to great lengths to defend a system of high technology, industrial development, regimentation of work and centralized planning. After presenting the fundamentally anti-Marxist thesis of the inherent laziness of human beings, he goes on to describe the system of militarism of labour which will be essential in order to compell such indolent creatures as humans to perform the work which will be required to raise production to the level necessary for their ultimate liberation. "The widest possible application of the principle of general labour service, together with measures for the militarization of labour, can play a decisive part only in case they are applied on the basis of a single plan covering the whole country and all branches of productive activity. This plan must be drawn up for a number of years, for the whole epoch that lies before us."[15] Needless to say, such a scheme can be achieved only if planning is in the hands of political leaders who are conscious of the laws of history (bureaucrats) and scientists who are knowledgable concerning the laws of nature (technocrats). In fact, as he observes in his presentation of *The Living Thought of Karl Marx*, "the programme of 'Technocracy' which flourished in the period of the great crisis of 1929-1932, was founded on the correct premise that the economy can be rationalized only through the union of technique at the height of science and government at the service of society."[16] The only error of the movement was its failure to see that the government must be a *Marxist-Leninist* one, that "only in unison with a proletarian government can the qualified stratum of technicians build a truly scientific and a truly national, i.e., a socialist economy."[17] It is not without justification that Castoriadis has called the Trotskyist movement "the bureaucracy in exile."

Where Trotsky is most informative is in his revelation of the epistemological assumptions underlying the Marxist view of technique. For he clearly shows that what we are examining is a theory based on a conception of knowledge as domination, lying at the heart of an instrumentalist view of both human society and nature. In *The Fourth International* he explains that "the need to know nature is imposed upon men by their need to subordinate nature to themselves."[18] This relation to nature is emphatically different from that envisioned by ecology, which is one of non-dominating interaction, the interrelationships of inseparable parts of an organic whole. Instead, his is the view of nature inherited from the enlightenment: nature as a field open for conquest by human rationality. Nature is conceived of instrumentally; it is a resource to be used, to be consumed. Trotsky is quite frank about this topic also. As he explains in *The Revolution Betrayed*, "the very purpose of communism is to subject nature to technique and technique to plan, and compel the raw materials to give unstintingly everything to man that he needs."[19] Science is the true vanguard of this revolutionary movement, the revolt against nature, and Trotsky is well aware of this. "Science," he says, "is knowledge that endows us with power."[20]

But nature, as every materialist knows, is not something merely external to humanity. We are a part of nature. Consequently, in dominating nature we not only dominate an "external world"—we also dominate ourselves. Trotsky accordingly foresees the development of a science of society which will permit the control of society, just as natural science permits the control of external nature. This matter is also discussed in *The Fourth International*, as follows: "Social life is neither a chemical nor a physiological process but a social process which is shaped according to its own laws, and these in turn are subject to an objective sociological analysis to foresee and to master the fate of society..."[21] Thus we move from an objectified and dominated nature to an objectified and administered society.

And make no mistake about it: this programme for domination and administration will not be carried out by "society." For wherever there are concentrations of power there will be social hierarchies and class domination. Marxist theory always contained the potentiality of performing ideological functions for technobureaucratic class power; it now has realized that potential. As such it performs an essential task in legitimating the project of domination—both within human society and over nature. Trapped within the confines of this project, it cannot escape the necessity of defending exploitative forms of technology. While orthodox Marxism can support the political tactic of a "united front" on some issues with the ecology movement, it cannot become *ecological*. For to do so would be to forsake its most fundamental principles concerning social change—to lose its orthodoxy.

All of this should be disquieting to anyone committed to the ecological perspective, for while ecology points to the necessity of decentralization, diversity in natural and social systems, human-scale technology, and an end to the exploitation of nature, orthodox Marxism must consistently opt for the reverse: centralization, uniform planning, high technology and an intensified domination of nature (all of which will, of course, lead to its opposite—in another epoch or two). So we are justifiably appalled when we discover that Trotsky writes that "radioactivity... is a magnificant triumph of dialectics," and that nuclear energy will offer us "unbounded technical possibilities."[22] Yet it is not his position on this *particular* issue which should be most disturbing to us. What should be our central concern is the fact that the ideology of domination can still be looked upon by some as a *revolutionary* theory, and that strategies of centralization, regimentation and productivist development can still be offered as a programme for human liberation. It is this which should impel us to further develop and propagate an ecological theory and practice, rooted in a vision of a non-dominating human community, and an organic unity with nature.

Notes

1. Leon Trotsky, *The Age of Permanent Revolution: A Trotsky Anthology* (New York: Dell Publishing Co., 1964), p. 355.
2. Karl Marx, *Grundrisse* (New York: Vintage Books, 1973), p. 705.
3. V.I. Lenin, *Selected Works* (Moscow: Progress Publishers, 1975), vol. 3, p. 529.
4. *Ibid.*, vol. 3, p. 530.
5. *Ibid.*, vol. 2, p. 620.
6. *Ibid.*, vol. 2, p. 529.
7. *Ibid.*, vol. 2, p. 635.
8. *Ibid.*, vol. 2, p. 596.
9. *Ibid.*, vol. 2, pp. 602-03.
10. *Ibid.*, vol. 2, p. 603.
11. *Ibid.*, vol. 2, p. 622.
12. Leon Trotsky, *The Revolution Betrayed* (Garden City: Doubleday Co., 1937), p. 45.
13. *Ibid.*
14. *Ibid.*, p. 8.
15. Leon Trotsky, *Terrorism and Communism* (Ann Arbor: Univ. of Michigan Press, 1972), p. 157.
16. Trotsky, *The Age of Permanent Revolution, op. cit.*, p. 225.
17. *Ibid.*
18. *Ibid.*, p. 343.
19. Trotsky, *The Revolution Betrayed, op. cit.*, p. 130.
20. Trotsky, *The Age of Permanent Revolution, op. cit.*, p. 344.
21. *Ibid.*, pp. 351-52.
22. *Ibid.*, p. 355.

Chapter 5

What is Anarchism?*

According to George Woodcock, one of the most judicious historians of anarchism, "the first thing to guard against" in discussing the topic is simplicity.[1] Unfortunately, most commentators on the subject, far from guarding against over-simplification, eagerly grasp at the most simplistic and non-technical senses of the term, and seem to have little interest in analyzing the *complex, historically situated* phenomena to which it refers. Thus, it is not unusual for academic "scholars" to gather no more evidence about the nature of anarchism than the derivation of the term, after which they can ascend to the heights of abstraction, paying attention neither to social history nor to the history of ideas. Since "anarchy" means "without rule," it is said, an anarchist is one who advocates a society in which ruling is abolished, and anarchism is the theory that such a society is necessary. In almost every case, the conclusion drawn from this superficial analysis is that such a goal is obviously beyond our reach, and that anarchism should therefore be dismissed as naïve utopianism. This will not do. As I hope to show, such an approach fails abysmally to do justice to an-

---

* Reprinted by permission of New York University Press from *Anarchism: Nomos XIX*, edited by J. Roland Pennock and John W. Chapman. Copyright © 1978 by New York University.

archism, as, in fact, does any definition which attempts to define the term by one simple idea. I would like to discuss such simple definitions further before pointing out additional difficulties in analyzing anarchism.

The assumption which underlies the sort of definition I am criticizing is that anarchism can be identified through one essential characteristic that distinguishes it from all other social and political positions. Most definitions of this type characterize anarchism in terms of some principle or some institution that it opposes. One such definition would see anarchism as a movement that is defined by its complete rejection of government. In fact, a great deal of evidence from the anarchist tradition could be pointed out in support of this view. Thus, in his *Encyclopaedia Britannica* article on anarchism, Kropotkin defines it as "a principle or theory of life and conduct in which society is conceived without government..."[2] Emma Goldman, in her essay, "Anarchism," defines it as "the theory that all forms of government rest on violence, and are therefore wrong and harmful, as well as unnecessary."[3] A well-known contemporary anarchist, Colin Ward (editor of the first series of the journal *Anarchy*), defines "anarchy" as "the absence of government,"[4] and "anarchism" as "the idea that it is possible and desirable for society to organize itself without government."[5] In some definitions, that which is rejected is identified not as government, but rather as the power that acts through government. In support of this position, one could cite Proudhon, who defines "anarchy" as "the absence of a ruler or a sovereign."[6] Or, the essence of anarchism is sometimes taken to be its attack on the state, which is often distinguished from government, as will be discussed in detail later. This can be supported by Bakunin's statement that "the system of Anarchism... aims at the abolition of the State,"[7] while Woodcock asserts that "the common element uniting all its forms" is its aim of "the replacement of the authoritarian state by some form of non-governmental cooperation between free individuals."[8] Other writers hold that it is not merely the state or political authority, but in fact authority itself which anarchists oppose. Sebastien Fauré proclaims that "whoever denies authority and fights against it is an anarchist."[9] Malatesta accepts the view that "anarchy" means "without government" but he expands the definition to mean "without any constituted authority."[10] Recently, Ward has said that anarchists oppose the "principle of authority,"[11] while Runkle, in his attack on anarchism, maintains that it "opposes authority in all its forms."[12] While Daniel Guérin is in most cases a perceptive commentator on anarchism, at one point he characterizes it in a way which is reminiscent of the most superficial and uncritical views. He goes so far as to suggest that the anarchist is one who "rejects society as a whole..."[13] A negative characterization which is probably the most adequate of all, if any is to be taken in isolation, is made by Malatesta, who holds that anarchists desire "the complete destruction of the domination and exploitation of man by man..."[14] Recently, Murray Bookchin has described anarchism in terms of its opposition to all forms of domination and all types of hierarchical organization.[15]

While fewer theorists (and especially non-anarchists) have attempted to define anarchism in terms of its positive side, there are examples of generalizations about its proposals. It might be seen, for example, as a theory of voluntary association. Kropotkin describes anarchism as seeking social order "by free agreements between the various groups, territorial and professional, freely constituted for the sake of production and consumption..."[16] Proudhon says that in anarchism "the notion of Government is succeeded by that of Contract."[17] This idea of voluntary association is also included in Woodcock's reference, cited above, to "cooperation between free individuals."[18] Anarchism might also be defined as a theory of decentralization. Paul Goodman notes that if "anarchy" means "lack of order and planning," then "most Anarchists, like the anarcho-syndicalists or the community-anarchists, have not been 'anarchists' either, but decentralists."[19] A closely related concept is federalism. Bakunin holds that anarchism proposes "an organization from below upward, by means of a federation."[20] Another way of defining anarchism is by its advocacy of freedom. Runkle holds that "the essence of anarchism is individual liberty."[21] A more specific but related conception is suggested by Bookchin, who describes the goal as "a situation in which men liberate not only 'history,' but all the immediate circumstances of their everyday lives."[22]

Thus, anarchism can be described not only as a theory that opposes such things as government, the state, authority, or domination, but also as a theory that proposes voluntarism, decentralization, or freedom. Yet to define anarchism in terms of its opposition or support for any or all of these would be inadequate. In fact, the anarchists who have been cited, while they sometimes present ill-considered, simplistic definitions, are aware of the complexity of the theory that they espouse, and their works, when taken as a whole, point to the necessity of a more comprehensive definition.[23]

Of all the critics and historians who have attempted to define anarchism, to my knowledge only one, Woodcock, clearly and concisely indicates the elements that will be taken here to constitute a minimum definition of anarchism. According to Woodcock, "historically, anarchism is a doctrine which poses a criticism of existing society; a view of a desirable future society; and a means of passing from one to the other."[24] In this discussion, the nature of these three criteria for anarchist theory will be elaborated upon, and a fourth, which is only implied by Woodcock, will be added.

Not all misunderstanding of the nature of anarchism results from over-simplification. One of the most serious faults of most discussions of anarchism is neglect of historical anarchist thought and practice. The paradoxical result is that we find political theorists attacking an anarchism that has existed primarily as a fiction in the minds of its opponents, and we find philosophers defending an anarchism that would be unrecognizable to the vast majority of anarchists throughout history (including the present). For example, Benjamin Barber, in his essay "Poetry and Revolution: The Anarchist as Reactionary" repeats the cliché of the irrationally utopian nature of anarchism. "The anarchists," he says, "manage to stand the naturalistic fallacy on its head: not that natural man, as he is, is what he ought to be; but that utopian man, as the anarchist conceives he ought to be, is in fact what man is."[25] Barber contends further that anarchism has no idea of political realities, and is concerned instead with a romanticist exhortation to revolution. "It must reject political theory itself in favour of poetry and revolution."[26]

Isaac Kramnick develops Barber's viewpoint further in his article "On Anarchism and the Real World: William Godwin and Radical England." Kramnick holds that "what replaces politics for the anarchist is either education or theater,"[27] and that, again, anarchists are totally out of touch with reality.[28] Runkle, in his book *Anarchism: Old and New*, asserts that "the student left, the radical right, and existentialism seem, at least superficially, to be contemporary forms of anarchism."[29] Runkle devotes half his book to the development of this view, which he correctly sees as superficial.

The writings of Barber, Kramnick, and Runkle exhibit very well the consequences of an ignorance of many elements of the anarchist tradition, and of the selective use of evidence about that tradition to construct misleading generalizations. Barber's charge of utopianism overlooks the many concrete and practical proposals that anarchists have presented, while his belief that the anarchist view of human nature is naïvely optimistic is a perennial half-truth that deserves to be critically examined. Kramnick's view that anarchist strategy has been limited primarily to education and theatrics shows an almost inconceivable disregard for the history of the anarchist movement. Finally, Runkle's careless attribution of relations between anarchism and recent political and philosophical tendencies is coupled with an apparent unawareness of the existence of a true "new anarchism," which has sought to synthesize the insights of classical anarchism with developments such as advanced technology and ecological theory.

While these various attacks on anarchism do a great deal to confuse the issue, some of its philosophical defenders succeed only in increasing the chaos. The work that has done most to retard meaningful analysis and criticism of the anarchist position is Wolff's *In Defense of Anarchism*.[30] As his critics have rightly pointed out, Wolff's argument that autonomy and moral authority are incompatible constitutes neither a defense of anarchism as a political theory nor a proof of the injustifiable nature of the state and government.[31] Whatever support Wolff's ethical position might give to anarchism is effectively undermined by his statement that he sees no practical proposals that follow from his theoretical acceptance of anarchism.[32] Anarchists have differed greatly on the issue of the degree of activism demanded by their position, but never before to my knowledge has any theorist claiming to be an anarchist presented no proposals for action at all.

The widespread misunderstanding of the nature of anarchism points to the need for a clear definition of the term. But before attempting that, two subjects about which there is particularly widespread confusion must be considered. The first of these concerns the anarchist view of government. Many writers about anarchism have taken opposition to government to be the most distinctive characteristic of the theory. This is, in fact, probably the most popular means of defining the term. Much of the present discussion brings into question a definition of anarchism that sees it exclusively in terms of its relation to one social institution, no matter how important it may be. However, there is further reason for questioning such a characterization: the distinction that some anarchists have themselves made between government and the state. While there runs through all anarchist writings an unmitigated contempt for the state, the anarchist position on government is far from unequivocal hostility.

A case in point is the thought of the American individualist anarchist, Albert Jay Nock. In Nock's book, *Our Enemy the State*, be distinguishes sharply between the state and government. Government, he says, consists of "strictly negative intervention" to secure the natural rights of the individual.[33] By this he means protection of life, liberty and property in the strictest Lockean sense. When society acts to prevent one individual from aggressing against a second individual who has acted peacefully, such government is perfectly justifiable. It is important to realize that Nock is not supporting governmental protection of huge concentrations of wealth, property or economic power. In fact, he argues quite vehemently that without the favourable treatment and protection through political means given to special interests, there can be no amassing of vast wealth. Much of his book, which shows individualist anarchism at its best, is dedicated to an analysis of state power in American history, and to a demonstration of the ways in which the state has supported certain mercantile interests, especially through land grants and protective tariffs. The state, according to Nock, arises when political means are used for the protection of exclusive interests. Following Franz Oppenheimer, he contends that the state originated historically as the tool of a dominant class.[34] According to this anthropologically questionable view, state power began with the conquest of a weaker (probably agrarian) tribe by a stronger (probably herding) tribe, the latter of which established a system of class rule in order to use the former for its labour power. The state, Nock says, has always maintained this class character, and state power has always been seen by special interests as an alluring means of gaining advantage over other groups in society.

Nock's use of the term "government" is quite atypical of that of anarchists in general, since most have not hesitated to use the term to refer to the abuses they attribute to the state. However, his ideas fit well into mainstream anarchist thought when examined in terms of the scale of the two systems he compares. He contends that if the state were replaced by "government" (in his unusual, limited sense of the term), something very close to Jefferson's proposal for "ward" government would result. Under such a system, the fundamental political unit would be the local township (for which I think we might also substitute the urban neighbourhood), which would be "the repository and source of political authority and initiative."[35] Action on a larger scale should be carried out, Nock says, through a voluntary federation of communities for their common purposes. He believes that the essential protective functions of government can be achieved through such a system, while avoiding the dangers of exploitation that exist in a centralized, large-scale state.

While Nock is not one of the most widely known anarchist theorists (although he is one of the most eloquent of the individualists), ideas similar to his can be found in the writings of the foremost exponent of anarchist communism, Kropotkin. While it is true that Kropotkin holds that anarchism aims at the production of a society "without government,"[36] nevertheless he sometimes praises some elements of government which could exist independently of the state. In his essay *The State: Its Historic Role*, he distinguishes sharply between the state and government. "Since there can be no state without government, it has sometimes been said that one must aim at the absence of government and not the abolition of the state."[37] Kropotkin correctly sees this strategy as politically unrealistic. The state in particular should be the object of immediate attention, for it entails not only the simple existence of political power, but additional elements, such as large territorial areas, centralization and the concentration of power in the hands of a few, hierarchical relationships, and class domination.[38] To such an institution, Kropotkin contrasts the medieval city, which he takes to be the best polity developed historically.[39] While these cities were not part of the nation-state, they certainly had governments; but far from lamenting their existence, Kropotkin has great praise for these governmental institutions. He enthusiastically approves of their assemblies, elected judges, and local militias, which are in accord with his own ideas about decentralized, participatory institutions. He also praises their belief in arbitration as opposed to authority without consent, and the subordination of military power to civil authority.[40] Thus, while he always kept in mind the ultimate goal of dispensing with government entirely, he was realistic enough to see that from an anarchist perspective decentralized community government was a considerable advance beyond the empires of ancient times, and would constitute progress beyond the modern nation-state. In view of this more complex view of government, it can be seen that a simple conception of anarchism as "opposition to government" does not accurately represent its position.

There is a further problem which, perhaps more than any other, underlies the widespread confusion about the nature of anarchism. It deals with the distinction between anarchism's vision of the ideal society and its view of immediate action. Stated differently, it is the question of the relation between utopian goals and practical possibilities. Several difficulties arise in regard to this question. Some would define an anarchist entirely in terms of a non-coercive, non-authoritarian utopia as the moral ideal. Thus, one who can describe what the ideal society might be like, express a belief that it might in some way be possible, and judge this ideal to be the only system which can be fully justified morally is called an anarchist.

I believe that this is a rather bad misuse of terminology, if traditional distinctions are to be maintained and contradiction avoided. Under such a definition it is clear that many (perhaps most) Marxists would qualify as anarchists, since they accept the ideal of the withering away of the state.[41] As many anarchists (for example, Bakunin) have pointed out, it is primarily on the question of practical strategies that anarchists and Marxists part company, rather than on their visions of the ideal society. Although differences do exist, in many ways Kropotkin's description of communism is similar to that of Marx and Engels. The anarchist's point is not necessarily that all aspects of the Marxists' goal are wrong, but that given the methods they advocate, they can be certain never to reach precisely those ends that they want. Methods of achieving change must therefore be considered if anarchism is not to be confused with Marxism (not to mention other socialist, and perhaps even liberal, positions that could, without contradiction, set up the same long-range goal).

While it is true that we often come across articles on Marx's "anarchism," we find that they do not reveal new information showing that Marx advocated decentralization, self-management, and voluntary association, nor that he was a secret admirer of Bakunin. Rather, they discuss one limited aspect of his position: his view of the final utopia. Robert Tucker's discussion of Marxism and anarchism in *The Marxian Revolutionary Idea* is a good example. Tucker holds that Marxism is "anarchist" in the sense mentioned, but "if we consider Anarchism not as an abstract political philosophy but as a revolutionary movement associated with a political philosophy, then we are confronted with the fact that Marxism was deeply at odds with it."[42] Although this view is superior to those showing no awareness of the relevance of anarchism to social realities, it is still inadequate, for there is no need to look for two anarchisms, one a political theory, and the other a social practice, which is what Tucker does when he asks how it is "that classical Marxism, while embracing anarchism as a political philosophy, disagreed with Anarchism as a socialist ideology."[43] This overlooks the essential anarchist principle that ends cannot be separated from means, nor theory from practice. There can be no "anarchism" in a full sense which does not, as an integral part of its theoretical framework, make distinctive proposals concerning practice, and take account of real historical conditions. Anarchist political philosophy implies anarchist activity in society. The interpretation of anarchism as a belief that utopia can be achieved immediately is erroneous. Because anarchists have accepted the ideal of a non-coercive, non-authoritarian society, some have assumed that they must automatically reject and destroy anything short of the ideal. The result is that anarchism is sometimes seen as implying a desire to destroy all established social institutions, preferably through violence. Yet none of the major anarchist theorists from Godwin to the present has held such as extreme view, and no anarchist popular movement has presented such a proposal as part of its programme. In spite of such lack of evidence, we often find even students of political theory confusing anarchism and nihilism, and scholars attending conferences on political philosophy questioning whether anarchist theory has any necessary link with bomb-throwing.

I would like to propose a definition of anarchism that is specific enough to be recognizable as a reasonable characterization of historical anarchism, as distinguished from political positions that have not traditionally been labelled "anarchist," and that is also general enough to take account of the wealth of diversity contained within the anarchist tradition.

There are four elements to this proposed definition, all of which must be involved in order to describe anarchism in a full sense. The founders of anarchist theory (Godwin, Proudhon, Bakunin, and Kropotkin) all fit this paradigm, and the principles embodied therein are implicit in the programmes of the anarcho-syndicalist and anarcho-communist movements, which constitute the mainstream of historical anarchist activism. Individualist anarchism in most forms also falls under the definition (although there are a few borderline cases).

For a political theory to be called "anarchism" it must contain: 1) a view of an ideal, non-coercive, non-authoritarian society; 2) a criticism of existing society and its institutions, based on this anti-authoritarian ideal; 3) a view of human nature that justifies the hope for significant progress toward the ideal; and 4) a strategy for change, involving immediate institution of non-coercive, non-authoritarian, and decentralist alternatives. Obviously, a "true" anarchist would exhibit all four characteristics, although someone who advocated anarchistic tactics without an explicit commitment to the anarchist ideal, or who accepted the ideal but proposed different strategies, could also be called an "anarchist" in a more limited sense.

The Ideal

Many anarchists are vague about the nature of this ideal for several reasons. One, which DeGeorge mentions, is that free, autonomous individuals will work out solutions that we can hardly, in the context of present society, foresee. The anarchist does not want to bind anyone to one vision of the ideal, since the acceptance of pluralism implies that various groups will create variations on the general goal. However, this argument concerning the authoritarianism inherent in such prescriptions can be overstated. There is certainly no contradiction in the idea of an anarchist proposing a description of a society that would meet the anarchist criterion for moral justification, so long as it is clear that the model is subject to criticism and modification, and that other models might also be found. As a minimum, one would have to show how to eliminate the need for the use of organized force, government and the state. This ideal must be at least plausible in its conception of human nature, which includes speculation about what people are capable of becoming, in addition to a description of what they are. The most convincing anarchist theories, while accepting the non-coercive, non-governmental, and, of course, non-statist nature of anarchy, deduce further characteristics of a society that has abolished domination. Examples often mentioned by anarchists include economic, social, racial, sexual, and generational equality, mutual aid, cooperation, and communalism.

Theorizing about "anarchy" creates an "anarchist" only in the most limited sense. Thus, the Marxist political philosopher might see this task as an integral part of a theory of transition from capitalism and socialism to full communism. A utopian novelist who enjoys dreaming about ideal societies, or a political philosopher who has a merely academic interest in the nature of the morally justifiable society, could also be called anarchists in this limited sense.

The Anarchist Critique of the Present

The distinctively anarchist critique of existing social institutions deals at its core with coercion and authoritarianism. Because the state and centralized political authority receives the most devastating critique on these grounds, any theory that on an anti-authoritarian basis questions the moral foundations of the state and government is acceptable. However, sophisticated and developed anarchist theory proceeds further. It does not stop with a criticism of political organization, but goes on to investigate the authoritarian nature of economic inequality and private property, hierarchical economic structures, traditional education, the partriarchal family, class and racial discrimination, and rigid sex- and age-roles, to mention just a few of the more important topics. In some varieties of anarchism, institutions such as private property and patriarchy are condemned at least as severely as is the state.

Most commentators on anarchism are well aware of the anarchist opposition to the forms of political organization existing in the modern nation-state. To a lesser degree, they grasp the anarchist critique of other authoritarian social institutions. What they often do not comprehend is the way in which this opposition to present social conditions fits into the total anarchist analysis.

The Anarchist View of Human Nature

Central to anarchism is its view of human nature, which asserts that there are qualities within human beings which

enable them to live together in a condition of peace and freedom. Most anarchists go on to describe the human capacity for mutual aid, cooperation, respect, and communal relationships, which are seen as the basis for social progress. While most anarchists hold a belief in such human solidarity, it is significant that some individualists reject it. Instead, they base their proposals for social organization on contract, rational self-interest, and, in the extreme case of Stirner, on ruthless egoism.[44] In both social and individualist anarchism, however, the view that people have a great potential for voluntaristic action and ability to dispose of the use of violence and coercion is central.

It is this view which provokes the frequent criticism that anarchism is excessively optimistic about human nature. In fact, it is not true that all anarchist views of human nature have been extremely "optimistic." In some ways, anarchists hold a quite realistic if not pessimistic view of human nature. It is the belief that power corrupts, and that people easily become irresponsible in their exercise of it, that forms the basis for much of their criticism of political authority and centralized power. Power must be dispersed, they say, not so much because everyone is always *good*, but because when power is concentrated some people tend to become extremely *evil*. The point is made not only in regard to political power, but other power as well, ranging from concentrated economic power on the level of society to concentrated patriarchal power on the level of the family.

There is, of course, abundant evidence of optimism in the anarchist tradition. Some of the greatest anarchist philosophers (for example, Kropotkin) have at times expressed a rather naïve belief in the capacity of people to act benevolently and to cooperate. Yet such optimism should not be taken as a given in the definition of anarchism. Much in the anarchist tradition points to a rejection of all dogmatic views of human nature (whether "optimistic," "pessimistic," or "realistic"), and to the acceptance of environmentalism. Godwin's thought is explicitly based on this outlook, and it is implicit in Bakunin's deterministic materialism. In such a view, people are inherently neither good nor evil, but rather behave and think in radically different ways under different circumstances. The problem for anarchists is to create the social conditions under which the libertarian rather than the authoritarian (and for social anarchists, the cooperative rather than the competitive) capacities of people are realized. What all anarchist positions have in common is that they accept this libertarian potential as a constituent of human nature.

The Anarchist Programme for Change

The final defining characteristics of anarchism are its practical proposals for change. An anarchist has a distinctive programme for action, a strategy for movement in the direction of the ideal, which is a response to the failure of existing institutions, and which is consistent with the anarchist view of human potentialities. Anarchism can have no meaning as a social and political theory if it says nothing about praxis, and it can have no clear meaning if it is defined in ways which confuse its proposals with those of theories known by other names. Thus, theories that say nothing about strategies for change, or which advocate centralist, authoritarian, or bureaucratic policies, cannot meaningfully be labelled "anarchist."

The distinctive characteristic of anarchist programmes is their immediate thrust in the direction of voluntarism and anti-authoritarianism. Examples of typical anarchist programmes include political decentralization, direct democratic or consensual decision-making, self-management of workplaces, maximum freedom of thought and expression, elimination of sexual repression, libertarian education, participatory communication media, non-authoritarian psychotherapy, non-dominating family and personal relationships, elimination of arbitrary distinctions based on sex, race, age, and linguistic usage, economic decentralization, and the development of technologies not requiring the domination and exploitation of nature and other species. Such anarchist proposals are practical in two senses. The most ambitious of those mentioned are within the power of a society to institute, were anarchist principles to become widely accepted within that society (as happened historically during the Spanish Revolution of 1936-39).[45] Furthermore, it is within the reach of anarchists in many societies in which anarchist theory is not yet widely accepted to put some of the proposals into immediate practice among themselves, as an alternative to the dominant institutions. In fact, the greatest energy of anarchists themselves (as opposed to writers about anarchism) has been put into this task, rather than into speculation about minute details of an ideal society.

It should now be clear how erroneous that view is which reduces the anarchist programme to an uncritical demand for the immediate abolition of government. What has confused many superficial observers is the demand by anarchists that the state be abolished, since in most cases anarchists do not propose that the nation-state be immediately replaced by an ideal anarchic society, but rather by a decentralized system, in which federation from below increasingly displaces centralized authority. As desirable as it is that primary groups which federate be as voluntary as is practically possible, there is no dogmatic demand that all vestiges of government, even in a decentralized form, be immediately destroyed. The guiding principle, to be applied according to historical conditions, is the replacement of coercive and authoritarian institutions by voluntary and libertarian ones.

A careful consideration of anarchist proposals shows that they differ markedly from those typical of other political ideologies. These proposals emphasize decentralization and voluntarism, while the Marxist, the non-Marxian socialist, the welfare statist, and the modern liberal have quite obviously come to rely increasingly on the state, centralized political authority, and hierarchical bureaucracy as a means toward social change. The anarchist differs from the classical liberal (who has been reincarnated in some elements of American conservatism and "libertarianism") in that the former rejects the use of government to protect any interests, including those based on private ownership of the means of production and class differences, while the classical liberal accepts the limited state as a means by which to preserve capitalism. In spite of these distinctions, there are no clear boundaries between the political positions mentioned, and they tend to merge at some points. Thus, leftist Marxism merges into anarcho-syndicalism. Daniel and Gabriel Cohn-Bendit, in their well-known book on the 1968 French revolt, call their position *Linksradicalismus* or *le gauchisme*, and describe it as being both Marxist and anarchist.[46] When leftist Marxists call for workers' councils and attack élitism and bureaucracy, they are in many ways close to the anarcho-syndicalists, who present similar proposals based on a similar class analysis.[47] On the other hand, the position of the individualists merges with that of classical liberals. As Benjamin Tucker, the great American individualist, claimed, "genuine [i.e., individualist] Anarchism is consistent Manchesterism."[48] The individualist anarchists hoped that the abolition of state interference would lead to a free and relatively equal society based on the labour theory of value. In this they have much in common with Locke, Adam Smith, Jefferson and, above all, Spencer.[49] In view of such similarities, while most of those who fall within the definition of "anarchist" presented here hold a position which is distinctive, and which constitutes an alternative to the standard political options, it is nevertheless the case that some who fulfill the criteria have viewpoints which are quite close to those of others who fit within other identifiable political traditions.

Is Anarchism Utopian?

Richard DeGeorge repeats the common misconception that the anarchist's "threshold of acceptance is so high, his faith in the rationality and morality of the ordinary person so little in accord with what many people experience in their dealings with their fellow man, and his schemes for bringing about his desired anarchist society so vague, that he is not a political realist but an idealistic utopian."[50] But a careful examination of the theories and practice of the best known anarchists will lead to the opposite conclusion.

Many well-known anarchists have been "pragmatic libertarians" (for example, Proudhon among the classical anarchists and Paul Goodman among the recent ones). Goodman defends "piecemeal change" in his article "The Black Flag of Anarchism," which drew a ranting, simplistic, and blatantly *ad hominem* reply from Mark Rudd, who interprets anarchism as conservative, because it attempts to change a variety of institutions instead of putting all its efforts into toppling the economic structure (assumed to be the sole basis for all the ills of society) at once.[51] Criticism like Rudd's makes DeGeorge's first accusation sound strange, and suggests that they might each be missing something important about the nature of anarchism.

Problems also arise in connection with DeGeorge's second point since, as has been explained, anarchists do not have an exclusively optimistic view of human nature. It has, in fact, become popular recently for liberals and unsympathetic socialists to condemn anarchism for the opposite quality: a lack of faith in the capacities of ordinary people. Barber, for example, accuses anarchists of having contempt for the masses and being élitists. Not being totally oblivious to history, he is forced to recognize that anarchists have indeed defended people's ability to determine their own destiny. Rather than questioning the accuracy of his previous contention, or considering the possibility that he is describing two conflicting factions within anarchism, he concludes that anarchists are "egalitarian élitists."[52] Kramnick, who relies heavily on Barber's analysis, goes a step further and depicts anarchism as unmitigated élitism. Through the method of selective quotation (when he bothers to cite evidence at all), he attempts to show that anarchists are extremely pessimistic about the abilities of the average person.[53] While such criticism does little to increase understanding of anarchism, it at least serves to point out that element of anarchist thought which exhibits scepticism about human goodness.

Finally, it should be noted that anarchists are not as vague about their proposals as DeGeorge claims. Bookchin, for example, includes practical proposals for designing eco-communities in *Toward an Ecological Society*[54] and other works, Hess and Morris present detailed sketches of decentralized community control in *Neighborhood Power* and *Community Technology*,[55] and George Dennison describes eloquently in *The Lives of Children*[56] how Tolstoyan libertarian educational principles can be applied in contemporary urban society. It is also useful to look at historical material dealing with anarchist movements. Descriptions of large-scale application of the anarchist programme in the collectivized factories and communal farms in which millions participated during the Spanish Revolution can be found in Dolgoff's *The Anarchist Collectives*.[57] In view of such evidence (of which there is an abundance) anarchist proposals cannot be called vague. Although some anarchists have been vague (whether out of principle or lack of imagination), others have not, especially in regard to immediate strategies for change. The desire not to impose one's will on others does not, as DeGeorge contends, demand vagueness. What it demands is that suggestions, which might be fully worked out, perhaps in terms of possible variations, should not be imposed through coercion, nor accepted uncritically by the community.

I would like to discuss one final topic that might help clarify the nature of anarchism: the various schemes of classifying anarchist positions. One such scheme divides anarchism into those varieties which put the greatest emphasis on personal autonomy and individual freedom, and those which stress participation in communal and intentional groups. Such a distinction can be made between individualist anarchism and social anarchism (although some figures, like Emma Goldman, seem to have an equally strong commitment to both individual freedom and social solidarity).

A more detailed classification based on theories of social organization divides anarchists into individualists, mutualists, syndicalists, and communists. Individualists (whose major theorists include Max Stirner, Josiah Warren, and Benjamin Tucker) are interested not so much in forming associations, as in enabling individuals to pursue their own ends without interference from others. They desire a society of self-reliant and largely self-sufficient individuals, achieving their ends through voluntary agreement, or contracts, with others. The mutualists, following Proudhon, see a greater need for new forms of social organization. Since economic and political power are concentrated, people must organize to defend their interests, and especially to eliminate such state-supported abuses as rent, profit, and interest. There is, for that reason, a need for mutual banks and producers' and consumers' cooperatives. The anarcho-syndicalists go one step further and propose large-scale organization of the working class into a single labour union as the essential means toward meaningful social change. The key to social transformation is the General Strike, which is to be followed by the re-organization of the means of production on principles of self-management. They are much in the tradition of Bakunin's collectivism. Finally, anarchist communism takes the commune, town, or neighbourhood as its basic unit. Decisions are to be made on the basis of communal needs, with production according to ability and distribution according to need. Kropotkin is the classical theorist of this variety of anarchism.

I would like to elaborate somewhat on the distinction between anarcho-syndicalism and anarcho-communism for two reasons. First, these are the two forms of anarchism which have been of the greatest historical importance, and have produced the most debate among anarchists themselves concerning practical proposals. Secondly, many observers of anarchism do not realize the fundamental importance of this division to anarchist theory. DeGeorge, for example, holds that "the strongest present-day position" consists of "an amalgam" of the two positions mentioned. He takes Guérin as the best exemplar of this position.[58] I believe that Guérin has made a significant contribution to libertarian socialist theory, and to the study of Marxism and anarchism, in his attempts to effect a synthesis between the two traditions. His important book on anarchism is a notable product of this endeavour. However, it is this synthesis of Marxism and anarchism that is the "amalgam" presented by Guérin, not the one mentioned by DeGeorge. There is still a fundamental opposition between the position taken by Guérin and that of anarcho-communists like Murray Bookchin, or of any of those who are "communitarians."

While it is true that communitarian anarchism has incorporated many elements of the anarcho-syndicalist position, the reverse does not seem to be true. We find in present-day anarchism a traditional division, in which the communitarians continue in the tradition of the communist anarchists (who did not deny the importance of the syndicalist emphasis on liberating the workplace), while others, like Guérin and Chomsky, preserve an essentially syndicalist approach.[59] The communitarian anarchists do not take the workplace or even the economy as the primary focus (as important as these may be), but rather the total community, with all its interrelated elements, such as work, play, education, communication, transportation, ecology, and so forth. They argue that to isolate problems of production from their social context might lead to the perennial

135

Marxist error of combatting economic exploitation while perpetuating and perhaps even expanding other forms of domination. Further, communitarian anarchists argue that the analysis of economics and class on which both classical Marxism and syndicalism are built is outdated, and that anarcho-syndicalism itself is therefore in many ways obsolete.[60] If anarchism is to be fully understood, the nature of this very important dispute must be understood: one alternative focuses on work, the other on life as a whole; one on economic relationships, the other on the totality of human relationships, and the relationships between humanity and nature.

As I will discuss in several essays in this book, it is my view that the anarcho-communist position as developed by Bookchin and others is the strongest contemporary anarchist position. In fact, it appears to be the social theory which is most compatible with such developments as the critique of Western technological rationality, the ecological view of human society and nature, and, on the highest level of generality, the organic and process view of reality, based in part on modern science. If anarchism is to be evaluated, it is this, its strongest and most highly developed form, which should be considered.

Notes

1. George Woodcock, *Anarchism* (Harmondsworth: Penguin Books, 1963) p. 7.
2. Peter Kropotkin, *Revolutionary Pamphlets* (New York: Dover, 1970), p. 284.
3. Emma Goldman, *Anarchism and Other Essays* (New York: Dover, 1969), p. 50.
4. Colin Ward, *Anarchy in Action* (London: Allen and Unwin, 1973), p. 11.
5. *Ibid.*, p. 12.
6. Steward Edwards, ed., *Selected Writings of Pierre-Joseph Proudhon* (Garden City: Doubleday Anchor, 1969), p. 89. With his usual penchant for paradox, Proudhon describes this condition as "a form of government."
7. G.P. Maximoff, ed., *The Political Philosophy of Bakunin* (New York: Free Press, 1964), pp. 297-98.
8. Woodcock, *op. cit.*, p. 11.
9. *Ibid.*, p. 7.
10. Errico Malatesta, *Anarchy* (London: Freedom Press, N.D.), p. 7.
11. Ward, *op. cit.*, p. 12.
12. Gerald Runkle, *Anarchism: Old and New* (New York: Delta, 1972), p. 3.
13. Daniel Guérin, *Anarchism: From Theory to Practice* (New York: Monthly Review Press, 1970), p. 13.
14. Paul Berman, ed., *Quotations from the Anarchists* (New York: Praeger, 1972), p. 28.
15. See *Post-Scarcity Anarchism* (Montréal: Black Rose Books, 1977), especially the title essay.
16. Kropotkin, *op. cit.*, p. 284.
17. Edwards, *op. cit.*, p. 98.
18. Woodcock, *op. cit.*, p. 11.
19. Paul Goodman, *People or Personnel* and *Like a Conquered Province* (New York: Vintage, 1968), p. 6.
20. Maximoff, *op. cit.*, p. 298.
21. Runkle, *op. cit.*, p. 3.
22. Bookchin, *Post-Scarcity Anarchism, op. cit.*, p. 41.
23. A definition of anarchism which differs from both types mentioned is put forth recently by Robert Wolff. According to Wolff, the distinctive characteristic of what he calls an anarchist is that he or she "will never view the commands of the state as *legitimate*, as having binding moral force." *In Defense of Anarchism* (New

York: Harper and Row, 1970), p. 18. The uniqueness of this definition lies in the fact that it commits the anarchist neither to support nor to opposition to any social and political institutions, at least in any obvious way. This point will be discussed further below.
24. Woodcock, *op. cit.*, p. 7.
25. Benjamin Barber, *Superman and Common Men: Freedom, Anarchy, and the Revolution* (New York: Praeger, 1972), p. 18.
26. The text reads "revelation," but presumably this is a misprint. However, those who are interested in the relationship between anarchism and revelation are directed to the *Catholic Worker*.
27. Isaac Kramnick, "On Anarchism and the Real World: William Godwin and Radical England," *American Political Science Review* 66 (March 1972): 114. I have dealt with Kramnick's contentions elsewhere in detail. See "On Anarchism in an Unreal World: Kramnick's View of Godwin and the Anarchists," *American Political Science Review* 69 (March 1975): 162-7, and also Kramnick's comment and my rejoinder, in the same issue. For a more detailed discussion of Godwin's contribution to anarchist thought, see my book, *The Philosophical Anarchism of William Godwin* (Princeton: Princeton University Press, 1977).
28. *Ibid.*, p. 128. Kramnick concludes that "utopian anarchism" is ultimately reactionary, since it has no effective strategy for change.
29. Runkle, p. 13. The idea of a professor of philosophy suggesting that existentialism might seem to be "a form" of anarchism is a bizarre one. The relationship between anarchism and existentialism is, however, a topic which deserves serious study (as opposed to Runkle's sensationalistic exploitation). Strangely, in order to find out whether existentialism really is "a form" of anarchism, Runkle examines the thought of Sartre, who, for most of his life, associated his thought with Marxism (although he did in his last years proclaim himself an anarchist). Runkle overlooks the fact that two well-known existentialists, Martin Buber and Nikolai Berdyaev, have been associated with anarchism. See Buber's *Paths in Utopia* (Boston: Beacon Press, 1955), and Berdyaev's *Dream and Reality* (New York: Collier, 1962), especially the epilogue; *The Beginning and the End* (New York: Harper and Row, 1957), ch. viii; and *Slavery and Freedom* (New York: Scribners, 1944), part III, section IA.
30. Robert Wolff, *In Defense of Anarchism* (New York: Harper and Row, 1970).

31. See Jeffrey Reiman, *In Defense of Political Philosophy* (New York: Harper and Row, 1972).
32. Interview with Robert Wolff, included in a radio broadcast entitled "The Black Flag of Anarchy" (Baltimore: Great Atlantic Radio Conspiracy, 1973). A catalogue of tapes on anarchism and related topics, including interviews with Wolff, Bookchin, and other well-known figures, is available from that group.
33. Albert Jay Nock, *Our Enemy the State* (New York: Free Life Editions, 1973), p. 22.
34. *Ibid.*, p. 20. See Franz Oppenheimer, *The State* (Montréal: Black Rose Books, 1975).
35. *Ibid.*, p. 57.
36. Kropotkin, *Revolutionary Pamphlets, op. cit.*, p. 284.
37. *Ibid.*, p. 10.
38. *Ibid.*, pp. 10-11.
39. *Ibid.*, p. 27. Had he been more familiar with non-Western and tribal societies, he might have judged differently. See Dorothy Lee, *Freedom and Culture* (Englewood Cliffs: Prentice-Hall, 1959), and any of the many works on stateless societies, including, perhaps most notably, E.E. Evans-Pritchard, *The Nuer* (Oxford: Clarendon Press, 1940).
40. Kropotkin, *Revolutionary Pamphlets, op. cit.*, pp. 26-7.
41. The authenticity of this ideal has been questioned by some. See Richard Adamiak, "The Withering Away of the State: A Reconsideration," *Journal of Politics* 32 (February 1970): 3-18.
42. Robert Tucker, *The Marxian Revolutionary Idea* (New York: Norton, 1969), p. 87.
43. *Ibid.*, p. 88. As a result, he feels he must use capitalization to distinguish between the two.
44. For a criticism of extreme individualist anarchism, see my book, *Max Stirner's Egoism* (London: Freedom Press, 1976).
45. For descriptions of revolutionary Spain, see Sam Dolgoff's *The Anarchist Collectives: Worker Self-Management in the Spanish Revolution (1936-39)* (Montréal: Black Rose Books, 1974), and Vernon Richards' *Lessons of the Spanish Revolution* (London: Freedom Press, 1972).
46. See their book mistranslated as *Obsolete Communism: The Left-Wing Alternative* (London: Penguin, 1968). The English title makes no sense. The French should be translated as *Leftism: A Cure for the Senile Disorder of Communism*, which, besides being less confusing, preserves the parody on Lenin's work, *Left-Wing Communism: An Infantile Disorder*.

47. DeGeorge holds that communist anarchists present a "Marxian analysis." Richard DeGeorge, "Anarchism and Authority," p. 11, unpublished paper given to the 1974 Annual Meeting of the American Society for Political and Legal Philosophy. This is partially true; however, such an analysis is more typical of anarcho-syndicalism, as will be discussed further.
48. Cited in Leonard Krimerman and Lewis Perry, eds., *Patterns of Anarchy* (Garden City: Doubleday Anchor, 1966), p. 34.
49. The case is perhaps different with the "anarcho-capitalists" of the present, who live in an era of entrenched economic power. Since they have not explained how all can be placed in an equal bargaining position without abolishing present property relationships, it seems likely that what they propose is a system in which the affluent voluntarily associate to use force and coercion against the poor and weak in order to maintain class privilege. The abuses of the state are thus perpetuated after the state is allegedly abolished.
50. DeGeorge, *op. cit.*, p. 37.
51. Paul Goodman, "The Black Flag of Anarchy" (Corinth, Vermont: Black Mountain Press, N.D.). The article originally appeared in the *New York Times Magazine*, July 14, 1968.
52. Barber, *op. cit.*, p. 25.
53. Kramnick, *op. cit.*, p. 114.
54. Murray Bookchin, *Toward an Ecological Society* (Montréal: Black Rose Books, 1980).
55. David Morris and Karl Hess, *Neighborhood Power: The New Localism* (Boston: Beacon Press, 1975); and Karl Hess, *Community Technology* (New York: Harper and Row, 1979).
56. George Dennison, *The Lives of Children* (New York: Vintage Books, 1969).
57. See especially Bookchin's introductory essay, which is a brief but masterly treatment, in historical context, of the relation between theory and practice.
58. DeGeorge, *op. cit.*, pp. 12-13.
59. It is the latter who have a Marxian analysis, not so much the communitarians, as DeGeorge contends. On this question, see "Syndicalism and Anarchism" in *Freedom* 35 (October 26, 1974): 4 and (November 2, 1974):6. The debate between Monatte and Malatesta concerning syndicalism and communism is reproduced. Even more important is George Woodcock's "Chomsky's Anarchism," *Freedom* 35 (November 16, 1974):4, in which the nature of the anarchism of Chomsky and Guérin is discussed in view of that historical division within anarchism.
60. Again, Bookchin's introduction to Dolgoff, *The Anarchist Collectives*, *op. cit.*, is relevant.

Chapter 6

Anarchism and the Present World Crisis

We are now at a point in history at which the need for a new political vision is becoming acutely evident. In the industrialized West, we find increasing dissatisfaction with traditional political options and a loss of faith in formal democracy. This dissatisfaction has manifested itself thus far primarily through a process of depolitization in which there has been a drastic loss of confidence in political parties and non-voting on a massive scale. In the East, we find a growing movement of dissent, which challenges the Marxist orthodoxy, often silently, through withdrawal of allegiance and cooperation, sometimes dramatically, in periodical revolt. And in both West and East we find in many countries and to varying degrees a cultural opposition which vaguely, yet perhaps prophetically, points to the need for a new unifying vision.

One premise of the present discussion is that this disillusionment with both liberal capitalism and state socialism is justified. The prevailing world systems, in this view, no longer offer us a hopeful prospect of resolving the vast social and ecological crises which now confront humanity. In fact, it is becoming increasingly clear that these systems, with their deep commitment to such values as industrialism, high technology, centralism, urbanization, and the state, have been instrumental in creating the social atomization and ecological imbalance which are at the core of these crises. For this reason, what is necessary is an alternative vision of society, the future, and indeed reality itself: a vision which departs from the traditional ideologies on all these fundamental questions. This vision, I will argue, is anarchism.

In discussing the anarchist approach to the present world crisis, I will focus on some of the objections which opponents of anarchism have raised to the view that it can be a viable global strategy. In particular, I will deal with the points made by Alan Wertheimer in his analysis of "the case for anarchy" in the recent *Nomos* volume on anarchism.[1] In his essay, Wertheimer contends that anarchism is unable to successfully deal with four presently existing world social conditions. These are: 1) that "the population of the earth is (perhaps) too large, but increasing at a rapid rate with no immediate prospect for a serious reduction"; 2) that "in much of the world, basic human needs are not being satisfied"; 3) that "the world's natural and human resources are not evenly distributed across the globe"; and, finally 4) that "the present level of subsistence is based on a high level of social and economic interdependence among various regions of the world and also within the regions themselves."[2] In addition, Wertheimer contends that anarchism is unable to cope with conflicts between individual self-interest and social needs, particularly as this relates to the question of defence.

In considering the anarchist response to these problems, it is important to understand the meaning of the term "anarchism." What I take here to be anarchism is a tradition of theory and practice which has developed and evolved within an actually existing historical movement (calling itself the "anarchist movement") over the past century and a half. I take this movement to have at its present stage of development such guiding principles as the rejection of all forms of domination; the acceptance of forms of human interaction based on cooperation, autonomy, and respect for the person; and insofar as its underlying ontological premises are systematically developed, an organicist, ecological view of society, nature, and reality in general. In practice (and this is the main focus of the present essay) these principles lead anarchists to propose such policies as the replacement of nation-states by federations of communal and workplace associations; replacement of corporate capitalist and state ownership by self-management of production by the producers; replacement of the patriarchal-authoritarian family by libertarian family and living arrangements; replacement of the megalopolis and centralized population distribution by decentralized, ecologically balanced population patterns; and replacement of centralized, high technology by more humanly scaled alternative technologies, which are compatible with decentralized, democratic decision-making, and which are not destructive of the social and natural environments. These principles have been developed considerably by the mainstream of anarchist theory, beginning with Bakunin and Kropotkin, and by the historical anarchist movement in its predominating anarcho-syndicalist and anarcho-communist forms. Yet an equally great contribution to this development has been made by a related libertarian tradition, which has been called "utopian" and "communalist," and is represented by such social theorists as Fourier, Gustav Landauer, and Martin Buber. These two lines of development have reached a synthesis and, I believe, their most advanced stage of theoretical development in contemporary communal-ecological anarchism, which is the form being defended here.[3]

Population Problems: Density and Growth

The population question poses several problems for the anarchist position. One of the most basic is the issue of whether anarchistic forms of social organization are even possible in societies with either absolutely large populations or high levels of population density. According to one line of criticism, systems of law (and indeed extensive ones) are unavoidable in highly populated societies. For this reason, anarchy, which assumes the absence of a legal system, cannot be workable in these societies.[4]

It is important to emphasize that anarchists recognize the necessity for *rule-making* in all societies. The important consideration is not whether there shall be rules, but rather the level at which the rules are made, the processes used to determine them, and the nature and extent of the rules themselves. Anarchists argue that whenever feasible, voluntary rule-making, through processes like arbitration and consensus, should be used. But since this is often not possible, the next step is to develop systems of rule-making through democratic processes at the communal level (although many decisions will no doubt be left to even smaller groups and to individuals if the community is to maintain its libertarian character). This communal democracy may be interpreted as requiring formal systems of local law which can, insofar as communities are in agreement, be extended in scope through federation. There is, however, a strong tendency to favour case-by-case consideration of issues by local assemblies and popular judicial bodies, much on the model of some aspects of the Greek polis and certain tribal decision-making processes. There do not seem to be any obvious reasons why such systems of decentralist and federative rule-making could not be developed in some form in highly populated societies.

But even if possible, can this decentralized decision-making be practical in such societies? In fact, there is evidence that the relative advantages may be greater in the more complex, highly populated societies. As value and interest conflicts multiply with population growth and urbanization, the centralized state apparatus becomes increasingly more inept as a means of coping with rapidly proliferating crisis situations. The typical tactic of the state is to expand bureaucratization and centralized planning, which results in further dissociation between the planning mechanism and social reality. Increasingly particularized problems are confronted in an increasingly generalized manner. Decentralized and federative decision-making, on the other hand, is inherently more capable of dealing with complexity since it is itself complex and diversified. Multiplication of loci of problems calls for a corresponding multiplication of loci of information-gathering, discussion, and decision-making.

There are, however, alternative approaches available to the centralized state. One is to incorporate more decentralized mechanisms into the overall centralized structure. Given the strong centralist economic and political tendencies of contemporary society, it is not surprising that such attempts are usually superficial and ineffective (note, for example, the degree of bureaucratization and economic concentration under supposedly "anti-bureaucratic" Republican administrations in post-war America). Another possibility is to resort to increased authoritarian and repressive controls, given the disintegration of traditional internalized controls and the failure of bureaucratic methods of problem-solving and control. This will become a more appealing option as social atomization continues its development and crisis situations become more severe. Significantly, the process of bureaucratization itself contributes greatly to the simplification and atomization of society. It could be argued that if this process were allowed to reach its perfection, then centralized bureaucratic processes would be the most appropriate structure for society. Yet this success for bureaucracy would be won at the expense of the complete dissolution of the organic fabric of society, a price that few would wish to pay. For the above reasons, anarchists argue that decentralized decision-making is a more adequate response to the size and complexity of society, and also that it is more desirable in terms of preserving what is of value in social complexity.

This should not be taken to imply, however, that the anarchist sees a high level of urbanization or high densities of population as in any way desirable. There are many kinds of social and ecological complexity. The cultural diversity of ethnically variegated urban areas may embody a social value which can be preserved during the process of deurbanization. On the other hand, the sort of complexity entailed in planning transportation systems, or protecting the environment in areas where over-concentration makes these problems virtually insoluble, is a complexity which is dispensable. So the problem of overpopulation must be solved, and anarchist decentralism is an attempt at a solution. The question of the anarchist approach to the problem of the numerically high level of population in relation to ecological constraints will be investigated shortly. This is necessary since anarchist strategies would be obviously unrealistic if they demanded a much lower *global* density of population than that presently existing, or could not cope with the high rate of growth that will be inevitable for some time. It should be noted first, however, that decentralization of population does not demand an overall low density of population. It is well known that many Third World countries, in which population is primarily dispersed in villages, have a higher density of population nationally than many other countries in which the population is concentrated in urban centres. Furthermore, there is anthropological evidence that societies with economic and political systems more loosely organized than those proposed by contemporary anarchists have had rather high densities of population.[5] It can be argued that decentralist policies increase the level of population that can be maintained within a given area, in view of the decreased ecological stress which results from dispersion of population, industry, waste production, etc. (assuming the practicality of decentralist technology).

This does not mean, of course, that anarchists look with equanimity at levels of population growth which threaten to rapidly strain the limits of our planet's capacity to support human life, or that they merely hope to increase this capacity through decentralization. So a second, and more important, question arises: can there be anarchist strategies to limit population growth so as to stabilize population at a level most conducive to human well-being and optimal ecological balance? As Wertheimer points out, "while we preach birth control, the Indian peasant continues to propagate children in order that he have help in working in the fields and in order that someone will survive to take care of him when he is too old and infirm to take care of himself."[6] Though he may understand the disastrous social consequences of his action, can we expect him to do otherwise than mitigate his own suffering? Consequently, the argument continues, a rational population policy with state powers of enforcement is necessary.

This argument is based, however, on a false dilemma. The apparent alternatives are anarchic reproduction (which is in fact not "anarchic" in the anarchist sense, but rather controlled by the prevailing hierarchical and inegalitarian socioeconomic system), and controlled reproduction (which is subject to the additional control of the coercive apparatus of the state). But these are far from the only alternatives and neither would be advocated by anarchists. They advocate instead that in societies like India the social and economic system be thoroughly transformed, although in ways which are more compatible with village population distribution and traditional methods of production than are centralist governmental policies. Furthermore, they maintain that state policies aimed at preservation of the existing economic system while instituting compulsory birth control (along with promoting urbanization and high technology, as under the Indira Gandhi regime) will only perpetuate the present level of misery and exploitation, while aggravating the damaging ecological effects of overpopulation. The anarchist approach to peasant societies in which tenancy or small-holding predominates requires the replacement of these forms by co-operative cultivation of the soil by associations of producers. When such a system is instituted, the members of the associations are in a position to overcome their previously quite understandable concern for maximizing the labour supply and they can then provide for their old age and undertake other social welfare measures by the cooperative regulation of their surplus production. This is, of course, based on the assumption that the technology for adequate cooperative production is available (an assumption that will be discussed shortly) and that if the surplus now diverted to native and external ruling classes is reclaimed, then the needs of the producers can better be fulfilled. The essential point in the context of the present discussion is that the anarchist approach to problems of overpopulation implies conscious social reorganization and cannot be equated with "libertarian" inactivity or mere moralistic encouragement.[7]

The Problem of Scarcity

Anarchism has always concerned itself with the problem of scarcity. Much of the appeal of anarchism to the peasants of Spain, the Ukraine, and other countries lay in its vision of greater abundance based on libertarian communalism and production for real needs. Recent anarchist theory, as exemplified by Murray Bookchin's classic *Post-Scarcity Anarchism*, has taken the question of scarcity as a central one for political theory. But, of course, the important question is not whether anarchists have at times convinced large numbers of people, nor whether they have been concerned with the problem, but rather whether they have evidence that their approach of decentralized production and alternative technologies is workable. Accordingly to Colin Ward, the proposals for labour-intensive, decentralized food production made by Kropotkin over a century ago have been shown by experience to be quite practical. As he has observed, "the Japanese experience—the evolution from domestic insufficiency, through self-sufficiency, to an embarrassing 'over-production'—illustrates the technical feasibility of Kropotkin's claims for the enormous productivity of labour-intensive agriculture. The modern horticultural industry in Britain and in the continental countries fully lives up to his expectations...."[8] E. F. Schumacher's Intermediate Technology Group has carried on the tradition of thinkers like Kropotkin and William Morris in developing so-called "appropriate technologies" which will allow developing societies to solve their problems of scarcity and unemployment while avoiding the disastrous consequences of heavy industrialization and urbanization. In the United States, groups like the Institute for Local Self-Reliance are exploring possibilities through which impoverished local communities can escape from the trap of dependence and economic exploitation by the development of community industrial and agricultural production. David Morris and Karl Hess present a rather detailed picture of some of these possibilities in their book *Neighborhood Power*,[9] which is based in part on their work with such experiments in the Adams-Morgan neighbourhood in Washington, D.C. Perhaps the strongest extended argument for the kind of decentralization of production advocated by anarchists since Kropotkin can be found in Lewis Mumford's half century of work on technology and mechanization.[10] As he writes in *Technics and Civilization*:

> In a balanced economy, regional production of commodities becomes rational production; and inter-regional exchange becomes the export of the surplus from regions of increment to regions of scarcity, or the exchange of special materials and skills.... But even here the advantages of a particular place may remain temporary.... With the growth of economic regionalism, the advantages of modern industry will be spread, not chiefly by transport—as in the nineteenth century—but by local development.[11]

These few citations do not prove the anarchist case. Yet they do show that the case must be examined, and that it is unconvincing merely to appeal to the reigning ideology of high technology, as if its validity were self-evident.[12]

In discussing the anarchist approach to questions like scarcity and the "standard of living," it is important to note that what is being called for is not mere subsistence, but rather a society of abundance. Anarchists argue that the seeming implausibility of achieving such a society through anarchist forms of production results from a failure to question the ideology of material consumption. If abundance must rely on infinitely expanding productivity and exhaustion of nature as a resource, it obviously can never be achieved. But for anarchists, abundance is to come from the development of social needs and from satisfaction of the desire for a creative and joyful existence. In this connection, they find inspiration for their vision in the richness of symbolic imagination, the depth of communal feeling and the joy of immediate experience in many traditional socieites.[13] Anarchists emphasize the inability of mere increases in production to raise the qualitative standard of living once the most basic material needs are provided for. To discuss this subject adequately, one would have to deal at length with such themes (common to anarchism and humanistic/libertarian Marxism) as the nature of a society based on the model of human being as consumer, the reduction of human values to commodity values in a consumerist society, and the destruction of the human and natural environments in a society obsessed with commodity production and quantitative growth.

Yet, recognition of these seemingly abstract themes should not lead to a failure to apprehend the practical concern for forms of technological development which combine levels of production sufficiently high to fulfill basic and higher needs with the requirements for a humanly scaled, non-bureaucratic, non-hierarchical social system. What anarchists reject is a simplistic, non-dialectical approach which isolates problems of production, for instance, from the totality of social relationships, or one which sees only the alternatives of continued development of present directions of technical evolution or the immediate destruction of all that has resulted from this development. This either/or approach ignores alternative lines of development of technology and also overlooks alternative strategies for abundance, such as greater sharing of social products as opposed to individualistic consumption, abolition of wasteful consumption resulting from manipulated needs and desires, and the creation of more social needs (in which the growth of needs themselves leads to abundance rather than scarcity) rather than material consumption needs.

In evaluating the relationship between the generation of needs and the nature of various modes of production, the experience of primitive societies is enlightening. Marshall Sahlins has shown that abundance is not something that humanity is just now achieving, or that it will only achieve in the future. Rather, given the prevailing relationship between the system of needs created and the level of production, primitive hunting and gathering societies were in fact the first affluent societies and had surplus production and abundant leisure by modern standards.[14] As Marx demonstrated in his analysis of the creation of needs under capitalist production, the industrial revolution under capitalism only aggravated conditions of scarcity and toil that had arisen with the development of agrarian societies. In view of such historical evidence, it is incorrect to assume that the existence of a society of abundance necessarily has a positive correlation with the existence of large quantities of the kind of consumer goods now produced.

It is true, as Wertheimer contends, that if anarchism "implies a 'polyculturism' in which individuals are free to choose their own values, it is possible that many persons will choose to value the goods which only industrialism makes possible."[15] However, people who live in an anarchist community will find that some such "goods" will only be available if the "goods" that they hold to be the highest ones (freedom, equality, humane relationships, harmony with nature, etc.) are given up. Anarchists certainly believe that people should not be *forced* to desire egalitarian work relationships over hierarchical structures, non-polluting transportation over powerful cars, alternative energy sources over nuclear power, decentralized ecological communities over throwaway suburbs, and so forth. But in no sense can a society in which people seek hierarchical power, maximum consumption of commodities, and fulfillment of needs produced by advertising be called an anarchist society. For this reason the anarchist analysis discards the liberal theory of wants which takes them as an unexplained given, or as the raw material for the development of social policy. Instead, it investigates the preconditions for "wanting," "desiring," or "needing" and the methods by which people can transform their wants as part of the process of creating a humanly fulfilling, cooperative society.

The Problem of Distribution

If the present line of argument has any merit, anarchist forms of production and "liberatory technology" are capable of fulfilling basic human needs and are compatible with those social forms which lead to the fulfillment of higher ones. But an additional objection arises: even if an anarchist society could reach an adequate level of production, it can be argued that such a society is incapable of achieving an equitable distribution of goods. It is argued, first, that if nation-states are unable to transcend their "narrowness of territoriality," then anarchist communities, with their local basis, can only be expected to be even more narrow; secondly, that inequalities between communities in resources or productivity would result in injustices that could not be rectified; and, finally, that anarchist reliance on "spontaneous" redistribution is hopeless in view of the severity of the world crisis.[16]

The argument that anarchism leads to narrowness based on local communalism relies on an exclusive direction of attention to the anarchist emphasis on community control and decentralization and a lack of acknowledgement of the principles of federalism and mutual aid. From the time of Bakunin and Kropotkin, anarchism has stressed the importance of local, regional, and global federations of communities and worker collectives. There are two sides to the anarchist rejection of the nation-state: one is communalism and the other is internationalism (if "nation" is taken in its cultural, rather than political sense). Anarchist decentralism is not a mechanistic formula for solving all "social problems." Rather, it is an integral part of a social practice through which humanity can recreate itself in a more personalized, self-conscious, and communal form. The anarchist "commune" is a community of people attempting to create relationships and institutions based on an organic, ecological, cooperative view of existence. The relationship between local communalism and global communalism is expressed well in the work of Martin Buber, who argues that unless the inhumane, bureaucratic, objectifying relationships created by the state, capitalism, and high technology are replaced by personalistic, cooperative relationships arising in the primary communal group, it cannot be hoped that people will have a deep concern for humanity as a whole. In Buber's view, unless we can see humanity in our neighbours it is impossible to expect us to overcome that "narrowness" which prevents us from acting with a concern for the entire species. But this is not a mere moral dictum; rather, it is a call for communitarian praxis. As Buber states it, "an organic commonwealth—and only such commonwealth can join together to form a shapely and articulated race of men—will never build itself up out of individuals but only out of small and even smaller communities: a nation is a community to the degree that it is a community of communities."[17]

Anarchists contend that to the extent that redistribution is a necessity, it will be encouraged more by the practice of mutual aid through free federation than by the continuation of action by nation-states or by the creation of a world state. Wertheimer never explicitly confronts the question of class; yet a central element of the anarchist case concerns the development of class interests in societies based on centralized bureaucratic forms of organization. The relevant question is whether statist or federalist forms of organization can contribute most to the development of cooperative patterns of thought and action and, to look at the other side of the same issue, whether power does indeed corrupt in proportion to the degree to which it is centralized or concentrated. Anarchist theory asserts that as long as concentrated political or economic power remains, we can expect it to be used in the interest of those who control that power. If we look at history, it might not seem an exaggeration to say that there is some evidence in favour of this view.

We might look, for instance, at the distribution of wealth in societies which have liberal democratic processes and a state to preside over the carrying out of the will of the people. (We will later consider briefly systems outside the liberal-democratic tradition.) In the United States, a nation with the greatest concentration of wealth and one of the longest traditions of liberal democracy, there appears to be virtually no redistribution taking place between economic strata and only a fraction of 1% of the GNP is devoted to aid to poorer countries.[18] It must be conceded that modern liberalism and social democracy have at times taken steps which have had a moderately redistributive effect and that the growth of these ideologies could be expected to lead to an expansion of these programmes. Yet, in view of the nature of these proposals (which is hardly a speculative theoretical question, given that liberal and social democratic regimes have been in power in numerous countries), redistribution will be for the foreseeable future primarily a gradual process *within* nation-states and can only be expected to be achieved on the global level over a long period of time. If, then, we are indeed in a period of crisis in which drastic measures producing redistribution are necessary (as Wertheimer claims), it hardly seems likely that these are the ideologies to which we should look for guidance.

For evidence of the nature of the alternative proposed by anarchists, we can examine the federations established by the anarcho-syndicalists in Spain in 1936. We find that the redistribution which has been largely absent over generations in liberal and social democratic countries took place in a period of a few months in collectivized areas, primarily as a result of the institution of self-managed industry and agriculture. In the short time that the collectives were able to act autonomously, they began to expand this egalitarianism beyond the limits of the individual collectives. According to Gaston Leval, perhaps the most careful student of the Spanish collectives, in areas like Castile and Aragon "the libertarian communist principle was applied not only within each Collective, but *between* all the Collectives."[19] Leval describes such programmes as disaster relief, redistribution of fertilizer and machinery from the wealthier to the poorer collectives, and cooperative seed production for distribution to areas in need. According to Leval, there was an awareness among the collectivists that "having risen above the communalist mentality, the next thing was to

153

overcome the regionalist spirit."[20] The Spanish anarchist experiments of the 1930's were, of course, short-lived and many of the projects initiated were undermined by the Popular Front regime and then crushed, first by the Stalinists (whose "Republican" armies actually invaded the Aragon collectives), and then by the Fascists. But the question still remains whether it is the organizational principles embodied in these collectives and federations, or the organizational principles of the state which deserve most to be developed and expanded to the global level. The guiding assumption behind anarchist proposals for social organization is that unless human beings develop patterns of life and values based on mutual aid at the level of small groups and local communities, one cannot expect them to go very far in the practice of mutual aid at any other level of social organization. This social psychological premise underlies all anarchist arguments for communal federation. Not only is this premise plausible on the basis of such theoretical analyses as Reichian mass-psychology, but it also seems to have the beginnings of a more direct historical verification in Spanish collectivist experience.

Thus far, the discussion has centred around the concept of "redistribution." Yet, this conception has been based, I am afraid, on inadequately critical presuppositions which must be examined further. As Marx points out, the problem of distribution is largely a problem of production. What is a problem of distribution under one system of production is no longer a relevant problem given different relations of production, while some problems of distribution are *insoluble* given certain systems of production. Wertheimer's formulation of the problem as "redistribution of the world's resources" assumes that the problems of poor societies will be solved by a flow of "resources" from societies of relative abundance to societies of relative scarcity. This hope might he questioned as being unrealistic in view of the nature of international politics, but, more fundamentally, the entire problematic of "redistribution" is based on the questionable assumption of the feasibility of seeking a solution to the problem while continuing a technological system founded on dependency and disproportions in economic power. Anarchists argue that since the technology for liberation now exists, the major problem for poor societies is the carrying through of the process of social transformation in these societies. This process, it is argued, necessitates their economic and political liberation from exploitation by imperialist powers and native ruling classes and their emancipation from patterns of domination transmitted through cultural tradition. The function of an anarchist movement in such societies is seen as the creation of a praxis adequate to displace these groups and structures and to institute liberatory forms in their place. Thus, the economic problem is not seen as the absence of enforced redistribution (which is unlikely to be endorsed by the classes and states which benefit from the exploitation), but rather as the destruction of the undesirable patterns of production which result in the maldistribution and of the ideologies which legitimate the process. It is true, as Wertheimer asserts, that redistribution (like production and distribution in general) will not occur "spontaneously" in the sense that they will occur without planning or strategy. But the point of the anarchist argument is that it is much more likely that more equitable distribution will occur as a result of the self-conscious cooperative efforts of the exploited to change power relationships, than as a consequence of the agreement of exploiting powers to subject themselves to the control of some higher political authority which is to enforce redistribution.

If this analysis is correct, then the real alternative to the anarchist approach appears to be, not a liberal or social democratic optimism about global democracy, but rather Marxism-Leninism, which has enough awareness of the realities of economic power to realize that such a shift in power relationships will inevitably involve a process of global class struggle. But although anarchists may agree that the Marxist-Leninist approach can succeed in significantly reducing the extremes of economic inequality, it is judged to be a failure as a praxis of liberation. Among the most important arguments for this conclusion are the following: 1) that the Marxist-Leninist view of social revolution, with its strong commitment to statism and centralism, results in a new state-capitalist and bureaucratic-centralist form of class domination perpetuating political and often economic inequality; 2) that Marxism-Leninism's uncritical acceptance of high technology leads to continued alienated production and the necessary development of a technocratic class interest and to continued domination of nature and destruction of the ecosphere; and 3) that the economistic and productivistic orientation of Marxism-Leninism blinds it to many important areas of the struggle for human liberation, not the least of which are the cultural, the aesthetic, and the erotic, and weakens its analysis of many forms of domination (including political, racial, sexual, and psychological ones).[21] These arguments are also directed at other statist and centralist positions and some of the analysis applies equally to technocratic liberalism.

The Problem of Transition

Another common argument against the anarchist position is that the transition to an anarchist society would have disastrous results, given the high degree of interdependence in the present world economy and the present level of urbanization. Anarchism is seen as implying cataclysmic change, the immediate destruction of all complex organization, and a regression to communal independence.[22]

But as has already been pointed out, anarchists do not advocate complete communal independence, but rather an organic interdependence beginning with the most basic social units and building, through federation, to humanity as a whole. Neither do anarchists propose that technological change and decentralization be taken as absolute principles to be dogmatically applied no matter what human needs may dictate. They therefore do not advocate that *all* technology be destroyed while we wait for liberatory alternative forms to be developed and instituted. They propose instead that research now be done on alternative technology and that people begin to use these liberatory forms to whatever degree possible, even while high technology continues to predominate. For example, while anarchists reject completely conversion to nuclear energy, they do not advocate that other energy sources be eliminated but that they be replaced progressively by solar, wind, methane, geothermal, hydroelectric, cogeneration, and other alternatives.

Similarly, anarchists do not advocate decentralization through annihilation or forced relocation of city dwellers. Many anarchists do, in fact, approve of cities of traditional scale and advocate such policies as neighbourhood assemblies, integration of work, play, and living spaces, community gardens and workshops, and similar approaches to transform the urban social and physical environment. There is a long anarchist tradition dealing with the humanization and democratization of city life, as illustrated by Kropotkin's observations on the Medieval cities and Bookchin's discussion of the Greek polis and the neighbourhood assemblies of the French Revolution in Paris.[23] Yet anarchists do foresee the scaling down of the inhuman megalopolis to the level of the city and an ongoing process of synthesis of town and country. What is called for as an immediate necessity is not the displacement of huge masses of people but the institution of small-scale direct democracy in the form of neighbourhood and workplace assemblies. Anarchists see such factors as personality structure, economic conditions, technological forms, population distributions, and political institutions as inseparably interrelated and they reject theories of change which fail to deal with all these factors as constituents of a social totality. Yet they are not so naïve as to propose that all aspects of social transformation will proceed at the same pace. Technological change and population redistribution will obviously present material obstacles which will require a long process of constructive activity. Much of this development will continue after changes in political and economic institutions have already occurred. But it is important to note that much of the development of technological forms which will make libertarian political and economic structures seem increasingly more realistic and necessary are already taking place.

A Note on Self-Defence

It is a fundamental principle of anarchism that if the community is to be defended, this must result from the voluntary action of the people. This leads to the criticism that the anarchist community could not effectively defend itself against the highly organized, compulsory militaries that ordinarily engage in warfare. In fact, it might not defend itself at all since, while each member might wish that the community be defended, they will each, because of self-interest, voluntarily choose that others be the ones to do the defending.[24]

Anarchists firmly believe that "war is the health of the state," and that consequently it always threatens to be crippling, if not fatal, to freedom. To militarize a society in order to fight authoritarianism means an automatic victory for authoritarianism. For this reason anarchists insist on the necessity of limiting military activity to communal self-defence through popular militias and they oppose hierarchical, centrally directed military forces. In this context, the argument that this approach will lack popular support is not a significant one. Communities do in fact defend themselves when there is a real danger to their freedom. The theoretical objection concerning non-participation overlooks the psychological elements of war and the pervasive effects of social pressure. A cohesive community (as, for example, a tribal society) does not have difficulty securing participation in defence, although the anarchist requirement of voluntarism becomes increasingly more difficult to fulfill as the threat to the group increases in magnitude. The crucial question is therefore whether the strategy of popular self-defence can be effective when utilized.

There now seems to be growing evidence that, at least under some conditions, such means can be successful. For example, the peasant anarchist Makhnovist movement in the Ukraine developed highly successful methods of guerrilla warfare against overwhelming odds in its battles against several armies from 1918-1921. The military success of the Makhnovists was only ended when their army, by then worn down by its victories against rightist forces, was attacked by its erstwhile "ally," the Bolsheviks.[25] The Spanish collectives also achieved a remarkable degree of mobilization of the population during the period of the people's militias. In fact, support and morale only declined significantly when the militias were militarized in the hands of the state.[26] Recent experiences such as the Indochinese wars and resistance to colonialism and neo-colonialism in many areas of the world (Afghanistan being the most recent instance) have brought into question the ability of powerful nation-states to successfully (or profitably) crush opposition in areas where guerrilla warfare is vigorously supported by local communities. The case for the effectiveness (as opposed to the moral necessity) of self-defence through popular militias or community-supported guerrilla warfare has not been conclusively made. However, it is not possible to dismiss it on grounds that it could not gain popular support, or that it would be immediately crushed by traditional military forces.[27]

Conclusions

In his final argument, Wertheimer notes that contrary to what he takes to be the anarchist position, "human suffering cannot always be attributed to states and their legal superstructures."[28] This comment illustrates well one of the most common popular misconceptions about the nature of anarchism, namely, that it can be reduced to mere antistatism or opposition to government. It is essential to understand that in spite of the manner in which they have been depicted by many opponents, anarchists reject such a simplistic analysis of human problems. Despite Wertheimer's denial, anarchists have always recognized that there are natural restrictions on human wellbeing. In fact, one of the most distinctive contributions of anarchist thought has been its movement in the direction of a decisive break with the Western rationalist and Enlightenment belief in liberation through epistemological-technological triumph over nature. In their critique of the concept of the domination of nature (which has become an increasingly prominent theme in anarchist thought), anarchists have argued that it is our tendency to deny our limitations over against nature that has led to a will to power which lies at the core of the authoritarian consciousness. In this sense anarchist theory aims at a fully developed naturalism which is *much more* than a fully developed humanism.[29] But this is only a part of what is overlooked in characterizations such as Wertheimer's. It is equally significant that in analyzing social limitations on human development, anarchists have not restricted their analysis to the effects of the state. Their critique deals with the entire system of domination, including not only its statist and bureaucratic aspects, but also such factors as economic exploitation, racial oppression, sexual repression, sexism, heterosexism, ageism, and technological domination.

Anarchism has a highly coherent and historically founded approach to the problems mentioned by Wertheimer. The case for anarchism is not discredited, and is, in fact, hardly touched by the kinds of criticism he and many other contemporary commentators offer. In their view, anarchism is an unwise strategy for social change because it presents little hope for gain but great risk of losses for humanity. Yet, anarchist theory presents considerable evidence that the reverse may well be the case. The scope of this essay has precluded any attempt to explore thoroughly the details of this evidence. Instead, this discussion has attempted to identify more carefully the nature of the anarchist position and to present some of the central arguments and empirical data which support some of its key claims. One of the most important of these claims is that reliance on the state or a global superstate for change will lead to a continuation of many of the patterns of domination that the state has done so much to develop and reinforce in the past. If this is correct, the anarchist strategy of change "from below" in people's everyday lives, in their families, in their work and community relationships, and finally, in society at large through associations rooted in these fundamental struggles, would seem much more promising.

Anarchists maintain that the roots of the present ecological crisis can be found in the prevailing systems of industrialism and centralist high technology. The anarchist programme is both a strategy for human liberation and a plan for avoiding global ecological catastrophe. While this programme obviously requires a great deal of further development, even in its present form it appears to be the only political practice which offers a viable synthesis between the values of human self-development and liberation, and those of ecological balance and global survival. It is for this reason that Richard Falk concludes that "the anarchist vision... of a fusion between a universal confederation and organic societal forms of a communal character lies at the very center of the *only* hopeful prospect for the future world order."[30] If this hope is ever to be realized, what is necessary is the development of a viable libertarian and communalist theory and practice. This will require the coming of a new epoch in social theory in which there is a decisive break with both liberal and Marxist ideology and a new era of global social experimentation in which the social form legitimated by these ideologies is transcended in a practice of social and ecological regeneration.

Notes

1. Alan Wertheimer, "Disrespect for Law and the Case for Anarchy," in *Anarchism: Nomos XIX* (New York: NYU Press, 1978), pp. 167-88.
2. *Ibid.*
3. For one of the most advanced statements of the contemporary anarchist position, see Murray Bookchin, *Post-Scarcity Anarchism* (Montréal: Black Rose Books, 1977), *Towards an Ecological Society* (Montréal: Black Rose Books, 1980), and *The Ecology of Freedom* (Palo Alto: Cheshire Books, 1982).
4. Wertheimer, *op. cit.*, pp. 182-83.
5. See "Elements of Amerindian Demography" in Pierre Clastres, *Society Against the State* (New York: Urizen Books, 1977), pp. 64-82.
6. Wertheimer, *op. cit.*, p. 184.
7. For a libertarian, decentralist view of the effects of industrialization and urbanization on Third World societies, see E.F. Schumacher, *Small Is Beautiful* (New York: Harper, 1973), Part III. On the Indian anarchist Sarvodaya movement, which carries on the Gandhian tradition of village cooperative production, see Geoffrey Ostergaard and Melville Currell, *The Gentle Anarchists* (New York: Oxford University Press, 1972).
8. Peter Kropotkin, *Fields, Factories and Workshops Tomorrow*, ed. by Colin Ward (London: Allen and Unwin, 1974).
9. David Morris and Karl Hess, *Neighborhood Power* (Boston: Beacon Press, 1975). See also Bookchin's "Towards a Liberatory Technology" in *Post-Scarcity Anarchism, op. cit.*, pp. 83-139.
10. See especially Lewis Mumford, *Technics and Civilization* (New York: Harcourt, Brace and World, 1934), and *The Myth of the Machine* (New York: Harcourt, Brace, Jovanovich, 1967-70).
11. *Technics and Civilization, op. cit.*, p. 388.
12. For one of the most detailed discussions of the practical feasibility of decentralized, communitarian technology see Peter Harper and Godfrey Boyle, eds., *Radical Technology* (New York: Pantheon Books, 1976).
13. See Dorothy Lee, *Freedom and Culture* (Englewood Cliffs: Prentice-Hall, 1959); Norman O. Brown, *Love's Body* (New York: Random House, 1966); Claude Lévi-Strauss, *Tristes Tropiques* (New York: Pocket Books, 1977), especially Part Seven, "Nambikwara"; Ashley Montagu, ed., *Learning Non-Aggression* (Oxford: Oxford University Press, 1978), and Bernard Rudolfsky, *Architecture Without Architects* (Garden City: Doubleday, 1964).

14. See Marshall Sahlins, *Stone Age Economics* (Chicago: Aldine Publishing Co., 1972).
15. Wertheimer, *op. cit.*, p. 183.
16. *Ibid.*
17. Martin Buber, *Paths In Utopia* (Boston: Beacon Press, 1958), p. 136.
18. See Christopher Jencks, *et al.*, *Inequality* (New York: Harper, 1973), especially the statistical analysis of income distribution on p. 210.
19. Gaston Leval, *Collectives in the Spanish Revolution* (London: Freedom Press, 1975), pp. 184-85.
20. *Ibid.*, p. 85. For the internationalist position of the Federacion Regional Española, developed as early as 1870, see Temma Kaplan, *Anarchists of Andalusia 1868-1903* (Princeton: Princeton University Press, 1977), pp. 61-91.
21. For the anarchist critique of the Russian Revolution, see Voline, *The Unknown Revolution* (Montréal: Black Rose Books, 1974); on China, see *The Revolution Is Dead* (Montréal: Black Rose Books, 1977).
22. Wertheimer, *op. cit.*, p. 184.
23. See Kropotkin's *The State* (London: Freedom Press, 1969); Bookchin's "The Forms of Freedom" in *Post-Scarcity Anarchism*, pp. 143-69; Paul and Percival Goodman, *Communitas* (New York: Random House, 1960); Murray Bookchin, *Limits of the City* (New York: Harper, 1974); Robert Goodman, *After the Planners* (New York: Simon and Schuster, 1971); and the continuing discussion of the "urban question" in the Canadian libertarian journal, *Our Generation*.
24. Wertheimer, *op. cit.*, p. 185.
25. See Peter Arshinov, *History of the Makhnovist Movement* (Detroit: Black and Red, 1977).
26. See Vernon Richards, *Lessons of the Spanish Revolution* (London: Freedom Press, 1972), and José Peirats, *Anarchists in the Spanish Revolution* (Detroit: Black and Red, 1977).
27. For one of the few theoretical treatments of the topic, see the works of the "anarcho-Marxist" Abraham Guillén. For selections from his writings, which have been influential in Latin America, see his *Philosophy of the Urban Guerrilla* (New York: William Morrow and Co., 1973).
28. Wertheimer, *op. cit.*, p. 184.
29. This is one of the points at which contemporary anarchist theory intersects most clearly with critical theory. Cf. Herbert Marcuse, *One Dimensional Man* (Boston: Beacon Press, 1964),

pp. 144-69; Max Horkheimer and Theodor Adorno, *The Dialectic of Enlightenment* (New York: Seabury, 1972), pp. 81-119; and Albrecht Wellmer, *Critical Theory of Society* (New York: Seabury, 1974), pp. 129-39. For an excellent discussion relating the critique of technology and domination of nature to major themes in Eastern thought, see Hwa Yol Jung, "The Paradox of Man and Nature: Reflections On Man's Ecological Predicament" in *The Centennial Review*, vol. XVIII, no. 1.

30. "Anarchism and World Order" in Pennock and Chapman, *op. cit.*, p. 75.

Chapter 7

Master Lao and the Anarchist Prince

The *Lao Tzu* is one of the great anarchist classics.* Indeed, there are good reasons to conclude that no important philosophical work of either East or West has even been so thoroughly pervaded by the anarchistic spirit, and that none of the Western political thinkers known as major anarchist theorists (Godwin, Proudhon, Stirner, Bakunin, and Kropotkin) have been nearly as consistent in drawing out the implications of the anarchist perspective.

These conclusions follow from an examination of two aspects of the philosophical position of the work. The first relates to

---

* The *Lao Tzu* or *Tao te Ching* is one of the great philosophical classics of world literature. Taoism, which takes much of its inspiration from the work, is one of the two predominant traditions of thought and practice spanning the history of Chinese civilization. The *Lao Tzu* has over the ages appealed to diverse groups of readers. Some have found in it philosophical enlightenment: others, a path to mystical experience; and still others, knowledge of the means for personal growth. In recent years, many Western readers have given it more careful attention, as the growth of ecological consciousness has uncovered fatal limitations in Western views of nature, and the Taoist philosophy of nature has been looked to as a more adequate alternative.

165

the most distinctive characteristic of anarchism: its opposition to all forms of domination. Classical anarchism made considerable contributions to the critique of several of these forms.¹ Its strengths lay in its analysis of the state and of economic exploitation, and in its modest but significant groundbreaking in the analysis of bureaucracy and technological domination. In the past generation the anarchist critique has expanded considerably. With the growth of feminism has come an awareness of the centrality of patriarchy in the origin and perpetuation of hierarchical society. Closely related has been the development of critical psychology, which has explored the relation between the institutional forms of domination, the processes of authoritarian conditioning, and the constitution of the psyche. Finally, the elaboration of the ecological perspective has led to a careful examination of human domination of nature. As a result of these advances there now exists an anarchist critique of domination which makes the classical anarchist position appear naïve and undeveloped.

The *Lao Tzu*, on the other hand, appears remarkably advanced theoretically if this contemporary critique is taken as the standard. It deals with *all* the dimensions of domination that have just been cited, and subjects them to thorough criticism.

While the critique of domination is an important aspect of the anarchist position, even more essential is the positive worldview that underlies it. What gives significances to the negation of domination is a vision of the self, society and nature that can give direction to the project of social transformation. In short, there must be a coherent metaphysics of anarchism. But far from working out such a worldview, classical anarchism was extremely traditional and uncritical in this area. While there was some awareness of the need to break with Western individualism and mechanism, none of the major figures ever formulated a metaphysics which could adequately ground the moral ideal of a cooperative, non-dominating society. It is in this fundamental realm that contemporary anarchism has made its greatest advances over that of the last century. While it is true that some exponents continue to defend its classical Western forms, a growing number have adopted an organicist, ecological anarchism which coherently synthesizes theory and practice, metaphysics and critique.²

I have described earlier in this book the nature of this tendency in contemporary anarchist thought, which increasingly

> has come to see the ecological perspective as the macrocosmic correlate (indeed, the philosophy of nature) of the libertarian conception of a co-operative, voluntarily organized society. It has been moving toward a fully-developed, organic theory of reality, a theory which proposes a distinct view of nature, of human society, of the group, and of the self or person... [T]he organic, ecological worldview delineates a reality in which the whole is a unity-in-diversity, in which the development and fulfillment of the part can only proceed from its complex interrelationship and unfolding within the larger whole. The universe is seen not as a lifeless mechanism but rather as an organic whole, a totality consisting of non-discrete, interpenetrating processes. Society must become, like nature itself, an organic, integrated community.... And underlying all must be a new vision of the self—a self which is itself organic, having the nature of a process. It must be a self which is not objectified, or divided against itself, but rather is a harmonious synthesis of passion, rationality, and imagination. Such a self is a social creation, an embodiment of our common human nature in its process of historical development, yet also the most individualized and unique self-expression of reality, and therefore the most ultimately creative process.[3]

This chapter will demonstrate that on almost every key point the *Lao Tzu* is in accord with organicist anarchism. First, it teaches that ultimate reality—Tao—is organic, that it is a unity-in-diversity, that it consists of interrelated processes of personal and universal self-realization, and that it is a system of natural order free from domination. Secondly, the Taoist virtues of compassion, frugality, and non-assertion will be discussed as the basis of an anarchist non-authoritarian personality and of corresponding non-dominating social relations. Finally, the *Lao Tzu's* conception of the ruler-sage will be shown to be founded on an anarchist political position which rejects the state, law, and coercion.

The vision expressed in the *Lao Tzu* is perhaps above all a vision of an organic unity-in-diversity. One of the most powerful metaphors in the work is that of "the Uncarved Block" through which we are called back to a deep, underlying reality which humanity has largely forgotten. Our customs, our social conditioning, our language, in fact the most fundamental categories by which we interpret the world, lead us to fragment reality, to invalidly shatter it into a system of disconnected, or, at best, externally related objects and egos. The problem of metaphysics is to create an awareness of the oneness which underlies this multiplicity, and to do this without resorting to illusions which deny reality by dissolving plurality into nothingness. Taoism in no sense seeks an escape from the diversity and complexity of the world. On the contrary, its unifying vision coexists with an almost Nietzschean affirmation of individuality.

Yet the concreteness of the Taoist vision goes beyond this. The perception of the gap between unity-in-diversity and unreconciled division is firmly rooted in historical reality. It is essential to understand the *Lao Tzu* as perhaps the most eloquent expression of society's recollection of its lost oneness, an evocation of the condition of wholeness which preceded the rending of the social fabric by institutions like the state, private property, and patriarchy. Significantly, the *Lao Tzu* encompasses a ringing condemnation of all three of these systems, and proposes their replacement by institutions much closer to those of tribal society. I would suggest that just as Stanley Diamond has called for an understanding of Plato which takes into account his relation to these world-historical transformations (that is, as annihilator of the remnants of tribal values), so we should see the place of the *Lao Tzu* in this conflict (as a re-affirmation of organic society and its values).[4]

What precisely does the *Lao Tzu* say about the nature of Tao as unity?[5] Often it is said to be the origin of everything, that out of which all arises, that on which all things depend. It is "the ancestor of all things" (Chan, 4) and "the mother of all things" (Chan, 1). These images can be somewhat deceptive if they are taken to imply any separation between Tao and the universe. For there is no division: Tao is all-inclusive and immanent in "the ten thousand things." "Analogically, Tao in the world (where everything is embraced by it), may be compared to rivers and streams running into the sea" (Chan, 32). There is thus a oneness which underlies the multiplicity of the universe.

This oneness is not, however, a static unity, but rather the unity of the interrelated parts of a creative process. This follows from the assertion that Tao consists of both being and non-being. "All things in the world come from being. And being comes from non-being" (Chan, 40). As the opening chapter of the work explains, both being and non-being are aspects of Tao, and a full understanding of reality requires knowledge of both the multiplicity of existing things and also of the process of generation, the coming out of non-being into being:

> 'Non-Being' names this beginning of Heaven and Earth;
> 'Being' names the mother of the myriad things.
> Therefore, some people constantly dwell in 'Non-Being'
> Because they seek to perceive its mysteries,
> While some constantly dwell in 'Being'
> Because they seek to preserve its boundaries.
> These two ['Non-Being' and 'Being'] are of the same origin,
> But have different names.... (Young and Ames, 1)

This view of Tao immediately brings to mind many similar concepts in both Eastern and Western metaphysics. Notable examples include the distinction in Vedanta between Nirguna and Saguna Brahman, Böhme's discussions of the divine *Ungrund* and *Urgrund*, and Eckhart's references to a *Gottheit* that is more primordial even than *Gott*. There have been numerous attempts to explain the ubiquity of this coexistence of negative and positive description in mystical and organismic thought of many traditions. One approach is to stress the fact that in view of the inadequacy of our objectifying, delimiting language, reality can only be grasped by contradictory predications. The concept of the ultimate as the totality captures one aspect of reality: the oneness of all things. Yet it is necessary to speak of the ultimate as nothingness or non-being, inasmuch as reality is not a mere collection of all things in the world, but a unity in which our conventional conceptions of "thingness" or individuation are negated.[6]

I think that this explains part of what is intended in the *Lao Tzu*. But further, the assertion of the ultimacy of both being and non-being is an assault on all static conceptions of reality. Taoism should not be confused with forms of organicist thought (or pseudo-organicism) that call for "identification" with a timeless, spaceless, motionless One. The whole, like each being, is a process of becoming in which both being and non-being are enduring presences. No doubt the mystery of birth was a tremendous influence in the shaping of this conception. Just as birth is a process in which a being emerges out of the vague and mysterious void, so the universe as being must arise out of nothingness. Yet this is not to be taken in a mere mythological or cosmogonal sense, for the process of generation is asserted to be without beginning. It is thus an explanation of the enduring structure of reality. The process is repeated in the development of each being in the universe:

> Man models himself after Earth.
> Earth models itself after Heaven.
> Heaven models itself after Tao.
> And Tao models itself after Nature. (Chan, 25)

There is thus a macrocosm-microcosm relationship between the universal Tao and each being, although this relationship in no way negates the individuality and uniqueness of each. For in both cases development is a process of creative self-realization.

According to the *Lao Tzu*, each being has its own Tao, in the sense of its own path of self-development and unfolding. While it is true, as David Hall argues, that Taoism rejects "principles as transcendent determining sources of order,"[7] and as Roger Ames contends, that it negates such "authoritarian determination" as "teleological purpose, divine design, Providence,"[8] I believe that it would be incorrect to conclude that Taoism dispenses with *all* teleology. In fact, Tao can perhaps be described best as the immanent Telos of all beings. It is not surprising that teleology should seem tainted by authoritarianism, given the character of teleological philosophy from

Plato and Aristotle to Hegel and Marx. But while teleological explanation has served such purposes as legitimating class domination, nationalism, and human exploitation of nature, there is no necessary connection between teleology and domination. Thus, in the *Lao Tzu* we find a teleology which recognizes that each being has its own process of self-development that should not be disturbed:

> To know harmony means to be in accord with the eternal.
> To be in accord with the eternal means to be enlightened.
> To force the growth of life means ill omen.
> For the mind to employ the vital force without restraint
>   means violence.
> After things reach their prime, they begin to grow old,
> Which means being contrary to Tao.
> Whatever is contrary to Tao will soon perish. (Chan, 55)

The point is that we should allow each being to follow its own ideal pattern of development, which we cannot "force," but only hinder, through our interference. Given the accompanying conditions for nurturing growth, fullness of being will be achieved, after which comes inevitable decline and dissolution. The image of the self as the "Uncarved Block" expresses the idea of wholeness entailed in this self-development. The view of Lau that it means "a state as yet untouched by the artificial interference of human ingenuity"[9] partly misses the mark, I think, since it implies that there can somehow be a pure, pristine Self independent of human society, and that there is something necessarily "artificial" about "human ingenuity." It is true that "carving the block" means distorting the self by interfering with its development according to its unique telos, but society does not *necessarily* have any such effect.

All human development takes place within the context of social relationships, and these can be the conditions for either self-realization or self-limitation. Consequently, "human ingenuity" can be just as much a means of preserving the "Uncarved Block" in its uncarved state, as a factor in distorting it. Thus, tribal societies which conceive of social relations primarily in terms of kinship, and which hold a vitalistic or panpsychist view of nature, tend to maintain a high degree of awareness of the social and natural roots of the self. Civilization, in identifying the self with social status (citizenship, class membership, property ownership, functional role, etc.) reduces the organic social self to a narrower individual or abstract ego. The *Lao Tzu* looks backward to the primordial unfragmented society and its social self, just as it points forward to a restored organic society and social person.

In the concept of the organic self, both Taoism and contemporary anarchism seek to transcend the narrow limits of "the individual." As Roger Ames notes, given the metaphysics of organism, the person "is understood as a matrix of relationships which can be fully expressed only by reference to the organismic whole," and for this reason "the expression 'individual' might well be ruled altogether inappropriate in describing a person."[10] For similar reasons there has been a tendency in recent organicist anarchist thought to explicitly reject "the individual" as the degraded self produced over millenia of social domination, and perfected in modern bourgeois, statist, technobureaucratic society. The term "person" is reserved for the developed social self that can thrive only in an organic community embracing humanity and nature.[11]

Two aspects of Tao have now been mentioned. First, it is an organic unity-in-diversity; and secondly, it is an ideal course of development or unfolding inherent in all things. The final aspect is in a sense merely the synthesis of these two. Given the organic connectedness of all beings, the totality of all processes of self-realization constitutes a harmonious system. Tao is thus a natural order in each being and in reality as a whole. If each being strives only to reach its own natural perfection, and refrains from seeking to dominate others, the greatest possible order will result. Thus, the ironic truth proclaimed in the *Lao Tzu* is that attempts to control lead to disorder, and that the more extensive the control, the more chaotic the world becomes. Spontaneity and order are not opposites, as is universally held according to political, technical, and economistic rationality, but rather they are identical. If each being is permitted to follow its Tao, the needs of all will be fulfilled without coercion and domination. Note the contrast between Tao and the patriarchal authoritarian God, who demands abject subservience from his creatures:

> All things depend on it for life, and it does not turn away from them.
> It accomplishes its task, but does not claim credit for it.
> It clothes and feeds all things but does not claim to be master over them. (Chan, 34)

The Taoist vision penetrates the illusion of inevitable natural scarcity (which arose with the political, economic and technical innovations of civilization), to apprehend the abundance of the outpouring of nature. Every society founded on domination and struggle within society has always perceived the human relation to nature as one of struggle, conflict, and conquest. No matter how much production may increase, scarcity persists or even expands. But in the *Lao Tzu*, as in the consciousness of pre-civilized humanity, nature is understood to be, rather than a collection of scarce resources, an infinite wealth, a plenitude:

> Heaven and earth unite to drip sweet dew.
> Without the command of men, it drips evenly over all.
> (Chan, 32)

When each follows his or her own Tao, and recognizes and respects the Tao in all other beings, a harmonious system of self-realization will exist in nature. There is a kind of natural justice that prevails, so that the needs of each are fulfilled:

> The Way of Heaven reduces whatever is excessive and supplements whatever is insufficient.

Whereas (as will be discussed later):

> The Way of Man is different.
> It reduces the insufficient to offer to the excessive. (Chan, 77)

According to Lau, in statements such as the above "heaven is conceived of as taking an active hand in redressing the iniquities of this world," and "this runs counter to the view of the Tao generally to be found in the book as something non-personal and amoral."[12] But there is no reason to find such an inconsistency, unless one minimizes the metaphysical implications of the work, and interprets it as a more or less eclectic anthology of traditional wisdom. For if the Tao is an all-encompassing natural order, a unity-in-diversity in which the immanent telos of each being is in harmony with that of all others and of the whole, then there is no need to posit any sort of personal agency in the universe responsible for rectifying injustice. Order and justice are assured when each being follows its appropriate path of development. All other systems of order are mere social conventions, and to the degree that they deflect us from our natural end, they produce only disorder and injustice:

> Therefore, only when Tao is lost does the doctrine of virtue arise.
> When virtue is lost, only then does the doctrine of humanity arise.
> When humanity is lost, only then does the doctrine of righteousness arise.
> When righteousness is lost, only then does the doctrine of propriety arise.
> Now propriety is a superficial expression of loyalty and faithfulness, and the beginning of disorder. (Chan, 38)

Insofar as morality means social convention, the *Lao Tzu* advocates a perspective of "amorality." But to the degree that it proposes a way of life founded on universal self-realization unrestricted by domination and instrumental rationality, it constitutes one of the most distinctive and significant moral theories ever propounded. In a sense the moral purpose of the *Lao Tzu* is its central one, for the emphasis in the work is never on mere description of the nature of things. The inquiry into ultimate reality is always firmly embedded in a search for a way of life, and a true understanding of the work requires that attention be given to the art of living that it describes. Fortunately, the author summarizes the essentials of this art very concisely:

> I have three treasures. Guard and keep them:
> The first is deep love,[13]
> The second is frugality,[14]
> And the third is not to dare to be ahead of the world.[15]
> (Chan, 67)

While the first Taoist virtue is compassion, some passages in the *Lao Tzu* give the impression that not only is it not virtuous, but that it is even contrary to nature. For example:

> Heaven and Earth are not humane (*jen*).
> They regard all things as straw dogs.
> The sage is not humane.
> He regards all people as straw dogs. (Chan, 5)

In asserting that the enlightened person regards all people as straw dogs—worthless ritual objects—the author seems to be rejecting both humanism and compassion. But this is only half true. While the *Lao Tzu* is predicated on anti-humanism (in fact, this is one of its great strengths), this does not imply a denial of the importance of compassion. Rather, it is only with a rejection of humanism that the greatest possible compassion can arise. To act "humanely" means, at worst, merely accepting the conventions of society concerning morality and goodness, and implies, at best, remaining within the biased perspective of the interest of our own species. To transcend this "humane" outlook means, as Chan says, to be "impartial, to have no favorites,"[16] but not in the sense of complete detachment. Rather, it is the *impartiality* that results from identification with the whole, an impartiality that allows one to respect all beings and value their various goods.[17] For this reason it is possible to assert that "the Sage has no fixed (personal) ideas. He regards the people's ideas as his own" (Chan, 49), and that "he has no personal interests" (Chan, 7).

The person who comprehends Tao is able to take the perspective of the other, and to overcome the egoism which treats the good of each as antagonistic to that of the other. This is certainly the implication of the famous passage stating that:

> ...he who values the world as his body may be entrusted
> with the empire.
> He who loves the world as his body may be entrusted
> with the empire. (Chan, 13)

Some commentators have stressed the implicit approval of a kind of selfishness in the concept of concern for one's body,[18] for unless one fully affirms his or her own existence and process of self-realization, there is no possibility of truly valuing other beings or of affirming reality. But a further important implication of the passage is that one should identify with the whole. Realizing one's own Tao is identical with participation in the universal Tao. Thus, all self-realization, one's own and that of all others, is valued by one who understands Tao. Compassion arises from a "self-love" that has nothing to do with egoism.

The way of life advocated in the *Lao Tzu* is thus based on love, respect, and compassion for all things. If such a life is to be lived, one must understand the bounds of one's own Tao: what is essential to one's own self-realization, what is unnecessary, and what undermines it and that of others. The *Lao Tzu* expresses this idea in its teaching that one should seek simplicity and frugality, and avoid luxury, extravagance, and excess.

Some interpretations of the *Lao Tzu* hold that it advocates "asceticism." If this term is defined as a kind of self-denial or self-sacrifice for the sake of some higher Good, then the truth is just the contrary. And even if it is construed as a kind of "renunciation" (to use Chang's unfortunate term) for the sake of one's own spiritual growth, this misses the point somewhat. The life of "simplicity" is in no way the impoverished life of one who seeks escape from the corrupt world and its temptations. Rather it is something much more affirmative: it is the consummate existence of one who has rejected whatever would stunt or distort growth and personal fulfillment.

Simplicity is not, however, a quality with implications for personal life alone. It refers also to social institutions which will promote rather than hinder self-realization. A society based on social status, or one glorifying the pursuit of wealth and permitting economic inequality, is inevitably destructive and produces conflict, disorder, envy, and crime:

> Do not exalt the worthy, so that the people will not compete.
> Do not value rare treasures, so that the people shall not steal.
> Do not display objects of desire, so that the people's hearts shall not be disturbed. (Chan, 3)

Rather, we should "discard profit" (Chan, 19). But in doing so, we are losing nothing, for the pursuit of wealth and social status only distracts one from the essential task of following one's Tao. Just as the New Testament asks "what does it profit a man to gain the whole world, yet lose his own soul," so the *Lao Tzu* places in question the value of wealth and prestige:

> Which does one love more, fame or one's own life?
> Which is more valuable, one's own life or wealth?
> ....
> He who hoards most will lose heavily. (Chan, 44)

But wealth and luxury are not condemned only because of their spiritually debilitating quality. There is also a recognition that they are unjust and contrary to the order of nature. The *Lao Tzu* attacks the institutions of civilization on the grounds that whereas nature "reduces whatever is excessive and supplements what is insufficient," society "reduces the insufficient to offer to the excessive" (Chan, 77). The criticism of political and economic institutions is sometimes made explicit:

> The courts are exceedingly splendid,
> While the fields are exceedingly weedy,
> And the granaries are exceedingly empty.
> Elegant clothes are worn,
> Sharp weapons are carried,
> Foods and drinks are enjoyed beyond limit,
> And wealth and treasures are accumulated in excess.
> This is robbery and extravagance.
> This is indeed not Tao (the way). (Chan, 53)

While this attack on economic and social inequality seems fully in accord with the Taoist outlook,[19] it might seem strange

177

to some that the *Lao Tzu* would go so far as to launch an attack on knowledge and wisdom in the name of simplicity.[20] Why would a work which itself attempts to transmit wisdom about life, and which has traditionally been attributed to an "old sage," counsel one to "abandon sageliness and discard wisdom" (Chan, 19)? The truth conveyed is not as obscure as it might appear initially. In an organic society, knowledge (like art, religion, and politics) is integrated into the life of the community, rather than reified by becoming the possession of the members of a hierarchical institution. The *Lao Tzu* is attacking knowledge as the *property* of an intelligentsia or a class of literati. Just as wealth sets one against another and seduces people away from their natural good, so knowledge can do likewise if it is reduced to a form of amassing power:

> True wisdom is different from much learning;
> Much learning means little wisdom.
> The sage has no need to hoard;
> When his own last scrap has been used up on behalf of others,
> Lo, he has more than before! (Waley, 81)

One final implication of the concept of simplicity: its requirement that certain forms of technology be rejected and that technical efficiency not be accepted uncritically as a justification for social change. The *Lao Tzu* exhibits an awareness that technological development, which has always been justified as fulfilling human needs, may in fact be destructive of human self-realization and of the social institutions most conducive to it. What is feared is that artificial wants and desires will be created, and that complex, hierarchical social institutions, accompanied by egoism, inequality, and disorder, will arise. Consequently, the community should reject such technology and preserve its simplicity:

> Given a small country with few inhabitants, he could bring it about that though there should be among the people contrivances requiring ten times, a hundred times less labour, he would not use them. (Waley, 80)

I hasten to add that there is nothing in the Taoist view that implies that new *non-dominating* forms of technology should be rejected. But given the fact that technical innovation in the epoch of the *Lao Tzu* served the purposes of power and control, it is not surprising that the work should emphasize the need for a more critical approach to technological change.

An important theme throughout the *Lao Tzu* is the necessity of avoiding competition and other forms of self-assertive and aggressive action. What is proposed instead is "non-action" (*wu-wei*), activity which is in accord with one's own Tao and with those of all others. Since one achieves the good life by following one's own unique path, there is no point in striving to place oneself "above" others. In fact, to do so is self-destructive, since in competing we subordinate ourselves to some external standard of goodness, virtue, or success. Even if we "win," we are defeated, since we have conformed to the alien values of those whom we have vanquished. Competition conflicts with the Taoist emphasis on individuality (a quality that excludes individualism, which is necessarily competitive), and with what David Hall calls the "polycentric" view. The Taoist sage will therefore "succeed" through eschewing the quest for power and prestige:

> He does not show himself; therefore he is luminous.
> He does not justify himself; therefore he becomes prominent.
> He does not boast of himself; therefore he is given credit.
> He does not brag; therefore he can endure for long.
> It is precisely because he does not compete that the world cannot compete with him. (Chan, 22)

In describing the non-aggressive, non-dominating personality that is the ideal, the *Lao Tzu* continually resorts to images of the female and the child. Roger Ames is entirely correct when he argues that the Taoist advocates a form of androgyny in which "the masculine and feminine gender traits are integrated in some harmonious and balanced relationship."[21] This is the clear implication of the statement that:

> He who knows the male (active force) and keeps to the
> female (the passive force or receptive element)
> Becomes the ravine of the world. (Chan, 28)

The concept of rigidly defined sex roles is totally alien to the Taoist sensibility, since this implies subordinating the unique person to social convention, and denying the diversity of human nature. It is another example of cutting the "Uncarved Block," or interfering brutally with Tao.

But there is a good reason why, in spite of its androgynism, the importance of the female is stressed heavily. The *Lao Tzu* is launching a direct (if non-aggressive!) attack on one of history's most entrenched and enduring systems of domination: patriarchy. Under a patriarchal system there is little need to emphasize the value of "masculine" qualities. What is required is a vehement defense of the "feminine." Furthermore, while it is true that "masculine" qualities are recognized in the *Lao Tzu* to be of value, those usually stereotyped as "feminine" seem to be the *more essential* ones to the Taoist perspective. In a revealing passage, creativity and love (in the non-possessive "maternal" sense) are identified as "feminine":

> Can you understand all and penetrate all without taking any action?
> To produce things and to rear them,
> To produce, but not to take possession of them,
> To act, but not to rely on one's own ability,
> To lead them, but not to master them—
> This is called profound and secret virtue (*hsüan-te*). (Chan, 10)

In a Taoist community, people are permitted to develop according to their own Tao, so that to the extent that "masculinity" and "feminity" exist (as *contrasting*, but not *opposed* qualities), they are spontaneous and natural. An infinite variety in combinations of qualities might occur. Without *imposed* sex roles, androgyny is the ideal. However, when we consider the strictly opposed sex roles of patriarchy, no reconciliation of the antagonistic roles is possible, and the "feminine" must be selected as being closer to the ideal.

For similar reasons the child is often taken as the model. This is also heretical from the perspective of patriarchal society. Since virtuousness is identified with the power and status of the adult male, to recommend that adults emulate infants appears ludicrous at best. Yet for anti-patriarchal Taoism, the child has two essential qualities in abundance: non-aggressiveness and spontaneity. While in a society based on power, strength is valued most as a personal characteristic, in the Taoist society founded on natural order one should seek "the highest degree of weakness like an infant" (Chan, 10). The infant is not ruled by inordinate desires, such as the longing for power, wealth, status, or luxury. Instead, all actions are natural and spontaneous. As the *Lao Tzu* states in an irrefutable argument:

> He may cry all day without becoming hoarse,
> This means that his (natural) harmony is perfect. (Chan, 55)

Just as in nature the softest and weakest thing, water, can overcome the hardest obstacle, so softness and weakness are the most effective qualities in personal development. Softness characterizes the organic, while hardness is typical of the inorganic and mechanistic. Rigidity, both mental and physical, is an attribute of the authoritarian. Rigid muscles and rigid categories are two closely related ways of futilely attempting to stop the flow of reality. As Wilhelm Reich explains, "character armor" is the means by which the authoritarian seeks to avoid the threat of feeling and experiencing too much.[22] The *Lao Tzu* states the same point:

> When a man is born, he is tender and weak.
> At death he is stiff and hard.
> All things, the grass as well as trees, are tender and supple
>   while alive.
> When dead, they are withered and dried.
> Therefore the stiff and the hard are companions of death.
> The tender and weak are companions of life. (Chan, 76)

What then can be said of a society obsessed with economic and political power, a society riddled with bureaucratic and technocratic organization, a society convinced that "security" comes from military strength (in short, of civilization in its most advanced state)? From the Taoist viewpoint such a society is striving to reduce people to a condition of living death. Our society, even more than the earlier stage of civilization known at the time of the *Lao Tzu*, possesses all the qualities that are the target of the work's devastating attack. The *Lao Tzu* illustrates well how out of organicist metaphysics flows an anarchist critique of both the inorganic society based on power relations and of the character structures which prevail in such a society.

In view of this critique, it is true, as Roger Ames argues, that Taoism should not be judged "quietistic," as it often is when its discussion of the feminine, the childlike, weakness, and softness are not analyzed carefully. When power is combatted by its own methods ("strength"), power inevitably prevails, no matter which side is victorious. But despite its rejection of aggressiveness, Taoism does not propose a quietistic withdrawal from the world. Rather, it contends that the foundations of power can be undermined by "rivers and streams flowing to the sea" (Chan, 32).

In spite of all its authoritarianism, one might conclude that what the *Lao Tzu* advocates is merely quasi-anarchistic, because the work is explicitly addressed to the ruler, and because the existence of the state is accepted. While Roger Ames argues for the coherence of the idea of Taoist anarchism, he contends that the *Lao Tzu* does not fully adopt this position, since it "sees the state as a *natural* institution, analogous perhaps to the family."[23] Frederic Bender goes even further, concluding that the work is "hardly anarchistic in the Western sense, since it retains, albeit in improved form, ruler, rule, and the means of rule (the state)."[24] My position is that it dispenses with all of these, if they are taken in their *political* sense. Its major divergence from classical Western anarchism is that, given its more thorough rejection of patriarchy, technological domination, and domination of nature, and given the greater coherence of its metaphysical foundations, the *Lao Tzu* is more consistently anarchistic.

The *Lao Tzu* expresses an entirely negative view of government. Occasionally it sounds as if only the *excesses* of political control are condemned:

> The people starve because the ruler eats too much tax grain.
> ....
> They are difficult to rule because their ruler does too many things. (Chan, 75)

Such a passage might mean that good rulers would tax less and control people less, but, in fact, "good rule" can only mean "no rule," that is, ruling without such measures as taxation and control. The idea of governmental "abuse" is absurd from the standpoint of the *Lao Tzu*, in view of the fundamental and absolute nature of its critique of government.

As the ego is to the organic self, so is political society to the organic community. In both cases the *Lao Tzu* uses the image of the carving of the block:

> Without law or compulsion, men would dwell in harmony.
> Once the block is carved, there will be names. (Waley, 32)

"Naming" refers to reifying dynamic processes, destroying natural unity, and reducing the organic to the inorganic. And this is indeed the transformation that took place with the rise of the state: the organic community was divided or "cut up" into a society of classes, of rulers and ruled, of rich and poor, of élites and masses, and, finally, of individuals contending for power, or, at worst, "survival." The *Lao Tzu* shows an acute awareness of the contrast between previous organic society and existing political society, an awareness which must have been heightened by the intense degree of strife prevailing in its time. Yet the central objection to government is metaphysical: it is a distortion of reality, a destruction of the natural order of society, the replacement of Taoist "non-action" by control and domination.

Government is the source of disorder. This is the political message of the *Lao Tzu*:

> The people are difficult to keep in order because those
> above them intefere. This is the only reason why they
> are so difficult to keep in order. (Waley, 75)

What is strange is not this seemingly paradoxical statement, but rather the fact that after over two thousand years of evidence to support it, it still seems paradoxical. If the *Lao Tzu* is correct, then the more laws there are, the more disorganized society will be; the more prisons are built, the more crime will increase; the more bureaucracy proliferates and experts are trained, the more social problems are aggravated; the more military power expands, the more conflicts occur and the threat of destruction looms larger. (Consequences such as these are predicted in Chapters 57 and 58 of the *Lao Tzu*.) And these have in fact been the results of the political organization of society. Every expansion of political control for the sake of maintaining order has only further destroyed the organic structure of society, thus advancing social disintegration and producing more deeply rooted disorder.

But can the proposed alternative to political society, a non-authoritarian, cooperative society, possibly exist? Frederic Bender thinks that it cannot, although it is not entirely clear what it is that he considers impossible (a non-coercive social system, a society "lacking entirely in institutionalized authority," a "social organism" without "someone exercising authority," or a society practising "unanimous direct democracy").[25] He argues that the fact that such societies never existed is evidence that they are not possible. However, there have indeed been societies without "institutional authority" in the sense of a separate, permanent stratum of officials holding coercive power. Bender cites the existence of the authority of "elders, chiefs, shamans, and the like" as evidence for "systems of authority" in all societies.[26] But to really understand the relevance of these phenomena to anarchism, it is necessary to analyze carefully the meaning of "authority" in each case and the sense in which it constitutes a "system."

I would argue that anthropology presents us with abundant evidence that "authority" in primitive society differs radically from that of political society. To give just one example, while the "chief" is often assumed by the European mind to be a political ruler, in fact, he (or sometimes she) is often primarily a ritual figure, or one with carefully delineated, non-coercive functions dealing with specific areas of group life. Discussions of societies without states or authoritarian political structures can be found in such works as Evans-Pritchard's *The Nuer*, Lévi-Strauss' *Tristes Tropiques*, Tait and Middleton's *Tribes Without Rulers*, Dorothy Lee's *Freedom and Culture*, and, above all, Pierre Clastres' *Society Against the State*.[27] Clastres' conclusions based on the study of many Amerindian tribes are especially striking:

> One is confronted, then, by a vast constellation of societies in which the holders of what elsewhere would be called power are actually without power; where the political is determined as a domain beyond coercion and violence, beyond hierarchical subordination; where, in a word, no relation of command-obedience is in force.[28]

To say that such societies have existed is certainly not to say that they fully embody the anti-authoritarian ideal of anarchism. Yet an exploration of the nature of organic societies of the past serves to show what was lost with the rise of civilization, and what could be regained in a more self-conscious form in the future. It also helps us understand that there are many kinds of authority, and that some imply neither membership in a special office-holding group possessing coercive power, nor even "authoritarianism" in any sense.

The Taoist ruler-sage is an example of one who exercises such non-dominating authority. This authority is, however, much closer to the anarchist ideal than is that of the tribal chief or elder. For whereas these figures often have no personal power at all, they may serve as vehicles through whom the restrictive force of tradition is transmitted. The Taoist ruler, on the other hand, imposes nothing on others, and refuses to legitimate his or her authority through the external supports of either law or tradition.

As is now clear, the *Lao Tzu* teaches that people should not (and, in fact, cannot) be coerced into doing "the right thing." This follows from the internal-development teleology of Taoism (which is opposed to the external-good sort of teleology of utilitarianism, or the transcendent-good teleology of Thomism, for example). The sage does not attempt to legislate or require the good:

> I take no action and the people of themselves are transformed.
> I love tranquility and the people of themselves become correct.
> I engage in no activity and the people of themselves become prosperous.
> I have no desires and the people of themselves become simple. (Chan, 57)

In view of this conception of the true ruler as one who does not interfere with the development of others, there is no reason to think that the sage is what is called in political terminology a "ruler." As Lau notes, "the sage is first and foremost a man who understands the *Tao*, and if he happens also to be a ruler he can apply his understanding of the *Tao* to government."[29] Where I would differ from Lau is, first, that the *Lao Tzu* never implies that only men can be sages, and, secondly, that it is essential to add that applying "understanding of Tao" to government means not governing. Attempts to interpret the *Lao Tzu* as a manual of strategy in the "art of governing" inevitably fail. They require a rather extreme literal-mindedness, in which "ruling" must always mean holding political office, and "weapons" must always mean military, rather than spiritual arms.[30] The meaning attributed to rulership in the *Lao Tzu* is clear: it is the nobility that comes from identification with Tao, and with successfully following one's path of self-realization:

> To know the eternal is called enlightenment.
> Not to know the eternal is to act blindly and to result in disaster.
> He who knows the eternal is all-embracing.
> Being all-embracing, he is impartial.
> Being impartial, he is kingly (universal). (Chan, 16)

The power of the ruler is thus not political; it comes from the force of example alone. It is for this reason that the *Lao Tzu* can assert that "the best (rulers) are those whose existence is (merely) known by the people" (Chan, 17). In fact, in several versions of the text the best rulers are "not" known by the people.[31] Presumably, they are not known as rulers or leaders in the ordinary sense, although they are known as models of personal development. In either case a subtle, non-coercive authority is attributed to the ruler. There is nothing in this kind of authority that is contrary to anarchism. It is neither imposed on anyone nor used to manipulate. On the contrary, it is the result of the most non-aggressive activity, and can only exist if "the people," seeing the sage following the path of non-dominating self-realization, freely choose to do likewise.

Thus, the *Lao Tzu* does not propose the continuation of political authority, but instead its replacement by natural authority. The "empire" which is ruled by the sage is not the political state, but rather the natural order which is attained by the acceptance of Tao. The *Lao Tzu* says implicitly what is stated explicitly in the *Huai Nan Tzu*: "Possessing the empire" means "self-realization."[32]

Notes

1. By "classical" anarchism I mean the tradition associated closely with the international workers' movement, and, especially, that beginning with the mutualism of the French labour movement in the 1840's and extending to the decline of anarcho-syndicalism with the defeat of the Spanish Revolution in the late 1930's.
2. The towering figure in this development is Murray Bookchin. As I have advised in previous essays, his works, *Post-Scarcity Anarchism* (Montréal: Black Rose Books, 1977), *Toward an Ecological Society* (Montréal: Black Rose Books, 1980), and, especially, *The Ecology of Freedom: The Emergence and Dissolution of Hierarchy* (Palo Alto: Cheshire Books, 1982), should be consulted. The latter is the most important book to appear so far in the history of anarchist thought. Those who, like Frederic Bender, suspect that anarchism remains psychologically naïve, should examine Paul Goodman's theory of the self in *Gestalt Therapy* (New York: Bantam Books, 1977). Finally, anyone interested in Taoism and anarchism should consult the work of Ursula LeGuin, who is perhaps the most widely read contemporary anarchist writer, and also a Taoist. For a study of Taoism in one of her best known novels, *The Dispossessed*, see Elizabeth Cummins Cogell, "Taoist Configurations: The Dispossessed" in Joe de Bolt, ed., *Ursula K. LeGuin* (Fort Washington, N.Y.: Kennikat Press, 1979), pp. 153-179.
3. "The Politics of Liberation: From Class to Culture" in *Freedom* (London), vol. 41, no. 17 (Aug. 30, 1980), pp. 9-11, 15-16. Reprinted as the first essay of this volume.
4. "Plato and the Defense of the Primitive" in *In Search of the Primitive: A Critique of Civilization* (New Brunswick: Transaction Books, 1974), pp. 176-202.
5. References to the *Lao Tzu* will cite the translator and the number of the chapter cited. Among the translations consulted were the following: Wing-Tsit Chan, "The Lao Tzu" in *A Source Book in Chinese Philosophy* (Princeton: Princeton University Press, 1963), which will be the primary source cited; R.B. Blakney, *The Way of Life: Lao Tzu* (New York: New American Library, 1955); Gia-Fu Feng and Jane English, *Lao Tzu: Tao te Ching* (New York: Vintage Books, 1972); D.C. Lau, *Lao Tzu: Tao te Ching* (Harmondsworth: Penguin Books, 1963); Rhett Y.W. Young and Roger T. Ames, *Lao Tzu: Text, Notes, and Comments (by Ch'en Ku-ying)* (Taiwan: Chinese Materials Centre, 1981); and Arthur Waley, *The Way and Its Power: A Study of the Tao te*

      Ching and Its Place in Chinese Thought (New York: Grove Press, 1958).
6. Cf. John Findlay, "The Logic of Mysticism" in *Religious Studies* (1972).
7. David Hall, "The Metaphysics of Anarchism," *Journal of Chinese Philosophy*, vol. 10, no. 1, pp. 58-59.
8. Roger Ames, "Is Political Taoism Anarchism?" *Ibid.*, p. 34.
9. Lau, *op. cit.*, footnote 5, p. 36.
10. Ames, *op. cit.*, pp. 31, 30.
11. As I have stated this point previously, the struggle for liberation today is not, as Marxism and classical anarchism argued, "the struggle of the socialist *worker* to succeed the bourgeois *individual* as the subject of history. Rather it is the emergence of the *person*, the organic social self, who must through social, communal self-realization combat those forces and ideologies which reduce this self to asociality (individualism, privatism) or being a producer (productivism)." "The Politics of Liberation," Chapter 1 of this book. For extensive discussion of the problem of the self, see the works of Bookchin cited above.
12. Lau, *op. cit.*, p. 24.
13. "Compassion," according to Lau, Chang, and Blakney; "commiseration," according to Young and Ames; and "pity" in Waley's translation.
14. Young and Ames, Lau, Chan, Waley, and Blakney are in accord on this rendering, while Chang proposes "renunciation."
15. What is rejected is variously translated as "to be first in the world," according to Chang and Young and Ames; "to take the lead in the empire," according to Lau; "to be foremost of all things under Heaven," according to Waley; and to "be the whole world's chief," in Blakney's rather unusual phrasing.
16. Chan, *op. cit.*, footnote 5, p. 142.
17. See Holmes Welch's excellent discussion of this passage in *Taoism: The Parting of the Way* (Boston: Beacon Press, 1957), pp. 44-45.
18. See Lau, p. 40, and Waley, pp. 157-158.
19. Taoism does not, of course, advocate "equality," but rather a society in which both equality and inequality have no meaning.
20. Note that a *reductive simplification* of the self can be the result of the growth in complexity of inorganic social institutions. The social self has a kind of rich complexity which is the goal of Taoist "simplicity."
21. Roger Ames, "Taoism and the Androgynous Ideal," in *Historical Reflections/Réflexions Historiques*, vol. 8, no. 3 (Fall 1981), p. 43.

22. See Wilhelm Reich, *The Mass Psychology of Fascism* (New York: Simon and Schuster, 1970).
23. Ames, "Is Political Taoism Anarchism?" *op. cit.*, p.35.
24. Frederic Bender, "Taoism and Western Anarchism: A Comparative Study," *Journal of Chinese Philosophy*, vol. 10, no. 1, p. 12.
25. *Ibid.*, p. 22.
26. *Ibid.*
27. E. E. Evans-Pritchard, *The Nuer* (London: Oxford University Press, 1940); Claude Lévi-Strauss, *Tristes Tropiques* (New York: Pocket Books, 1977); Tait and Middleton, *Tribes Without Rulers* (London: Routledge and Kegan Paul, 1958); Dorothy Lee, *Freedom and Culture* (Englewood Cliffs: Prentice-Hall, 1959); and Pierre Clastres, *Society Against the State: The Leader as Servant and the Humane Uses of Power Among the Indians of the Americas* (New York: Urizen Books, 1977).
28. Clastres, *op. cit.*, footnote 27, p. 5.
29. Lau, *op. cit.*, footnote 5, p. 32.
30. The *Lao Tzu* does, however, have many fascinating insights on the nature of war and on the distinction between legitimate self-defence and destructive militarism. This topic must be passed over for the sake of space, but see Chapters 31, 36, and 69.
31. Chan, *op. cit.*, footnote 5, p. 148. This is the reading adopted by Chang.
32. Cited by Roger Ames, "Is Political Taoism Anarchism?" *op. cit.*, p. 36.

Chapter 8

Ecology, Technology, and Respect for Nature

According to a classic formulation by the philosopher Immanuel Kant, "everything has either a price or a dignity. Whatever has a price can be replaced by something else as its equivalent; on the other hand, whatever is above all price, and therefore admits of no equivalent, has a dignity." For Kant, the thing that pre-eminently has such a dignity is the moral law, and human beings, who are capable of participating in and acting according to this law, share in this quality of dignity. For this reason we, as rational beings, ought always to be treated as ends and not as mere means. We are worthy of respect. Other beings have no such worth.

What are the implications of such a division of reality, especially as it relates to our conception of humanity and the environment? According to such a view, nature can be separated into two parts, one of which (our own species) is deserving of moral consideration, while the other ("external" nature) is of purely instrumental value. While the theorists like Kant who helped formulate the modern conception of the relation between humanity and nature had little awareness of its historical portent, the consequences are now clear. Nature as *physis*, an abundant outpouring of life, a myriad play of forms, is transformed into "natural resources," a stockpile of "raw materials" or potential commodities to be cycled and then recycled when demanded for purposes of power, profit, consumption, and, in general, the satisfaction of human needs or wants.

This conception of reality raises important questions concerning our view of technology. Technology is, in theory, a system of means for achieving the material transformation of nature according to human purposes. Such a system includes those tools and machines, skills, techniques, and procedures required for this task of transformation. As technology develops, this system of means expands. And as it grows, the world, as its object, is increasingly transformed and appropriated within this sphere of instrumentality. In short, a growing segment of reality (both materially, through transformative practice, and symbolically, through instrumental rationality) is absorbed into what we might call, paraphrasing Kant, "the kingdom of means."

The question I wish to raise is whether there are any grounds for granting non-human nature any moral status, so that it cannot legitimately be assimilated entirely into this realm of instrumentality. Most defences of concern for nature rely ultimately on humanistic foundations. We are all familiar with arguments that we should preserve natural resources because they are necessary for our survival, because they are aesthetically pleasing, because they have recreational value, because they will be beneficial for future generations, or because doing so will maximize profit or economic growth in the long run. In other words, our regard for nature is grounded in its potential for use by human beings for various human purposes. Such arguments are no doubt successful. Even from the limited perspective of species egoism the project of unlimited exploitation of nature turns out to be indefensible. The systems of high technology arising out of the industrial revolution—those which Mumford labels "paleotechnics"—have indeed led to such a degree of degradation of both ecological and sociocultural systems that human self-interest alone would justify their abolition. Yet let us assume that somehow our voracious will to power could be restrained sufficiently for us to master our *self*-destructive impulses. This will to power would then only be directed outward toward "external" nature. The aim of the

Western tradition to use the "conquest of nature" as a means to our own survival and mutual self-realization would then be achieved. Let us assume the validity of this false abstraction of humanity from its organic place in nature, and of this rigid compartmentalizing of consciousness into instrumentalizing and non-dominating spheres. Even given these assumptions there remains the question of whether this idealized species egoism would itself be justified.

The attribution of a moral status to a being depends on the recognition that it has a good which can be more or less attained. The Western tradition, from the classical Greek philosophers to modern Liberalism, has usually interpreted such a good in terms of rationality, and thus limited it to human beings (or sometimes also to superhuman beings). More recently, advocates of "animal liberation" have recommended expanding the moral realm to include beings having consciousness, often on the grounds that conscious beings can experience pain and pleasure, or that they can have an interest. Such arguments have contributed significantly to moral discourse, insofar as they have sought to bring our treatment of other species more in line with the principles that we assume in justifying our dealings with other human beings.[1] Thus, if we value the experience of humans in part because of the sort of rationality exhibited in language use, we are unjustified in treating primates which are capable of learning human language as if they were mere things, or in annihilating whales, which seem to have a kind of linguistic ability. Similarly, if we believe that we must justify any physical suffering that we impose on humans, it cannot be morally legitimate to impose enormous suffering on animals raised in factory conditions, and at times to resort to procedures amounting to torture, without demonstrating the necessity of this imposition.

Where the discussions by "animal liberationists" and other advocates of "animal rights" have usually fallen short is in the limitations of their theoretical framework, which tends to take our common sense intuitions about morality as their starting-point, and never really subjects these perceptions to thorough critical analysis. What is needed is a more systematic examination of moral value developed within the context of a comprehensive understanding of the relationship between humanity and the rest of nature at all levels of development. The hope is then that as we come to understand more adequately the relation between ourselves and the rest of nature we can better understand the meaning of our perceptions of value and goodness and better comprehend their place in the scheme of things. The present discussion cannot, unfortunately, go very far in achieving the comprehensiveness and systemization that I am calling for. Its task is a very modest one: to suggest the direction in which we should be moving if we wish to give our moral judgements a firm foundation in an adequate view of the universe.

Several tendencies in modern thought have been making important contributions to the development of such a view. These include ecological thought, process philosophy, and systems theory, to mention some of the most notable examples. While much of the argument in this book proceeds from an analysis founded on the richer organicist outlook of the ecological perspective and the more adequate comprehension of interaction and development found in process philosophy, at present I want to examine the striking implications of the least holistic and organicist of these tendencies—systems philosophy. Laszlo summarizes the characteristics of all natural systems as follows: 1) they have a systemic state property; that is, they constitute ordered wholes; 2) they exhibit system cybernetics, engaging in self-stabilization and self-organization in order to maintain their identities and structures as systems, and 3) they have what Koestler calls the "holon property," participating in intersystemic and intrasystemic hierarchies (in other words, they possess at once the characteristics of parts and wholes).[2] These characteristics are found in all natural systems, including not only the human organism or person, but extending from the atom to human society. We may add that natural systems exhibit to an increasing degree as we move higher in degree of complexity, *an ideal pattern of development*, so that self-organization becomes a dynamic process within the parameters of self-stabilization.

What is described in these rather abstract terms corresponds to what we perceive in our experience as a *good*. All beings in nature share the characteristic of possessing such a good. Minimally this good entails self-preservation. From the point at which life emerges it also increasingly involves an organized pattern of growth and development. And at the highest levels of organization there occurs the possibility for realization of diverse potentialities—in humans, complex thought, creative imagination, personality, etc.

If we are to attribute moral value to the attainment of our good, that is, if we are to recognize it not merely as a natural process, but also as an end perceived as having the value or quality of goodness, then we are required by the demands of consistency to give moral recognition to the similar goods existing at all levels of nature. There is then no reason to limit moral consideration (or even a concept like "interest," to the extent that it is analytically helpful) to human beings, to self-conscious beings, or even to living beings. Good must be recognized wherever it exists. This is not to say that we should never interfere with the realization of any such good, a goal which is, in any case, impossible to achieve. Rather, the appropriate conclusion is that even if (as I think we have good reasons for holding) the good of a self-conscious being should be given precedence over that of one without self-consciousness, and that of a sentient being over that of one without sentience (given a condition of *necessary* conflict between these goods), there is still a burden of moral justification which must be borne. Whenever our good can be achieved without the destruction of the good of another being, it is our moral responsibility to do so. No being should therefore be reduced to a *mere* means, although many will often necessarily be treated as means.

A further conclusion follows from the above reasoning. It has been stated that all natural systems have the quality of being both wholes and parts. While this "holon property" is more strongly evident when we consider the relation between atoms and molecules, molecules and cells, cells and organs, organs and organisms, and the human person and society, it also describes in some important ways our relation to the biosphere. If, as we are assuming, we are to give precedence to those goods realized at higher levels in the hierarchy of nature, then there is reason to give *highest* consideration among natural systems with which we have a practical relationship to that of the biosphere. If we can recognize a good for the biosphere, we should grant it priority over less comprehensive goods, and guide our actions accordingly. Environmental biology or ecology has demonstrated that the biosphere is indeed an ordered whole performing adaptive self-stabilization and self-organization. Observation of biological and social evolution shows that there are patterns of long-term development taking place within the parameters of adaptation. The emergence of self-consciousness has posed the possibility of a process of coordination of self-stabilization and self-organization of the system with the maximum harmonious realization of its constituent goods. Yet the result thus far has been quite to the contrary. The possibility instead confronts us that the striving for particular goods may not only fail to achieve a harmony between these aims and the larger good, but it can finally even come into conflict with the requirements of the larger system for adaptation and stabilization. Thus, perceived goods such as accumulation of capital, expansion of power, and consumption of commodities clash not only with a multitude of particular human and non-human goods, but also with the good of the biosphere itself. The moral problem, then, converges with the ecological problem. If the ecological crisis has resulted from our lack of recognition of the continuity between human social, cultural, and technological systems and the ecosystem within which these have evolved, a moral crisis has arisen from our failure to recognize the relation between our own good and the system of goods of which it is a part.

What, then, are the consequences of this conclusion for our view of technology? It is evident to me that it implies a break with systems of so-called "high technology" which are predicated on maximum human control and utilization of the environment, on the breaking down of complex natural systems and simplification of the biosphere, and on an administrative view of reality. A belief that human beings are beings within nature, rather than above it or apart from it demands the development of what Illich calls "convivial tools,"[3] Schumacher labels "intermediate technology,"[4] and Bookchin (perhaps most adequately) describes as "liberatory technology," or "ecotechnology."[5] Besides being more compatible with human cooperative self-development and even human survival, such technologies offer the possibility of achieving human goods

which life emerges it also increasingly involves an organized pattern of growth and development. And at the highest levels of organization there occurs the possibility for realization of diverse potentialities—in humans, complex thought, creative imagination, personality, etc.

If we are to attribute moral value to the attainment of our good, that is, if we are to recognize it not merely as a natural process, but also as an end perceived as having the value or quality of goodness, then we are required by the demands of consistency to give moral recognition to the similar goods existing at all levels of nature. There is then no reason to limit moral consideration (or even a concept like "interest," to the extent that it is analytically helpful) to human beings, to self-conscious beings, or even to living beings. Good must be recognized wherever it exists. This is not to say that we should never interfere with the realization of any such good, a goal which is, in any case, impossible to achieve. Rather, the appropriate conclusion is that even if (as I think we have good reasons for holding) the good of a self-conscious being should be given precedence over that of one without self-consciousness, and that of a sentient being over that of one without sentience (given a condition of *necessary* conflict between these goods), there is still a burden of moral justification which must be borne. Whenever our good can be achieved without the destruction of the good of another being, it is our moral responsibility to do so. No being should therefore be reduced to a *mere* means, although many will often necessarily be treated as means.

A further conclusion follows from the above reasoning. It has been stated that all natural systems have the quality of being both wholes and parts. While this "holon property" is more strongly evident when we consider the relation between atoms and molecules, molecules and cells, cells and organs, organs and organisms, and the human person and society, it also describes in some important ways our relation to the biosphere. If, as we are assuming, we are to give precedence to those goods realized at higher levels in the hierarchy of nature, then there is reason to give *highest* consideration among natural systems with which we have a practical relationship to that of the biosphere. If we can recognize a good for the biosphere, we should grant it priority over less comprehensive goods, and guide our actions accordingly. Environmental biology or ecology has demonstrated that the biosphere is indeed an ordered whole performing adaptive self-stabilization and self-organization. Observation of biological and social evolution shows that there are patterns of long-term development taking place within the parameters of adaptation. The emergence of self-consciousness has posed the possibility of a process of coordination of self-stabilization and self-organization of the system with the maximum harmonious realization of its constituent goods. Yet the result thus far has been quite to the contrary. The possibility instead confronts us that the striving for particular goods may not only fail to achieve a harmony between these aims and the larger good, but it can finally even come into conflict with the requirements of the larger system for adaptation and stabilization. Thus, perceived goods such as accumulation of capital, expansion of power, and consumption of commodities clash not only with a multitude of particular human and non-human goods, but also with the good of the biosphere itself. The moral problem, then, converges with the ecological problem. If the ecological crisis has resulted from our lack of recognition of the continuity between human social, cultural, and technological systems and the ecosystem within which these have evolved, a moral crisis has arisen from our failure to recognize the relation between our own good and the system of goods of which it is a part.

What, then, are the consequences of this conclusion for our view of technology? It is evident to me that it implies a break with systems of so-called "high technology" which are predicated on maximum human control and utilization of the environment, on the breaking down of complex natural systems and simplification of the biosphere, and on an administrative view of reality. A belief that human beings are beings within nature, rather than above it or apart from it demands the development of what Illich calls "convivial tools,"[3] Schumacher labels "intermediate technology,"[4] and Bookchin (perhaps most adequately) describes as "liberatory technology," or "ecotechnology."[5] Besides being more compatible with human cooperative self-development and even human survival, such technologies offer the possibility of achieving human goods without morally indefensible domination of other species and of the biosphere.

The characteristics of these technologies include the following: low consumption of resources; utilization of widely dispersed, renewable energy sources; minimal disturbance of ecosystems; human scale; comprehensibility; compatibility with aesthetic values; feasibility of continual reassessment and fundamental redesign in relation to analysis of needs; multifunctionality; capacity to fulfill basic human needs; tendency to reduce artificial scarcities; incompatibility with technocratic and bureaucratic structures; compatibility with democratic control of society, decentralized decision-making, and non-hierarchical social structures; conduciveness to production processes involving enjoyment, creativity, and human development.[6]

Such a conception of technology implies a rejection of the dominant path of technological development in the modern world; yet it avoids the sort of Stoical resignation bordering on despair adopted by "technological pessimists" like Ellul. These critics of technology urge us to heroically persevere in upholding moral values and spirituality in the face of the inexorable domination of the world by the technological system. The vision of a new technology can inspire us instead to expand those technological possibilities which allow us to affirm our aspirations for autonomy, mutuality, joyfulness, and harmony with nature.

Yet inspiration will not, of course, produce on its own any far-reaching social change. A technology such as that described will not be created by monumental acts of good will, or even by tremendous sales of the *Whole Earth Catalog*. Technological change can only be understood in terms of the interaction between economic, political, cultural, and technological systems. Technological evolution must be accompanied by parallel changes in other social institutions. Therefore, I must conclude that whatever promising beginnings we may make, the full development of a technology conducive to considerably expanded human freedom and self-development and compatible with a respect for nature is not likely to take place under the predominating systems of economic and political power. For it is these systems, corporate capitalism and state socialism, which have inevitably engendered the techniques of domination of humanity and nature. In saying this I am not merely noting a historical correlation between these systems and systems of technology which are morally unacceptable. Rather, I am claiming that if we investigate the nature of societies which increasingly find their organizational basis in systems of economic and political power (as opposed to kinship, cultural tradition, or many other alternative principles of organization), a strong dialectical interaction will be discovered between the various subsystems of the system of domination.

Consequently, a new technological practice aimed at ecological regeneration and founded in a respect for nature must be accompanied by a new political practice aimed at social and cultural regeneration. Such a practice will seek to transform all social institutions by replacing mechanistic, power-based structures by organic social forms. It will oppose centralization with decentralization, hierarchical control with self-management, manipulation with mutuality, atomistic individualism with community, and domination with cooperation. And, eschewing a narrow conception of the political, it will seek transformation at all levels of interaction, including all spheres of personal and civic life. If such a new politics can be achieved, the political will become for the first time in actuality what it has been in theory since Aristotle described it as the "master art" which aims at the realization of a good of all which embraces all the particular goods. It is only on the basis of such a politics that "respect" (whether for other human beings or for nature) can find its fulfillment in an ethical world order.

Notes

1. Some will no doubt judge harshly any concern for "animal rights," not to mention seemingly bizarre concerns like "wilderness preservation," in a world in which *human* rights are so blatantly trampled upon—a world in which there is widespread malnutrition, poverty, illiteracy, brutal repression, torture, and the proliferation of weapons designed to annihilate billions of members of our own species. Yet the hostility and contempt which are directed against the partisans of "nature" are badly misplaced. Any consciousness of the nature of domination in any of its forms can be a pathway to understanding the entire system. Respect and mutual aid are not scarce commodities to be carefully allocated. Fortunately, the more they are distributed, the more remains to be dispensed.
2. Ervin Laszlo, *Introduction to Systems Philosophy: Toward a New Paradigm of Contemporary Thought* (New York: Harper and Row, 1973), pp. 35-53; and Arthur Koestler, *The Ghost in the Machine* (Chicago: Regnery Co., 1967), pp. 45-58.
3. See Ivan Illich, *Tools for Conviviality* (New York: Harper and Row, 1973).
4. See E. F. Schumacher, *Small is Beautiful: Economics as If People Mattered* (New York: Harper and Row, 1973), and George McRobie, *Small Is Possible* (New York: Harper and Row, 1981).
5. See Murray Bookchin, *Post-Scarcity Anarchism* (Montréal: Black Rose Books, 1977), and *Toward an Ecological Society* (Montréal: Black Rose Books, 1980). Bookchin's proposals are the only ones of those mentioned that incorporate technological change into a comprehensive ecological outlook and a coherent and elaborated view of human communal self-development. Illich and Schumacher do, however, present important insights into the possibilities for advances in labour-intensive, self-managed technologies of moderate scale in "non-advanced" societies. Bookchin, on the other hand, stresses the possibilities for a non-dominating, post-scarcity society based on more automated alternative technologies.
6. Many of these values inspire the view of technology presented in *Radical Technology*, edited by the editors of *Undercurrents* (New York: Pantheon Books, 1976).

Chapter 9

The Social Ecology of Murray Bookchin

Despite more than a decade of widespread public discussion of "ecological crises" and "environmental problems," authentic ecological thinking has had only the most marginal influence on contemporary society. The widespread tendency to trivialize ecology is not limited to its recycling by media, industry and politics for inclusion on their endless lists of "issues," "concerns," and "items on the agenda." More disturbing is the uncritical treatment of ecological concepts by virtually all the prevailing currents in social theory, including even the allegedly most radical varieties.

In *Toward an Ecological Society*,[1] Murray Bookchin launches a vehement attack on all attempts to dilute ecology into an innocuous form of "environmentalism," and he continues his efforts at constructing a comprehensive ecological social theory. In fact, though, he does much more than this, for there are several major tasks taken up in this wide-ranging work. First, Bookchin exhorts us to harken back to the Greeks, seeking to recapture the promise of classical thought and to comprehend the truth of the Polis. In doing so, he attempts to focus more clearly on the ways that the possibilities for human liberation and community are dependent on our success in developing an adequate solution to the problem of the self. Secondly, he seeks to expand critical theory into a fully developed critique of *all* forms of domination and ideology. This implies for him not only a definitive break with the more blatant species of productivism and oeuvrierist ideology that continue to masquerade as "radical theory," but also a clear rejection of the most subtle and advanced mystifications of hierarchy and domination. Thirdly, Bookchin attempts to incorporate the contributions of ecological and organicist thinking into an adequate philosophy of nature. In this regard the neo-Hegelian aspects of his thought now come more prominently into the foreground. Finally, he continues his formulation of what must be judged to be the first elaborated and theoretically sophisticated anarchist position in the history of political theory. To put it bluntly, anarchist thought has remained at best a mélange of brilliant insight and theoretical niaiserie prior to the work of Bookchin and those who are building on his foundations. For that reason, "anarchist theory" in the future will have to come to grips, above all, with this emerging organicist and ecological anarchist position.

Bookchin's single most important contribution to social theory is his effort to ground social analysis and practice in a coherent and comprehensive philosophy of nature. It has now been nearly two decades since he eloquently argued for the far-reaching implications of ecological theory for social and political thought in his essay "Ecology and Revolutionary Thought," carried further in this present work. The neo-Hegelian character of his standpoint now becomes more apparent. Bookchin comprehends deeply the irony of the movement of radical social theory since the Young Hegelians. While it has claimed since Marx's generation to have broken decisively with idealism in order to advance the project of uncovering the real development of the concrete material world, instead it has grounded itself in an abstraction from reality, which has meant a loss of some of Hegel's most crucial insights. Above all, it has never successfully come to terms with the category of totality. This failing vitiates even the most heroic attempts to construct an Hegelian Marxism, as in the case of Lukács' ultimately limited and inadequately critical conception of "social totality as a concretely historical totality." What has been lost is what

Bookchin seeks to recapture in his concept of a "new animism" which interprets all aspects of nature, not as a mere means toward human development, but rather as "manifestations of a larger natural totality, indeed, as respiritualized nature" (p. 93). History may not be the record of the overcoming of its own self-alienation by a transcendent *Geist*, but neither is it the story of humanity's struggle to abolish alienation through a replacement of an illusory conquest of nature by the achievement of real domination over natural agencies. Instead we find in Bookchin's account a "sweeping drama in which we split from blind nature only to return again on a more advanced level as nature rendered self-conscious in the form of creative, intelligent, and spiritually renewed beings" (p. 96). Yet this ecological naturalism is not merely another form of humanism in disguise. Ecology comprehends and takes seriously the whole. It "sees the balance and integrity of the biosphere as an end in itself.... Diversity is desirable for its own sake, a value to be cherished as part of a spiritized notion of the living universe" (p. 59). Western philosophy has seldom been conscious of nature as such a unity-in-diversity, at least since the early Greeks (mere traces of this outlook remaining by the time of Plato's *Timaeus*). Modern radical social theory has only more radically affirmed the division between humanity and nature, and has proposed entirely illusory solutions (usually reducing to more effective appropriation) to the problem. As a result, even its most liberatory currents have been almost entirely oblivious to the problem of human domination of nature and to the connection between this kind of domination and all other forms.

The promise of ecology is, however, a truly dialectical view of reality which "stresses differentiation, inner development, and unity in diversity" (p. 272). The project of radical social theory, according to Bookchin, is to draw out the social and political implications of this outlook. All his prescriptions concerning social practice (decentralization, the new urbanism, liberatory technology, affinity groups) are but the reconceptualizations of social categories in terms of this ecological, holistic, framework.

Bookchin's concern for applying ecological principles to all realms, and for avoiding the trap of false abstraction, is perhaps most evident in his discussion of one of the most enduring themes in his works: the nature of the self and "self-activity." It is a key premise of his critique that radical thought has predicated its analysis on an inadequate conception of the self, and that this has undermined its emancipatory and communal strivings.

For Bookchin, no mere form of organization can assure non-domination, no matter how admirable this form may be, as in the case of self-management, communalism, or direct democracy. In order to be successful, liberatory structures must be forms within which develops an authentic "selfhood." The problem of the self is the problem of "the individuation of the 'masses' into conscious beings who can take direct, unmediated control of society and of their own lives" (p. 256). The "unmediated" point should not be taken too literally, for what he means is the absence of mediation by externally imposed, inorganic structures, while the appearance of the developed self is certainly mediated by a long process of *paideia*. As he notes in his discussion of "spontaneity," the "spontaneous" action of a responsible self requires internal control, self-discipline, and the capacity for self-directed social activity (p. 259). Indeed, Bookchin's treatment of "spontaneity" can be considered a radicalized version of Hegel's conception of "liberty" as opposed to "caprice": it is not *arbitrary* action, but rather self-creation through self-conscious free activity.

Bookchin finds his inspiration for the process of self-formation in the educational ideals of the Greeks. The creation of the self requires an educational practice designed to produce persons capable of acting effectively and cooperatively in society. They must develop a capacity for "shared social practice," and attain such classical virtues as "personal fortitude and moral probity," or else the self becomes degraded into a "hollow" ego (p. 120). His demands for a politics of "direct action" and his call for an explicitly "anarcho-communist" movement can best be understood as proposals for a practice suitable for the formation of such a self, and its expression in an embryonic community and culture.

Bookchin thus wishes to recapture the ideal of "the people" as a community of selves, rather than the degraded class of workers or mass of consumers championed in Marxist or liberal theory. This ideal is most vividly depicted in his conception of the decentralized ecological community, his call for the rebirth of social creativity, and his analysis of the formation of the social person through libertarian primary groups. Again, his inspiration is the Polis, with its assemblies of citizens, rotation of offices, and citizen courts and militias. The functioning of these institutions, he argues, relied on the existence of citizens possessing an "art of political judgement" which assumes humanity to be essentially a cooperative species, having a sociality based on natural human feelings of solidarity and justice. The basis for social life is not interest, contract, or right, but rather *philia* (which he also compares to the concept of *agape* in the young Hegel), a "mutuality" which transcends individual interest and even individual need. Bookchin universalizes Aristotle's conception of the human being as *zoon politikon* and draws out the implications of the young Marx's identification of the "greatest wealth" for a human being as "the *other* human being." For Bookchin, human beings distinguish themselves most not through the process of material transformation "as they begin to produce their means of subsistence," but rather as they develop a self rooted in shared experience and common values, in "community life or *Koinonia*" (p. 238).

No one has been more aware than Bookchin of the implications of the question of how the "educators" must themselves be educated. According to his analysis, no "seizure of power," no "revolutionizing" of political and economic institutions can be successful without a concomitant process of *self*-transformation. Yet the left has failed to confront the problem, clinging instead to the fetishism of "the Revolution," mythologizing authoritarian regimes as "liberation," ignoring the seeds of domination which have lain within even the most libertarian movements, and spawning "militants" and ideologues in whose character structures are embedded hierarchy and authoritarianism.

For Bookchin, revolutionary movements will continue to be condemned to failure until they succeed in developing a deeply, rather than superficially, libertarian structure, and an authentic practice of direct action. It is important to understand that "direct action" in this sense does not mean more extreme, more violent, or more "militant" action. In fact, these qualities are more often characteristic of varieties of the vanguardism that Bookchin deplores. Instead it means a practice which expands our ability "to manage every aspect of our lives" (p. 53). Accordingly, he does not see any hope for such a practice in the machinations of various leftist sects, but rather in such embryonic developments as the growth of block committees, tenant associations, neighbourhood self-help groups, cooperatives, neighbourhood housing movements, and so forth (p. 183). While these tendencies must pale to insignificance beside the revolutionary fantasies of any hard-core leftist, Bookchin plausibly argues that these are among the few indications in advanced capitalist society of a growth in awareness of the need for direct self-management. He admits that these institutions range in character from counter-cultural to élitist; yet he contends that they present the possibility of a base for a "new body politic." Perhaps he exaggerates the chances for significant progress in this direction in the near future (and I believe that in the case of the anti-nuclear alliances he vastly overestimates their potential in view of his own analysis of the preconditions for change). Still, the test of an analysis is not the extent to which it gives us grounds for great optimism. If it is true that the possibility of creating a good society depends on the regeneration of an organic social fabric, then there is reason to believe that the most "advanced" industrialized societies, with their advanced degrees of social atomization and their advanced stages of replacement of traditional culture by commodity values, will have a more difficult project of regeneration than will some more "backward" societies. The same might be said in regard to the possible movement to more liberatory alternative or "intermediate" technologies from high or "low" systems of technology, respectively.

Yet given that the path toward social regeneration will be a long and difficult one, it is essential to know the direction in which progress can be made. Here lies the importance of Bookchin's argument that a libertarian and communitarian movement must find its roots in affinity groups which embody "a permanent, intimate, decentralized *community*" (p. 47), rather than in parties, unions, cells, chapters, study groups, think tanks, or whatever other units might be the alleged focus of "revolutionary" activity. Bookchin holds that if the structures we create in order to transform society reflect the structure of existing society, albeit as their mirror images, we can only reproduce that which exists, unless we succeed in further entrenching domination by mystifying it as "liberation" and "revolution."

Bookchin may be unrealistic in thinking that authentic affinity groups could form the "real cellular tissue" of anti-nuclear alliances, for example, given these organizations' character of being incoherent coalitions of liberals, environmentalists, counter-culturists, Trotskyists, anarchists, alternative politicos and adventurists. Yet the important point that Bookchin makes is that *only* entities like affinity groups could form the "real cellular tissue" of the kind of libertarian communitarian society that he envisions—the "ecological society" of his title. Such groups are "ecological" in the deepest sense: they embody within themselves the principles of organicism, unity-in-diversity, mutual interdependence, and non-domination that Bookchin sees as necessary at all levels of organization. Unless such a transformative practice can be achieved at the most basic level of human interaction, grandiose visions of social revolution will remain what they have been in the past: either another "sigh of the oppressed" or another ideology of the oppressors.

One of Bookchin's most significant achievements in his earlier work was his analysis of "liberatory technology." He presented evidence that human liberation is not advanced by the further development of high technology of the kind Mumford called "paleotechnics" (classically industrial technology), but that, instead, the overcoming of domination and hierarchy requires the utilization of technologies which are more decentralist, more comprehensible, more subject to democratic control, and more compatible with ecological values. The present work continues this line of analysis.

Bookchin rejects the view, which he attributes to most of the Marxist and syndicalist tradition, that technology can be looked upon instrumentally, as a means toward either liberation or domination, depending on how it is used. He thus rejects not only the orthodox Marxist view that liberation can be achieved through the unfettered development of the productive forces collectively owned by the "proletariat," but also the neo-Marxist and anarcho-syndicalist conception that it can be achieved by "self-management" of these same means of production. He dismisses as simplistic the idea that the system of domination can be undermined by, for example, workers electing managers, as long as the remainder of that system, with its hierarchical technology, its manipulative media, its urban sprawls, and, ultimately, its commodified system of values, is not concurrently revolutionized.

If for Bookchin the technological system is not a neutral instrument that can be used for good or evil ends, neither is it an autonomously evolving determinant of social change in all other institutions. He rejects the thesis of some "technological pessimists" that technology has become a self-contained system which is completely beyond control, so that humanity is condemned to being enslaved to it. This outlook is, in a sense, the mirror image of the Marxist/capitalist vision of human liberation through the removal of the fetters on technological development (by means of proletarian revolution or *laissez-faire*).

In Bookchin's analysis, tools, machines, and techniques "are immersed in a social world of human intentions, needs, wills, and interactions" (p. 128). He recognizes that the technological system can never validly be abstracted into a system of objects. All social institutions contain sedimentations of the symbolic, and cannot be understood through a bracketing or forgetting of their character as a system of meanings. Thus, Bookchin manages to get beyond even the view that posits a dialectic between "the path of technological development" and the development of other social structures. Neither the technics of domination nor the technics of liberation are the product of any inexorable path of technological evolution. For Bookchin, there are alternative lines of development, as he long ago described in "Toward a Liberatory Technology." The question of which will be followed will depend on our ability to develop adequately critical consciousness and liberatory practice, which implies that the struggle against domination will take place in areas that were once considered pre-eminently superstructural: the realms of values, judgements, perception, affect, sensibility, symbolization. As he concludes concerning the possibility of abolishing scarcity, a key factor in the perpetuation of domination, "we have the means available," but what we lack is "the freedom, values, and sensibility to do so" (p. 25). Why, though, have we failed to establish these non-technological preconditions for achieving a non-dominating post-scarcity society? According to Bookchin, the great revolutions have failed to the extent that "they had no material basis for consolidating the *general* interest of society to which the most radical elements staked out an historic claim" (p. 255). Even the proletarian revolutions failed because "the technological premises were *inadequate* for the *material* consolidation of a 'general will,' *the only basis on which the dominated can finally eliminate domination*" (p. 255). Yet even granted that Bookchin is claiming that these "technological premises" are merely necessary and not sufficient conditions for liberation, this explanation does not seem entirely convincing, and, in fact, seems to be a retreat from other aspects of his analysis of the relation between technics and social change. Kropotkin and others long ago outlined the nature of a decentralist, communitarian technology. Obviously, the existence of "the technological premises" cannot be equated with the actual social installation of such a system of technology, since this would presuppose the existence of the liberatory society (especially if we remember that technology is to be looked upon not merely as hardware, but as a system embodying meanings and values). But if the "technological premises" are interpreted as technical *possibilities* which might be utilized in an actual technological system, then the failure of 20th century revolutions cannot be attributed to the absence of such premises. Rather, we must conclude, as I think Bookchin himself sometimes does, that the true basis for these failures lies in the existence of "premises" that are more political, psychological, and ideological, and their interaction with the technological ones.

Bookchin finds evidence for optimism concerning the emergence of a more advanced consciousness in the developing contradiction between actuality and possibility. Accordingly, "the real proletariat resists... reduction of its subjectivity to the product of need and lives increasingly in the realm of *desire*, of the *possibility* to become other than it is. Concretely, the worker resists the work ethic because it has become irrational in view of the possibilities for a non-hierarchical society" (p. 241). The hierarchical worldview is thus "waning" as a result of a new vision made possible by productivity which does not require domination (p. 41).

But is the "real" proletariat described here any more "real" than the abstract proletariat elected by Marx to be the final revolutionary subject? Is not the "resistance" by workers (especially in the advanced Western societies here being discussed) more a consequence of their socialization into the commodity system of late capitalism and their acceptance of the values of consumption? The real proletariat seems to adopt increasingly the system of desires which long ago began to undermine the work ethic even among the bourgeoisie itself. Its vision is one of maximum consumption with minimum effort. Capitalism has itself eroded historically obsolete ideas of the spirituality and morality of work, and what remains is that empty rhetoric occasionally called upon to lend an air of legitimacy to the real values of status, power, and privileged consumption. Unfortunately, even as productivity has expanded, the inspiring vision of non-hierarchical society has succeeded in arousing the passions and imaginations of only a few, and even these few are seldom "workers." Perhaps a yearning for this ideal lurks near the surface of consciousness and is ready to burst forth; yet, we can hardly use it as an explanation of worker resistance, or even have much hope for what it might accomplish, until it achieves a more explicit, consciously developed form. Unconscious yearnings are notoriously amorphous, and can be channeled into either authoritarian or libertarian directions, depending on the state of the entire social system. This is the lesson of Reich's mass psychology (insofar as it can be disentangled from the positivism that blunts his critique). Bookchin recognizes the need for such analysis, yet he sometimes appears to hope for an almost automatic transition from unconscious need to conscious liberatory practice.

An example is the discussion of the May '68 "events" in France. He argues that "owing to the unconscious nature of the processes involved, there is no way of foretelling when a movement of this kind will emerge—and it will emerge only when it is left to do so on its own" (p. 261). Perhaps it is true that the preconditions for such events make prediction impossible. This should not lead us to believe that the preconditions for a thorough transformation of the type envisioned by Bookchin could be similarly unconscious. It was the lack of previous *conscious* libertarian and communitarian developments that made inevitable the failure of the '68 events to fulfill the hopes of the most advanced imaginations. The revolution, as Bookchin contends, can be no better than the revolutionaries, and the actors in '68 were the students reacting against the rigid French educational system, the militants of the CGT and the other unions, the adherents of the political parties of the left, the readers of leftist publications, the members of political sects. Given that the level of conscious liberatory practice was so low, it is surprising that unconscious desires, the enduring libertarian undercurrent in French culture, and the very exhilaration of rebellion itself, took the movement as far as it did go. Yet even in a relatively politicized society like France it could be but a beginning. The importance of the events in the personal histories of perhaps millions of people should not be minimized; yet it is certain that conscious developments of the sort Bookchin himself mentions (self-creative activity, libertarian primary groups, mutualistic institutions) will be necessary before many more socially creative "events" will transpire.

There is a similar problem with Bookchin's hopes, based on North American experience in the late 60's, that rapid change in consciousness is possible in that society. It is true that, among many, significant development did take place. But if the generation of the 60's is carefully analyzed, does it not appear that what we have witnessed over the past two decades is the capacity of a consciousness lacking a foundation in a developed personality and a developed perception to adapt superficially to changing circumstances with astounding uncreativity?

Whatever our aspirations for humanity, we must be haunted by the spectre of Nietzsche's "last man" as the inheritor of the earth. It is not only the *Übermenschen*, the "allsided individuals," or Bookchin's developed selves who have no need for traditional authority, and who might rebel against the constraints of the work ethic, but also the soulless egos, the creatures of the moment. It is possible that the present malaise of humanity results from its being in travail with earthly divinity;

more likely it is suffering from a possibly terminal case of Saturday Night Fever (or whatever we will come to call the latest variety of this Protean malady).

If Bookchin's hopes for change sometimes seem a bit exaggerated, given his own perceptive presentation of the preconditions for social progress, his critique of other theories of change seldom misses the mark. As should be apparent from this discussion, there runs through his work a constant, sometimes explicit, often implicit, critique of Marx and Marxism. It is true that he devotes some attention to other traditions, like liberalism and anarcho-syndicalism; but as often as not he dismisses them as being theoretically beneath contempt. On the other hand, Marx is recognized to be one of the few great theorists of human liberation, and among the towering figures in the development of human self-consciousness. In fact, the lineage of Bookchin's thought is found less in the *anarchist* tradition (as conventionally defined) than in the tradition of critical theory in the broadest sense, running through the classical Greeks, German idealism, Marx and the Young Hegelians, and, finally, the Frankfurt School and its successors. It is easy to allow Bookchin's critique of Marx and the Marxists (a critique which sometimes rises, or falls, depending on your point of view, to the level of invective) to obscure the degree to which he shares their problematic, and the extent to which he has even, in some cases (such as in the discussion of technology and consciousness) perhaps failed to break adequately with some Marxian presuppositions.

For Bookchin, Marxism is "the culmination of the bourgeois Enlightenment." Its values of "economic rationalization, planned production, and a 'proletarian state'" lead either to an ideology of state capitalism or one which is capable of "complicity with the stabilization of a highly rationalized era of state capitalism" (p. 195). Whatever Marx's concern may have been for recognizing the importance of subjectivity, de-alienation, self-consciousness, self-creative practice, and the overcoming of domination, his philosophy of history ultimately leads to a politics legitimating centralism, bureaucracy, the system of high technology, statism, and the domination of nature.

According to Bookchin's interpretation, Marxism "elucidates the function of... cultural, psychological, and ethical 'forces' in terms that make them contingent on 'laws' which act behind human wills," and which "by their mutual interaction and obstruction, 'cancel' each other out and leave the 'economic' factor free to determine human affairs" (p. 198). Actually, this account is a better description of Hegel's "cunning of reason" than of Marx's economism, if *Geist* is substituted for "the economic factor." Yet Bookchin's critique of the "scientism" of the Marxian dialectic is still valid, insofar as even Marx's recognition of the place of culture and values as superstructural factors having their place in the process of mutual interaction between social determinants coexists with his tendency to reduce them "in the final instance" to responses to the course of technological and economic development. Marxian theory is thus "captive to its own reduction of ethics to law, subjectivity to objectivity, freedom to necessity" (p. 199). As a result, it fails to establish an ethical critique of domination, relying instead on an analysis of historical development in which "objective laws" of history render domination finally obsolete. Marx, it is true, moves in several directions which undermine the ethical basis for his position. To the extent that he tends to identify the good with the pattern of unfolding of history he is necessarily doomed to failure in this regard, and even when he adheres to a human self-realization theory of goodness his position is fragmentary and inadequately critical (despite almost desperate attempts by the most advanced Marxists to find satisfaction in his "critical theory of needs").

But Bookchin goes too far in his claim that Marx judged domination purely "in terms of technical needs and possibilities" (p. 203), thus entirely overlooking the ethical. This may be true to the degree that Marx concerns himself with elaborating a positivistic philosophy of history; nevertheless, the ethical dimension remains implicit in his thought to the extent that he retains the concern with self-realization and needs mentioned above. While, on the one hand, domination is seen as being necessitated for the development of the technical structure under a given mode of production, the entire course of historical development ultimately gains its justification as a positive *value* as a consequence of its liberatory *end*. The revolutionized relations of production unchain the restricted forces of production, abundance is achieved through production for use and real need, the realm of freedom is vastly expanded, and human creative self-development becomes possible for the first time. In this highly imaginative historical drama moral value and historical reality are reconciled. Of course, even if one finds the plot to be believable, the reconciliation is largely undermined by Marx's tendency toward a reductionist view of knowledge, so that critique never gains a really firm foundation.

Much of Bookchin's attack on neo-Marxism is an incisive analysis of various attempts to cling to Marxism as an adequate theoretical framework while trivializing key principles, overlooking embarrassing implications, and stealthily (or sometimes heavy-handedly) smuggling in alien conceptions. He argues that given Marx's view of liberation through technological and productive development, the factory remains part of the realm of necessity which must fully carry out its role in history before the realm of freedom can emerge. Thus, those neo-Marxists like Gorz, who expound theories of Marxist self-management, betray the spirit of Marx's thought. One can only wonder, in view of Bookchin's devastating dissection of Gorz's muddle-headed eclecticism, why he bothered to devote 24 pages to what must be perceived as critical overkill.

While Bookchin's critique of Marcuse is also pointed and cogent, there is an unfortunate neglect for Marcuse's insights concerning the relation between human liberation and the erotic, aesthetic, and cultural realms, and his tendency toward a "new animism" that has much in common with Bookchin's own speculations. Bookchin effectively demolishes such instances of Marcusean political naïveté as his belief in the existence of Leninist anti-bureaucratic regimes, his reinterpretation of the Third World as the external proletariat, and his defence of European Communist parties as "potentially revolutionary forces" (pp. 219-220). Still, it is highly questionable whether Marcuse always "falls on the side of centralization, delegated power, councils and authority, as against decentralization, direct democracy, popular assemblies, and spontaneity" (p. 220). Rather, he never falls on *either* side, never admitting (or developing an awareness of) the contradiction between the two sets of alternatives. Perhaps this is, for a political theorist, a worse sin. Yet it allows for the possibility that there is a much more libertarian Marcuse than the one Bookchin often quite successfully attacks.

There is a similar analysis of other neo-Marxists, especially those who are consciously in the critical tradition. One can hardly dispute Bookchin's contention that they have not developed any promising liberatory practice, and, at their worst, they may indeed become "increasingly disengaged from society" (p. 213). Still, these thinkers are the source of some of the most incisive social analyses available, especially in the case of their synthesis of systems theory, critical theory, and other traditions in diagnosing the crisis tendencies in advanced societies. If Marxist theory has really done as awful a job as Bookchin claims in helping us with *changing* the world (a thesis with which I heartily concur), then perhaps it's not such a bad idea if it limits itself to more adequately *interpreting* it.

Toward an Ecological Society is a provocative work which gives abundant evidence of its author's position at the centre of contemporary debate in radical social theory. Some of the ambiguities and apparent inconsistencies which have been mentioned are no doubt the result of the work's character as a collection of essays written over a decade, and show the evolution of Bookchin's position. The need for a fuller discussion of some theoretical issues has been more than satisfied by the appearance of his *magnum opus, The Ecology of Freedom.*

The Ecology of Freedom[2] is the culmination of Bookchin's efforts to construct a comprehensive ecological social theory. It is a major achievement, destined to become a classic of contemporary social thought. A work of sweeping scope and striking originality, it towers over a field dominated by epigones, virtuosos, and tenure-seekers. It carries on the great tradition of political thinking.

Bookchin's perspective, as is clear from his earlier works, is deeply rooted in ecology. In this book he expands his ecological analysis to a full-scale teleological, organicist interpretation of reality. The result is a coherent, comprehensive, metaphysical position which is capable of integrating successfully his theories of the self, society, and nature.

Much of the significance of Bookchin's work lies in the depth and radicality of his critique. He places in question the direction in which Western thought has moved at crucial points in its evolution. From its beginnings, it bore the marks of the growth of social domination. While the pre-Socratics retain traces of the values of previous organic society that preceded the rise of patriarchy, the state, and private property, by the time of Plato and Aristotle the rationality of domination was already deeply rooted. Hierarchical authority is reflected in the idea of a transcendent source of order, class values are intruded into conceptions of human nature, and nature itself is denigrated or accorded merely instrumental value. This hierarchical, dominating view of reality is inherited by the tradition.

In the modern period, as society begins to fragment with the rise of Protestantism, the nation-state, and capitalism, the unity of the hierarchical worldview is itself shattered. As the dichotomy between society and "the individual" becomes clearly defined, and the gap between self and other widens, Western thought becomes increasingly incapable of sustaining an integrated vision of reality. Cartesian dualism posits separate subjective and objective realms, and is unable to give a firm basis to either. Materialism and positivism opt for the objective, and yield a spectral subjectivity, if any at all, while idealism and subjectivism degenerate into irrationalism and egoism.

Bookchin seeks to go two steps back—beyond the fragmentation of modern thought, and beyond the hierarchy introduced in the classical period—in order to reconstruct the tradition. The result is an attempt to liberate Western philosophy from its limitations, so that it can fulfill its original promise: to reveal the Logos of the world and to guide us in the art of living.

The beginning of this project is a re-examination of the concept of reason. Bookchin argues that we must restore to reason the significance that it had at the beginnings of Western thought: reason as Logos, as "an immanent feature of reality; indeed, as the organizing and motivating principle of the world" (p. 10). From the epistemological standpoint, reason means speculative knowledge, comprehension of the nature of this Logos. Yet such knowledge is only possible because of the rationality inherent in reality itself. This "immanent world reason" signifies "the self-organizing attributes of substance; it is the latent subjectivity in the inorganic and organic levels of reality that reveal an inherent striving toward consciousness" (p. 11). The conception that subjectivity somehow emerges full-blown from a purely objective world is a highly problematic one, and its implausibility is no doubt responsible for many capitulations to idealism or positivism. Yet the alternative of coexisting objectivity and subjectivity at all levels of existence has always been present. Spinoza made a good case for such a view, and contemporary systems philosophy and process philosophy point strongly in the same direction.[3] In Bookchin's version of this solution, Hegel's dictum that "substance is subjectivity" is divested of its idealist implications, and reinterpreted in terms of a naturalistic monism. "The term subjectivity expresses the fact that substance—at each level of its organization and in all its concrete forms—*actively* functions to maintain its identity, equilibrium, fecundity, and place in a given constellation of phenomena" (p. 275). Bookchin argues that reductionism (and, he might have added, subjectivism) denies "the high degree of nisus, of self-organization and self-creation inherent in nonhuman phenomena" (p. 275). This immanent teleology within all of nature is not interpreted as implying a rigid determinism. Rather, it signifies that each being has a coherent path of development which must be understood in relation to its dialectical interaction with other beings. The conceptions of organic totality and dialectical unfolding thus gain a much more comprehensive foundation than they had in Hegel's idealism or Marx's historical materialism, since they are rooted in the rationality of nature itself.

Nature, according to this view, is an organic unity-in-diversity in a process of self-development. Thus, "the true lies in the self-consummation of a *process* through its development, in the flowering of its latent particularities in their fullness or wholeness" (p. 32). This implies a concept of an "active nature" which is not a mere framework for *human* creative activity. The project of human domination of nature is illusory not only because human subjectivity reaches its limits over against the impervious objectivity of nature as other. Rather, it is more deeply illusory because it overlooks the inclusiveness of humanity in the underlying unity of an organic totality pervaded by activity and subjectivity.

In the scheme of the evolutionary development of subjectivity, humanity is "nature rendered self-conscious," an idea developed extensively in both Hegel and Marx. But for those thinkers the conception of humanity as universal self-consciousness is corrupted by the ideology of domination, and what Bookchin calls the "epistemology of rule." For Bookchin, our function is not to place ourselves above nature (whether as thinkers or producers), but rather to cooperate in the process of teleological development of which we are such a significant part. We should "make the implicit meanings in nature explicit," and "enhance its inner strivings toward greater variety" (p. 316). We must comprehend "the hidden desiderata of natural evolution," and thus "render nature more fecund, varied, whole, and integrated" (p. 342).

At this point the connection between the metaphysics of ecology and ecological ethics and politics becomes evident. The conceptions of self-development and unity-in-diversity which emerge from a consideration of the rationality of nature must be given a concrete significance in relation to the self and social institutions. The call for an "ecological society" is not, therefore, a proposal for a better solution to certain "environmental problems" that have arisen in modern society. Rather it is a thorough metaphysical and moral critique of civilization, and a proposal to put an end to its rebellion against nature. But for Bookchin, in order to understand a phenomenon critically, it is necessary to understand its origin and development. As he implicitly recognizes, it is also essential to understand its other. The understanding of civilization thus requires a comprehension of those societies out of which it arose, and about whose persistence "World History" has remained silent: tribal, or, as Bookchin calls them, "organic societies."

The organic societies discussed by Bookchin are "spontaneously formed, non-coercive and egalitarian" (p. 5). Their merit does not consist in their spontaneous formation (which is, in fact, the basis for their limitations), but rather in the fact that their social institutions and value systems embody the principles of non-hierarchical unity-in-diversity implied in the ecological worldview.

Relying on the work of Paul Radin, Dorothy Lee and other anthropologists, Bookchin argues that these societies held social values emphasizing the uniqueness of each person, and stressing a cooperative mode of existence. Fundamental to the social structure is the requirement that the basic material and social needs of all be fulfilled. There is an "irreducible minimum" which is accorded to each merely on the basis of being a member of the community (p. 56). Leadership exists, but is non-coercive and functional in nature, and thus does not imply the existence of an institutionalized hierarchy. Given their moderate demands on nature and the emphasis on fulfillment of basic needs, such societies were able to avoid the generation of contradictory pleasure principles and reality principles. Thus, harsh instinctual repression was unnecessary and polymorphous perversity could be allowed relatively broad social expression. Finally, the cooperative nature of the community reflected the importance of the "nurturing sensibility" of women, who occupied a social and economic position of great consequence. The importance of woman increased with the coming of the "fixed-soil community" in which food-gathering imagery, identified with the feminine, displaced hunting imagery in the symbolic repertoire of society (p. 58). In revering the feminine, the community paid homage to such values as nurturance and non-objectifying love.

It is Bookchin's view that all societies derive their image of nature through a projection of their social structures. With their cooperative mode of existence and non-hierarchical values, these societies accordingly saw nature as a harmonious community of which the tribal community is an integral part. This outlook was made possible by the existing system of needs, which precluded the necessity of struggle with nature. As a consequence of these material, social, and imaginary factors, organic societies had a structure and consciousness which were "ecological." Still, they did not possess the self-consciousness and reflectiveness that Bookchin attributes to the "ecological society" that should be the goal of social transformative practice.

Bookchin emphasizes not only the merits of "the outlook of organic society," but also its severe restrictions. He is very careful to avoid idealization of primitive society, as he exhibits in his criticism of the thesis that it was "affluent." He contends that a reduction of scarcity to a question of "needs and resources" ultimately "capitulates to the very economistic stance it is meant to correct" (p. 67). Such criticism, directed at Sahlins in particular, seems unduly harsh, since his analysis of primitive "affluence" can serve an important critical function in uncovering the inadequacy of concepts of civilized "affluence," and it does not necessarily imply any desire to "return to the primitive" in a simplistic sense. Yet Bookchin's point concerning primitive society is an incisive one. Whatever their achievements, one should never overlook their relative poverty of needs, and their failure to develop "humanity's obvious potentialities for producing a rich literary tradition, science, a sense of place, and a broad concept of shared humanity" (p. 67).

One of the most intriguing questions taken up by Bookchin is the process by which hierarchy and domination arose out of the organic societies that he describes. He contends that previous theories of the origin of systems of domination have usually been simplistic, whether they have posited an economic basis (e.g., that ruling classes arose when a sufficient surplus was generated to allow appropriation by a segment of society), or a political basis (e.g., that ruling classes established themselves through conquest, after which they were able to continuously extract a surplus from the labour of the subjected group).[4]

Bookchin argues that instead a complex theory of the gradual emergence of social hierarchy and the state is necessary. He concedes that certain material preconditions are necessary, and that phenomena like the development of the plough and the use of animal labour must be given due recognition. Yet there is no simple correlation between technical development and the growth of hierarchy or the rise of the state. Some societies with relatively greater technological advances retained much of their traditional structure, while others, like the Aztecs, developed class systems in the absence of many such technological changes. Similarly, the idea of conquest does not explain why societies in which centralized rule was established developed different degrees of hierarchy, and partial or full formation of a state. Bookchin contends that an adequate theory must recognize the emergence of class society and the state out of organic society to be the result of a complex dialectic, and must consider all the technical, political, economic, cultural, psychological, and epistemological factors that conditioned such a development. Most previous theories of the rise of hierarchy have strongly emphasized the "objective" factors, in the sense of the technical, economic, and political ones. Yet, in Bookchin's view, "rulership rested less on proprietorship, personal possessions, wealth, and acquisition—in short, the *objects* that confer power—than it did on the symbolic weight of status, communal representation, religious authority, and the disaccumulation of goods....." (p. 73). Overlooking this cultural context makes the specific modes of development of hierarchy incomprehensible, and creates the illusion of greater discontinuities between social forms than actually existed. What the simplistic position ignores is the persistence of values carried over from organic society, and their frequent manifestation in reactions against the rationalization and politicization of social relations. There is thus a long history of the evolution of the system of domination, and an accompanying history of resistance to it on behalf of freedom and communal values.

While Bookchin's wide-ranging discussion of the emergence of hierarchy cannot be fully outlined here, some of the key points should be mentioned. He notes the potential for generating power relations inherent in the early division of labour, in which the male specialized in hunting and defence. Society "tended to assimilate his temperament as a hunter, a guardian, and eventually as a warrior" (p. 78). A second source of power is in the tendency of the old to transform their natural authority into hierarchical social position, in order to gain security and self-protection. They desire social power as a substitute for their declining physical power; consequently, their precarious position produces "seeds for the hatred of eros and the body" (p.82). Shamanism intensifies hierarchical development, since it concentrates the power of the gerontocracy in the hands of an exclusive segment of society which has a "specialization in fear" (p. 83).

While these phenomena could be contained within the structure of organic society, leaving its kinship-based communal organization and its delicate interrelationship with nature relatively undisturbed, the growth of a true class system effects a more thorough social transformation. To account for such vast changes one must examine such phenomena as "the emergence of the city, the State, an authoritarian technics, and a highly organized market economy" (p. 89). But it also demands that attention be given to the mechanisms producing "a repressive sensibility and body of values" in which reality was reconceptualized "along lines of command and obedience" (p. 89). Bookchin calls such systems of valuation "epistemologies of rule."

The ensuing analysis of the rise of class society exhibits the complex dialectic between objective and subjective factors (factors which are, indeed, so interrelated that they can only be separated for purposes of analysis, as Bookchin later shows in his analysis of technology). In the realm of religion, anthropomorphic deities begin to displace remaining animistic values, and a formalized priesthood and priestly class replaces Shamanism. The values of priest and warrior increasingly become the dominant symbolic forces in society, but while the priesthood could exist within a prescribed realm, the ascendency of the warriors and their values meant true class dominance over the whole of society, and required fundamental transformation of its character. For Bookchin, the rise of the city as a contributing factor in these developments "can hardly be overemphasized." The city "provided the territory for territorialism, the civic institutions for citizenship, the marketplace for elaborate forms of exchange, the exclusivity of quarters and neighbourhoods for classes, and monumental structures for the state" (p. 97).

While Bookchin's analysis of the rise of hierarchy is impressive, there is a tendency to burden the theory with some hasty generalizations about its applicability. Granted that an adequate explanation requires consideration of an ensemble of factors that are usually over- or underemphasized, is it necessarily true that the relative weight attributed to the factors (which militates against the thesis of rapid emergence) is necessarily correct for all cases. Granted, for example, that Oppenheimer was wrong when he concluded that conquest of sedentary agrarian societies by predatory nomadic groups is the basis for the rise of "the state" and class society, is it not possible that conquest can be a revolutionary transforming force in some cases in which other factors have been relatively "underdeveloped"? Similarly, while Carneiro's theory seems simplistic, Bookchin might have devoted more attention to demographic questions. Clastres, for example, while rejecting the idea of a transition from the chieftainship to the state based on population influences, attributes to population increase much of the responsibility for expanded hierarchical tendencies *within* the chieftainship.[5] Further exploration of topics such as these could strengthen Bookchin's analysis, which nevertheless advances considerably the project of constructing a critical theory of the origins of social domination.

Bookchin's recent work has moved consistently in the direction of a comprehensive analysis of systems of technics in their political, economic, cultural, and ecological context. The present work is particularly illuminating in the area of the cultural context of technology. Bookchin emphasizes the extent to which meanings and symbols are embedded in the sphere of "the technical," and he explores the relation between technics (as objective social forces) and technical rationality (both as a system of organization and as a way of knowing) in the constitution of that realm.

The discussion of meanings and technics notes the permeation of all activity by cultural reason. Bookchin argues, for example, that to understand the nature of "skill" in Inuit society, conceptions of technical proficiency and instrumental action are not sufficient. In addition, one must understand the highly developed conceptions of community and person that underlie the process of production. The narrow view of the technical leads to invalid generalizations concerning the effects of technological development. Surface similarities may disguise underlying diversities in meanings, and dissimilar social forms may be confounded. While technological determinism encounters numerous empirical difficulties, this explanation helps explain its theoretical inadequacy.

An understanding of the "technical" in any historical period requires attention to many phenomena other than tools, machines, or "technologies" in any narrow sense. If, as Ellul and other "technological pessimists" have argued, technique has indeed become an increasingly dominant force in modern society, it is not merely because of the size, or even the complexity and incomprehensibility of technologies. Neither is it because technology is inherently "dehumanizing." Rather, it is in large part a consequence of the fact that capital and the bureaucratic state, the final products of the long evolution of hierarchy, have intruded technical rationality into every sphere of human existence, so that the "technical sphere" ultimately invades consciousness, personality, and the most intimate human relationships.

Any assessment of the destructive and liberatory effects of such developments as capitalism, the modern state, and advanced technology must take into account both the expansion of possibilities which has taken place, and the corrosive effects on the self, human culture, and nature. Bookchin cautions capitalist and Marxist devotees of the dogmas of "progress" and "modernity" against their ill-considered propensity "to elevate a deadening, homogenizing mass media over the spiritual yearning elicited by religious ceremonies, a mechanistic scientism over a colorful mythopoeic sensibility, and an icy indifference to the fate of one's immediate neighbors over a richly intertwined system of mutual aid" (p. 216). No doubt some will find in passages like this one further evidence of the existence in Bookchin's thought of a "Jewish Messianic" outlook that delights in overdrawn oppositions between Good and Evil, and betrays an "atavism" that is truly "regressive." Yet such attempts to dramatically point out the magnitude of the loss of cultural richness and organic interrelationship should not simple-mindedly be equated with rejection of any advances in modern society. In fact, Bookchin argues that "the material dispensation of capitalism" presents us with the potential for "the broadest conception of freedom known thus far: the autonomous individual's freedom to shape material life in a form that is... ecological, rational, and artistic" (p. 218).

In short, the realm of freedom is within reach. The material basis, in the sense of the technology for freedom and abundance, is within our grasp, yet the social forms and consciousness to realize such a goal are as yet lacking. Bookchin fears that an obsession with technical development, including "alternative technologies," will obscure this issue. The key question is not scale, but rather the creation of an emancipatory society which can incorporate the technology appropriate to it. Small is not necessarily beautiful, and there is no "appropriate technology" *tout court*. Technology cannot be separated from culture, and the creation of liberatory technology therefore implies not only the generation of "new designs," but also "new meanings." The former can easily be assimilated into the system of instrumental rationality.

What, then, is Bookchin's conception of freedom? In large part, it is a reconstruction of the Hegelian view, in which freedom is seen as "uninhibited volition and self-consciousness" (p. 36). But while Hegel vitiated the conception through idealism, Bookchin wishes to save its organicist content (lost in later radical thought) while giving it concrete psychological, cultural, and political meaning. The goal of social practice is the creation of the developed person who can participate actively in a community of self-realizing beings. Such a process of self-formation is the means by which the historically conditioned contradictions between individual will and desire and social need (or pleasure principle and reality principle) can finally be overcome. This requires a movement from the "fetishism of needs" to a situation in which needs become consciously directed, so that a truly rational society can finally be achieved.

As in his previous work, Bookchin finds in past historical experiments much evidence concerning human possibilities. Here, however, he goes further and presents an extensive "history of freedom," which is counterposed to the "legacy of domination" which is so much more prominent in world history. Many familiar examples appear: the Greek Polis, the sections of the early French Revolution, the New England town meetings, the Commune of Paris, the collectives of the Spanish Revolution, and so forth. Where the discussion is most enlightening, though, is in the presentation of evidence of a continuing tradition of libertarian and communal strivings throughout the Middle Ages and the early modern period. Here we find a submerged tradition of freedom, in which Medieval heretics, peasants, and, finally, radical Protestant sects, rebelled against the established order. While most studies of political thought and practice in the West recognize this tradition (if at all) merely with a perfunctory comment on Winstanley and the Diggers, Bookchin shows it to be quite extensive, and to include an astounding variety of groups with hedonistic, egalitarian, communitarian and anarchistic values. In the course of this discussion, he demonstrates the complexities of the religious consciousness, which contains not only the conservative, repressive, and ideological elements usually emphasized by the orthodox left, but also a critical and utopian dimension with vast revolutionary potential.

Bookchin continues to recognize the Polis to be superior in many ways to other historical models, insofar as its democratic aspects can be extricated from its basis in class domination. What he admires most is its success in nurturing a highly individualized social self by cultivating a balance between values like civic duty, developed personality, and freedom. A responsible self and an active citizenry were consciously created ("by design") through the system of assemblies, councils, courts, and other institutions in which direct democracy, rotation of offices, and other participatory processes prevailed.

Bookchin argues that our task today is to recreate such a social self and active citizenry, on a universalistic rather than a class basis. He contends that liberatory politics must be based on the "unmediated control over public life" that can only issue from direct action and direct democracy. Direct action is not seen as a *tactic* that can be judged on purely instrumentalist criteria. Rather, it is a process of training for "selfhood, self-assertiveness, and sensibility for direct democracy" (p. 132). It should be recalled that "direct action" does not signify a romanticist idealization of flamboyant deeds. Instead, it connotes a deep and enduring commitment to the immediate creation of modes of thought, feeling, and action which are alternatives to those conditioned by the system of domination. Daily life, says Bookchin, must be accepted as "a calling," in which liberatory institutions founded on cooperation, mutual aid, and personalism are created to replace those based on bureaucratic and market values. The hope for a total transformation of society must be maintained. Yet even when there is no immediate prospect of rapid dissolution of hierarchical institutions it is necessary to "defend society's molecular base" in whatever way possible, whether through the creation of non-dominating personal relationships, the development of communal and cooperative institutions, or by active resistance to the domination of humanity and nature. Without such direct action there will be no "body politic" in the sense of a community of selves capable of managing society, and terms like "democracy" and "revolution" will be only hollow slogans.

Bookchin is one of the few radical social theorists today who continues to offer a hopeful vision of fundamental social transformation, while remaining critical of the problematic of "revolution" as it has been presented in the past. While he continues to use the term, his conception of social change is qualitatively different from the standard "revolutionary" ideologies, which succumb to varying degrees of mechanism, instrumentalism, and reification. Given his conception of the ecological society, the true project of humanity must be the *regeneration* of the organic fabric of both society and nature—as mind, desire, and imagination are liberated from the legacy of domination.

The Ecology of Freedom is an eloquent, erudite, and highly ambitious work. Because of its bold aspirations, it often leaves gaps in its arguments. Its monistic metaphysics requires a more sophisticated confrontation of the intricacies of the mind-body problem. The theory of the formation of the self demands a deeper analysis of the processes of psychological development. Ecological ethics must deal more forthrightly with the issue of the fact-value dichotomy and how to avoid it. The nature of liberatory practice must be given a great deal more specificity. But no single book can take on all these problems, and an important function of this one is to give further research in these areas a sense of direction and of social purpose.

If radical social theory is to have today any of the vitality that it possessed in the past, Bookchin's attempt to ground it in a comprehensive view of reality, and to relate it authentically to movements like ecology, community organization, and feminism, will have made an enormous contribution to this renewal. But even more, for those who are disillusioned with the reigning traditions of materialism, idealism, and dualism, and who find in ecological, organicist, and process thought some intimations of an escape from the limitations of Western humanism and scientism, Bookchin's social ecology will signify a major breakthrough in contemporary social theory.

Notes

1. Montréal: Black Rose Books, 1980.
2. Palo Alto: Cheshire Books, 1982.
3. See Ervin Laszlo, *Introduction to Systems Philosophy* (New York: Harper and Row, 1972), especially Chapter 5, "Empirical Interpretations," pp. 55-117; and Arthur Koestler, *The Ghost in the Machine* (Chicago: Regnery, 1967), especially Chapter XIV, "The Ghost in the Machine," pp. 197-221.
4. Bookchin might also have referred to Carneiro's more recent "social circumscription" theory of the rise of the state, in which population pressures are said to lead to conflict, conquest, and political and economic domination. See "A Theory of the Origin of the State" in *Science*, vol. 169, 733-38, August 21, 1970. While the theory claims to be "ecological," it overlooks the complexities of social ecology stressed by Bookchin, and lapses into naïve empiricism.
5. See *Society Against the State: The Leader as Servant and the Humane Uses of Power among the Indians of the Americas* (New York: Urizen Books, 1977), pp. 180-83.

Chapter 10

The Labyrinth of Power and the Hall of Mirrors

Since the dawn of civilization cast its harsh light on a world of domination, humanity has been haunted by its remembrance of the dark primaeval night from which it emerged. It has lived the reality of division, separation, and power; while it has dreamt of reunion, reconciliation, and harmony. The dominant images throughout history have been the images of power, whether they gave expression to the ancient view of a universe ruled by a supreme patriarch, king, and judge, or to the modern conception of a quantifiable, manipulable world reduced to a stock of resources for technological domination. Yet the human spirit has also been troubled and inspired by other images which betray the bad conscience with which we have accepted the system of power.

While civilization has driven ruthlessly toward the appropriation of all of reality within its domain, it has inevitably encountered an Other which it has been unable to assimilate. It has responded politically with millenia of oppression and annihilation, and psychologically with a long epoch of repression and denial. But while civilized Man triumphed—as all the history books testify to—the Other has constantly surrounded him, invaded his very being, and sometimes driven him to madness. This Otherness has confronted Man in the form of the Primitive, of Woman, of the Child, and of Nature, and has established its Third Column within him, in the body, in instinct, in the imagination. Occasionally, it has broken into history, in anarchistic peasant revolts, in utopian experiments, and in the creative outpourings of artists, poets, and visionaries. In its enduring resistance to absorption into the order of domination it has faithfully awaited the inevitable twilight of civilization.

The true negation of power requires a reaffirmation of the integral nature of this Otherness. It must not be seen merely as the retreating shadow of civilization, and even less as a vain but heroic protest against the triumphant march of domination. Since the system of domination is itself the negation of organic social relations and an organic relationship with nature, the "negation of power" is therefore a negation of the negation, and implies the affirmation of a positive reality. In its negative theoretical moment it requires a fully critical analysis of the metaphysical, epistemological, and axiological foundations of civilization, while in its positive, speculative moment it demands their supersession in a non-dominating, organicist worldview. Furthermore, it demands careful analysis of the specificity of contemporary forms of power and the rationality which generates them. In the present preliminary sketch of such an analysis, I will suggest that an adequate conception of power in our present historical era presupposes an understanding of the dialectic between two forms of consciousness— a productivist rationality and a consumptionist one—which prevail in contemporary economistic society. Furthermore, I contend that the locus of determination of power relations has been shifting in the direction of the latter form, although much of even the most critical social analysis has lagged behind in its apprehension and theorization of this evolution. Finally, I argue that as a result of this development, it becomes increasingly more evident that the economic problem, the political problem, and the problem of technique must all be situated within an analysis of cultural reason which takes into account the centrality of the social imagination in the constitution of power and in any possible path toward its negation.

Most radical social theory throughout the modern period has failed to undertake a thorough critique of civilization and to investigate adequately the cultural and psychological dimensions of power (until recently some varieties of utopian thought and radical psychoanalysis were almost the only exceptions). Especially in the orthodox Marxist and anarchist traditions, there has been an obsession with the most overtly economic and politicial forms of power, so that a more complex analysis has been blocked. According to the received conception, power is depicted as a relation of domination in which the powerful subject the powerless to control in order to exploit the latter. In both classical Marxism and anarchism this exploitation is conceived of as being essentially economic. Thus, for Marx, "political power, properly so called, is merely the organized power of one class for oppressing another."[1] Other forms of power are, in the last instance, similarly traceable to the system of class oppression. Despite all the suggestiveness of the Marxian concept of ideology, forms of consciousness are also finally reduced to reflections of the conditions and contradictions that prevail in the economic structure.

For Bakunin, things are even clearer. "Together with the state must perish all that is known as law, the whole structure of law-making and government, from the top downwards, for its sole aim has been the establishment of the systematic exploitation of the people's labour for the benefit of the ruling classes."[2] The assumptions behind such views of power are that it is something that some have and others lack, that it is exercised by those in positions of economic and political privilege, and that it can be "negated" through the abolition of economic classes, political hierarchies, and other institutional sources of concentrated power. Thus far the theory; the rest is strategy.

While the faithful still cling to and repeat these eternal verities, they sound more and more like cultic incantations, since they have an ever-dwindling appeal (and perhaps more significantly, an ever-diminishing *meaning*) to the oppressed masses. This alone (not to mention the persistence of hierarchy and power relations even within anti-authoritarian social movements) should be enough to suggest that there is much more to the story, and that the classical model fails to grasp essential aspects of the foundations of power.

As a result of these increasingly obvious shortcomings, contemporary social thought has no paucity of attempts to reveal other hidden dimensions of power. Among recent analysts, Foucault has gained the most recognition for his efforts to move from a purely negative ("power-sovereignty," "juridico-discursive") view of power to one that grasps the positive dimensions of the phenemenon, showing the ways in which it creates realities and generates possibilities. In *Discipline and Punish* he describes a society in which power operates and reproduces itself through processes of discipline and surveillance. He argues that by the late 18th century there existed three competing "ways to organize the power to punish": "the monarchical system," in which "punishment is a ceremony of sovereignty," that of "the reforming jurists," who wished to use punishment as "a procedure for requalifying individuals as subjects," and the penitentiary system, in which punishment consisted of "a technique for the coercion of individuals." He argues that the dispute at this juncture in history was over three "technologies of power," and that the triumph of the third marked the ascendency of a technology of discipline and training.[3] The crucial development of the 18th century was the expansion of techniques of "hierarchized, continuous and functional surveillance," in order to constitute disciplinary power as an "integrated system."[4]

Foucault's analysis of disciplinary technique reveals an important dimension of power in the modern period. He notes that discipline has been essential to the formation of a certain type of individuality characteristic of our society. It is an analytical process which—in order to produce an individuality which is "cellular," "organic," "genetic," and "combinatory"— "draws up tables," "prescribes movements," "imposes exercises" and "arranges 'tactics.'"[5] The criteria for regulating these processes include efficiency of operation, judged both in economic terms and in relation to social resistances, maximization of range of applicability, and integration of techniques into the institutional structures of society.[6] It is appropriate that the conception of Panopticonism should have such a central role in this discussion, since Foucault describes a system of power which so clearly embodies the rationality of classic Benthamite utilitarianism. Yet despite the close connection between

Benthamite techniques of control and classical political economy (a connection which Foucault perhaps fails to fully explore, as Melossi and Pavarini note[7]), the early "philosophic radicals" had only a rudimentary awareness of the nature of the system of power they were helping to create. Bourgeois liberalism retained a liberatory moment in relation to the traditional authorities that it assaulted, and few 18th century minds (excepting some romantic conservatives) had even intimations of the fate of the new technologies of power. To understand their vicissitudes, we must look carefully at subsequent history. Their significance becomes much clearer as they are incorporated into Taylorism, with its analytical systemization of time, space, and motion, its aims of maximization of efficiency, utility, and productivity, its institution of processes of quantification that make Bentham's "hedonistic calculus" look primitive, its adherence to an explicitly economistic and reductionist view of human nature, and its open dedication to the service of the concentrated power of capital. While Foucault does not trace the transformations which led from classical utilitarianism to scientific management and beyond, he is helpful in uncovering aspects of the genesis of this general path of development.

Perhaps if Foucault has been content with describing a crucial historical epoch—in short, if he had remained within his chosen realm of the archaeology of knowledge—he might have been less misleading as a social theorist. However, he claims not only that he has uncovered some of the historical foundations of the system of disciplinary technique, but that in doing so he has discovered the key to understanding power in the modern period:

> Our society is one not of spectacle, but of surveillance; under the surface of images, one invests bodies in depth; behind the great abstraction of exchange, there continues the meticulous, concrete training of useful forces; the circuits of communication are the supports of an accumulation and a centralization of knowledge; the play of signs defines the anchorages of power; it is not that the beautiful totality of the individual is amputated, repressed, altered by our social order, it is rather that the individual is carefully fabricated in it, according to a whole technique of forces and bodies.[8]

Typically, Foucault presents us with an either/or approach to social theory, an approach in which every new hypothesis constitutes a definitive break with all that preceded it. But if we leave this exhilarating but insubstantial world of permanent theoretical revolution we must recognize that we do indeed live in a society of *both* spectacle *and* surveillance, and that comprehension of the two moments of domination is essential in order to have an even minimally adequate understanding of the system of power. True, the individual is "fabricated" by "a whole technique of forces and bodies." But even more profoundly, the individual is generated by the social imagination. "Fabrication" grasps an element of the process, but is an impoverished metaphor for the whole of it. The subordination of "image," "exchange," "communication" and "sign" to the species of knowledge entailed in the mechanisms of surveillance and discipline is a serious distortion.

In the end, the rejection of dialectical analysis of the formation of the self is a fatal flaw in Foucault's approach. It is true that there is no "beautiful totality" of the self that is merely repressed, but must naïveté be met by an equal and opposite naïveté? Subjectivity cannot be dissolved into a purely "fabricated" individual. The individual of modern bourgeois society is a being with both internality and externality, both of which are the product of long processes of evolution (both cultural and biological) which are embodied in the self. As Bookchin has pointed out, following Hegel, the nature of a phenomenon is in an important sense equivalent to the history of the phenomenon.[9] The self can only be understood as an organic totality within the larger organic totalities of human culture and of nature, and with which it has a dialectical relationship of growth and development. True, the self cannot be thought of as having *any* character apart from its natural and social relationships; yet it can at the same time have its own immanent, historically shaped telos, which is integral to its self-creative dialectical interaction with the rest of nature and society. Within this context, Foucault's discussion of disciplinary technique elucidates one aspect of the formation of the modern individual, but it scarcely grasps the nature of social being in this period.

Perhaps even more significant than the questionable concept of the "society of surveillance" is Foucault's discussion of "normalizing power" in modern society. He develops this conception to a certain extent in *Discipline and Punish* when he interprets the penal system as part of a "carceral network" which operates through such "judges of normality" as "the teacher-judge, the doctor-judge, the educator-judge, the 'social-worker'-judge."[10] This network, "with its systems of insertion, distribution, surveillance, observation, has been the greatest support, in modern society, of the normalizing power."[11] There is an apparent advance here, in that "normalizing power" would seem to be a more comprehensive concept that might bridge the gap between subjectivity and objectivity in a way that concepts like "discipline" and "surveillance" are incapable of doing. Yet it can be argued that the process of normalization, even at the height of the developments Foucault describes, had a quite different basis. The system cohered and functioned primarily because of the "ethical capital," the inherited sedimentation of cultural values that had been passed down, albeit in distorted form, through the bourgeois epoch. The individualizing, atomizing disciplinary mechanisms thus become not only the source and support of new relations of power and domination, but also the medium which begins to dissolve what we might call the cultural infrastructure supporting the disciplinary institutions themselves. "Normalizing power" can thus appear at the same time as "denormalizing power."

Yet such contradictions cannot become evident, given Foucault's usage of the equivocal term "normalizing," a usage which must be clarified if we are to see the limitations of his discussion. In *The History of Sexuality* he explains that "law operates more and more as a norm,"[12] a statement that might appear puzzling, given his assertion that society has increasingly come under the rule of utility—a tendency which results in reduction of law to punitive sanction, and thus undermines its functioning as norm. Yet law for Foucault is a "norm" only in a very limited sense: it has power to "qualify, measure, appraise, and hierarchize."[13] It acts *upon* the population, rather than *through* it, as part of the cultural tradition (and is thus the diametrical opposite of primitive "law"—as a consequence, both primitive society and modern society are in a significant sense the most "lawless" societies imaginable). Thus, when he describes the incorporation of law into "a continuum of apparatuses... whose functions are regulatory,"[14] he means this more in the liberal sense of a "regulatory agency" than in the ethical sense of "regulation" of practice by a standard of moral judgement. Obviously, we can deduce from the nature of the disciplinary processes certain "norms"--i.e., sanctioned behavioural characteristics that they tend to produce. Yet a fundamental question still remains: what is the nature of normative *value* in a society, and how can disciplinary institutions possibly produce or alter it? Foucault gives us little help in this matter.

On the other hand, he is most convincing when he demonstrates the interaction between penal and other disciplinary institutions and other social institutions, particularly the economic ones.[15] The "failure" of the prison is explained to be in reality its successful functioning as a process of differentiation of illegalities and transformation of the nature of crime. Hence, "the differential administration of illegalities through the mediation of penalty forms part of [the] mechanisms of domination,"[16] and crime is rendered socially marginal and economically less explosive through the manufacture of "delinquency."[17]

Despite Foucault's strictures against the negative view of power as mere constraint, coercion or repression, passages such as many of those discussed above indicate that he still remains within the confines of a largely negative conception of power, and that he has failed to grasp its profound positivity, especially in contemporary society. *The History of Sexuality* might therefore seem to be an advance toward such an understanding. There he argues that the mechanisms for the regulation of sexuality have a positive dimension also. They "have a double impetus: pleasure and power. The pleasure that comes of exercising a power that questions, monitors, watches, spies, searches out, brings to light; and, on the other hand, the pleasure that kindles at having to evade this power."[18]

At this point Foucault indicates an important truth about power. Its nature cannot be understood if it is reduced to something that is "held" by some so that others can be excluded from its "possession." He gives the processes of power more concreteness and specificity by suggesting how they *constitute* patterns of life. Power differentiates itself and consolidates itself by generating a multitutde of strategies and tactics on the part of both those who administer the controls and those who are subject to them—and these are often overlapping groups. Since power is in a sense a hierarchical network—indeed a labyrinthine structure with many dimensions—the relation of any individual to the entire system will depend on his or her positioning on a number of axes. The strategic model proposed by Foucault thus has a distinct advantage over the legalistic one in grasping the dynamics of power. Had he been able to overcome his biases against subjectivity, he might have considered the relation between this strategic view of power and the constitution of the *Lebenswelt*. In any case, the deaf ear which the oppressed often turn toward messages about their possible liberation becomes more understandable. Vague images of fulfillment in a possible future world must contend with immediate and constant satisfactions flowing from the strategies and tactics integral to one's existing form of life.[19] Foucault should be given credit for his contribution to this analysis. As he rightly concludes:

> The omnipresence of power: not because it has the privilege of consolidating everything under its invincible unity, but because it is produced from one moment to the next, at every point, or rather in every relation from one point to another. Power is everywhere; not because it embraces everything, but because it comes from everywhere.[20]

In the discussion of pleasure and its place in strategic action, it might seem that the subjectivity that was so noticeably absent in the "society of surveillance" of *Discipline and Punish* finally arrives on the scene. But this is not Foucault's intention, for he holds the concept of the subject to be a "theoretical drawback,"[21] and he contends that resistance against power must be founded not in the subject, but rather in "bodies and pleasures."[22] And, indeed, what does intrude is a rather meagre subjectivity in any case. The psychological dimension, the symbolic, and the imaginary have little place in Foucault's analysis. The family, we are told, must be seen as the locus for the interaction between strategies and tactics, as for example in the context of "the great 'maneuvers' employed for the

Malthusian control of the birthrate, for the populationist incitements, for the medicalization of sex and the psychiatrization of its non-genital forms."[23] Granted, the family must be understood in its relation to these technologies, not to mention the conceptualizations of experience that constitute the problematics underlying the techniques. Yet there is no reason to conclude, as Foucault does, that "the father in the family is not the 'representative' of the sovereign or the state; and the latter are not projections of the father on a different scale."[24] It is not only the critics of patriarchal authority (beginning with Reich, in *The Mass Psychology of Fascism*) who have pointed out the close connections, and indeed the symbiotic relation between the patriarchal family and political authoritarianism. Authoritarian ideology has only explicitly proclaimed what authoritarian cultural tradition has embodied in both its symbolic expressions and concrete practice. Psychoanalytic findings serve to demonstrate the depth in which patriarchal-authoritarian values underlay both the authoritarian family and state before the culturally and psychologically corrosive effects of late capitalism took their tool on both.[25] Unfortunately, the significance of both the original phenomenon and its contradiction in late capitalist culture escape Foucault's analysis.

Foucault's most concise delineation of the nature of power appears in *The History of Sexuality*:

> It seems to me that power must be understood in the first instance as the multiplicity of force relations immanent in the sphere in which they operate and which constitute their own organization; as the process which, through ceaseless struggles and confrontations, transforms, strengthens, or reverses them; as the support which these force relations find in one another; and lastly, as the strategies in which they take effect, whose general design or institutional crystallization is embodied in the state apparatus, in the formation of the law, in the various social hegemonies.[26]

Without a clear explanation of the meaning of "force relations" it is difficult to judge the adequacy of this analysis. Yet whatever plausible meaning might be attributed to them, this conception seems incapable of explaining the relation between the system of power and the meanings and values which must be understood if one is to have any comprehension of the *world* in which power, hierarchy, and domination exist. Foucault has contributed much to contemporary thought by helping focus on certain aspects of the relation between power and knowledge. Where he has fallen short is in his failure to explore at all adequately the roots of power in the very structure of rationality and in the imagination.

In this respect, Foucault's work represents a regression from the analysis of the Frankfurt School, which sought the basis for power and domination not only in the structure of contemporary rationality, but also in the evolution of reason since the beginnings of Western civilization:

> The true critique of reason will necessarily uncover the deepest layers of civilization and explore its earliest history. From the time when reason became the instrument of human domination of human and extra-human nature by man—that is to say, from its very beginnings—it has been frustrated in its own intention of discovering the truth. This is due to the fact that it made nature a mere object, and that it failed to discover the trace of itself in such objectivization, in the concepts of matter and things not less than in those of gods and spirit.[27]

With these words Max Horkheimer describes the foundation of the prevailing mode of rationality in civilization: instrumental reason. In formulating this conception, Horkheimer and the Frankfurt School subjected civilization to a devastating critique. Lévi-Strauss's relatively modest claim that the "primary function of written communication is to facilitate slavery"[28] is integrated into a more far-reaching indictment: that the entire rationale of civilization is domination.

For Horkheimer, the alternative to instrumental reason is "objective reason," the kind proclaimed by the philosophical tradition to be the supreme form of knowing. It is reason which seeks "concrete principles" that impart theoretical knowledge of reality.[29] To the extent that it is practical, it consists of the regulation of activity through theoretically established principles.

Reason in this form has always constituted critique, in that it implied the need for transcendence of actual, socially conditioned modes of thought and activity. This relative independence of reason in relation to prevailing reality constituted its objectivity. Enlightenment has, however, undermined this autonomy of objective reason by associating it with "dogmatism" and "superstition." Reason becomes "completely harnessed to the social process,"[30] and is accorded a new "objectivity" insofar as it is subordinate to the dominant reality. Critical reason is banished to a subjective realm in which relativism prevails.

Horkheimer and Adorno argue in *The Dialectic of Enlightenment* that this development signifies the reduction of reason to a tool of domination. The triumph of instrumental reason means that reality is perceived as a radical division between knowing subject and alien object and knowledge becomes a means of appropriation, control, and domination. Reason accomplishes "the preparation of the object from mere sensory material in order to make it the material of subjugation."[31] The end is the subordination of all of reality "to the rule of computation and utility."[32] The modern form of instrumental reason is, moreover, an expression of bourgeois society. It therefore presupposes the principle of "exchange of equivalents," which requires that objects be reduced to quantifiable, efficiently manipulable units. Qualitative distinctions are therefore reduced to matters of subjective perception, quantitative ones become the intersubjective basis for determining objective reality.

Marcuse elucidates this evolution of reason by relating it to the Weberian analysis of rationality. The general concept of instrumental reason is then given particularity in its modification under the system of industrial capitalism. Marcuse contends that as the system evolves, domination increasingly adopts the form of "total bureaucracy," and instrumental reason as technical rationality becomes the predominant mode of knowing.[33] Weberian "rationality," which deals with both institutions and forms of consciousness, has three elements. First, it entails universal quantification, a process which begins with the new science and technology of the Enlightenment, and eventually pervades all of reality, including "the conduct of life." Secondly, there is the rejection of all knowledge which is not subject to its narrowly defined, usually empiricist, procedures of rational proof. And finally, there is a concentration of knowledge in a "universal, technically trained organization of officials."[34] By these means, reality is reduced to a system of quantifiable objects and, more particularly, given the economistic ideology of the age, to exchange values.[35] By thus reducing "man and nature to fungible objects of organization," technical rationality permits the emergence of a system of "total administration."[36] The government of persons is replaced by the administration of things, but ironically, as persons are reified, transformed into things.

The Weberian concept and its development by the Frankfurt School have aided the understanding of power mechanisms in advanced societies. In particular, some theorists have employed the analysis in order to look behind the façades of liberal democracy and proletarian socialism to find technobureaucratic structures that have profoundly conditioned both systems. In addition, the analysis has social psychological import in suggesting the ways in which the quantification and reification in technical rationality have deeply penetrated into subjective life-processes. (Both the philosophy of culture of Adorno and Horkheimer and the philosophical psychology of Marcuse and Fromm are relevant in this connection.)

Yet this account of rationality remains inadequate. Powerful as it may be as theory of institutional rationality, it is less sufficient as a representation of individual consciousness, even in segments of society in which quantitative values and bureaucratization are apparently most firmly entrenched. Furthermore, it does little to explain the possibility of integrating human subjects into such a technological system. The most relevant Frankfurt School category in this connection, "the culture industry," succeeds primarily in explaining the pacification function of commodified culture, and aids little in the exploration of the positive dimension of this phenomenon. While it avoids the simplistic, though ubiquitous, analysis that Foucault calls "the repressive hypothesis" concerning the structure of power relationships, it nevertheless says much more about how liberatory possibilities are eliminated than about how new non-liberatory possibilities are generated. Nor does it indicate how central cultural production has become to the entire social system and its reproduction and growth.

If the orthodox Marxist economistic reduction of all forms of consciousness to superstructural excrescences was inadequate, so is the neo-Marxist analysis of reason insufficient, insofar as it fails to fully explore the cultural and symbolic dimensions of the "instrumental." Critical theory from Horkheimer to Habermas has tended to misconstrue the boundaries between instrumental, technical, or purposive rationality, on the one hand, and the cultural or communicative realm, on the other. The problem has been not so much one of correctly demarcating the two domains, as a failure to appreciate the inclusive character of the more comprehensive cultural or symbolic realm.

Meaning is fundamental to any social order. While functional explanations can succeed on their own terms, they are inadequate as a means of understanding social phenomena. Just as comprehension of purposive action cannot be predicated merely on descriptions of states of matter and energy, so meaning cannot be understood through mere description of functions and purposes. This is necessarily the case since, as Sahlins argues, "there is no other logic in the sense of meaningful order save that imposed by culture on the instrumental process."[37] It is not only societies in which "social control" is exercised through "cultural tradition" that the symbolic is fundamental. "In the last instance," *all* rationality is cultural, including that of capitalist society (whether market or state regulated varieties). Capitalist society is, of course, a unique social formation or cluster of formations. Yet its uniqueness, to cite Sahlins again, "consists not in the fact that the economic system escapes symbolic determination but that the economic symbolism is structurally determining."[38] The mechanism by which action is regulated is thus "a symbolic code, figured as the meaningful differences between products, which serves as a general scheme of social classification."[39]

Examination of the symbolic code reveals a tendency toward the priority of use-value, though in a very particular sense. In state-capitalist society the principle of use-value was purposefully implanted as part of the dogma of Marxian socialist ideology. In liberal capitalist society it emerges with the maturing of the culture of commodity consumption. In both cases ideology must increasingly adapt itself to the replacement of previous productivist values with those of use values. In the former case, the contradiction remains latent (if explosive), given the authoritarian monopoly on public discourse and the economically parasitical nature of the stratocracy.[40] In the latter case, the dissolution of obsolete value systems advances rapidly, and use-value begins to transform itself. With the evolution of the affluent society, the objective capacity of the system to generate commodities as images of use-value exceeds the subjective ability to use objects through traditional consumption. Consequently, "use" must be redefined to include the reception and projection of increasingly more ephemeral commodity-images, as opposed to the physical depletion of any material or structural substrata of the commodity-object.

The conversion of the social arena into pure spectacle accelerates increasingly in contemporary society.[41] The critique of the social division public/private had significance, in that it pointed out the magnitude of the loss of authentic social being involved in such a split. Yet even this division allowed the possibility of a refuge from the domain of power, as ideologically flawed as that sanctuary may have been. Today, social being invades the alleged sanctity of the private sphere ("in the privacy of your own home"!) to establish a new unity predicated on an even more radical separation. The private sphere can no longer legitimate itself ideologically as an autonomous sphere, as the entirety of social existence becomes incorporated in a social imagery encompassing processes of domestic consumption of images in a thoroughly "publicized" private realm, and the collective, if atomized, consumption of images in public space. The fundamental binary opposition public/private is progressively replaced by the opposition between the individual consumer operating under the sign of the commodity-image and the technobureaucratic system operating under the sign of utility, or technical rationality. The two systems interact dialectically. Spectacular consumption depends upon the continued functioning of the technobureaucratic system, and the converse is equally true. There is thus a material basis of the imaginary and an imaginary basis of the material.

Yet granted the necessity of the material basis, in the subjective acts of valuation the appearance of the image constitutes its reality and accounts for its exigency, and its legitimation follows from its ordering in the socially articulated hierarchy of symbols. If the essential aspect of the object of interest thus consists in its appearing, does this signify the ascendency of the aesthetic? Quite to the contrary. Aesthetic appreciation, which requires focused attention to form and expressiveness, is necessarily contemplative, and always preserves a moment of transcendence, is itself replaced by an obsession with *style*, an external relationship to patterns of consumption.

In accord with the general movement of transformation of the object into commodity-image, the subject itself becomes absorbed into the spectacular system. As our language indicates, "life" is progressively replaced by "life-style." Internality erodes as the self is identified with an aggregate of images to be presented for narcissistic auto-consumption, or for inter-subjective exchange for other images. As the persona of the recent Calvin Klein ad poses the question: "Am I really me, or am I just what I seem to be?"

It is in this context that Goffman's social anthropology of contemporary society must be appreciated. According to Goffman, the "the very structure of the self" is explained by its activity of "presentation" to others, or "performance." In his analysis,

> the performed self [is] seen as some kind of image, usually creditable, which the individual on stage and in character effectively attempts to induce in others to hold in regard to him. While this image is entertained *concerning* the individual, so that a self is imputed to him, this self does not derive from its possessor, but from the whole scene of his action, being generated by that attribute of local events which renders them interpretable by witnesses.[42]

The acute insight here is the perception that the self is externally derived from the imaginary context of action. What must be added is that this context is the economistic code reproduced through the commodification system. And while the "crucial fact" about the self as "dramatic effect" is "whether it will be credited or discredited,"[43] the determination of the possibilities of creditability by the code of commodity values must be shown to be the foundation of the process.

Baudrillard contrasts this bondage to the imaginary with forms of creative embodiment of the self in the manifestations of its own self-activity. The former gives rise to

> the identity that man dons with his own eyes when he can think of himself only as something to produce, to transform, or bring about as value. This remarkable phantasm is confused with that of representation, in which man becomes his own *signified* for himself and enjoys himself as the *content* of value and meaning in a process of self-expression and self-accumulation whose form escapes him.[44]

Nietzsche anticipated a century ago the path of development of modern selfhood. Throughout history, he says, the essence of enslavement and inauthenticity has been the failure of the enslaved to conceive of any values other than those imposed by the master. But without value-creation the self is a mere phantom: "the ordinary man *was* only that which he *passed* for."[45] More striking, though, is his judgement of the character of modernity and the selfhood it engenders:

> Sensibility immensely more irritable...; the abundance of disparate impressions greater than ever: cosmopolitanism in foods, literatures, newspapers, forms, tastes, even landscapes. The tempo of this influx *prestissimo*; the impressions erase each other; one instinctively resists taking in anything, taking anything deeply, to 'digest' anything; a weakening of the power to digest results from this. A kind of adaptation to this flood of impressions takes place: men unlearn spontaneous action, they merely react to stimuli from outside.... Artificial change of one's nature into a 'mirror''; interested but, as it were, merely epidermically interested...."[46]

In view of the process of hollowing out or "epidermalizing" of the self, the locus of contradiction in advanced society changes. It is true that the long-developing contradiction between the self as producer and self as consumer continues to intensify. As productivist character structures formed in superseded historical eras crumble, a serious motivation crisis develops, and poses a continuing threat to the healthy reproduction of the system. Still, the possibilities for technological integration have been far from exhausted, both in the realm of production (humanization, flex-time, codetermination, theories Y, Z, Z'...) and in the realm of consumption (where an infinity of images still remain somewhere in the think-tank). The crucial contradiction in advanced society is not the economic one, assuming the invalidity of Marxian economistic crisis theory (revolutionary praxis as waiting for the Dow-Jones to hit bottom). According to Baudrillard, the major contradiction is the failure to permit "participation," in the sense that "the system is structurally incapable of liberating human potentials except as *productive* forces, that is, according to an operational finality that leaves no room for the reversion of the loss, the gift, the sacrifice, and hence the possibility of symbolic exchange."[47]

The potential of the new social movements lies in their expression of demands that are not readily translatable into the economistic code. They augur a possible leap to a mode of interaction not predicated on the prevailing principles of calculation, consumption, and accumulation (as in Baudrillard's "symbolic exchange"). Radical feminism, for example, traces instrumental reason to its origin in the patriarchal proprietary family, explores submerged or disparaged modes of perception, and entertains the possibility of non-dominating forms of rationality. Ecology posits a reciprocal relation between humanity and the rest of nature, founded on an organicist conception of the totality. Today the very existence of a concept of nature constitutes radical critique, in view of the fact that "nature," even as object of domination, is an obsolete conception, and has been replaced by a bifurcated diffusion of images (industrialized "natural resources" vs. humanized "nature" as vacation spots, scenery, emblems). The possibility persists that these and other social movements will contribute to what Marcuse called a "new sensibility"[48] and which Bookchin elaborates more successfully as "symbiotic libertarian rationality."[49]

Ironically, the degree of failure of contemporary social movements to constitute a significant threat to the order of domination is in direct proportion to their degree of "success." They are silenced precisely to the extent that they are given a voice, since the speech that they are granted consists of the repetition of the sanctioned discourse which is necessary for the reproduction and maturation of the cultural system. As Baudrillard states, "the system now plays on the economic reference (well-being, consumption, but also working conditions, salaries, productivity, growth) as an alibi against the more serious subversion that threatens it in the symbolic order."[50] The failure of Marxism and all orthodox socialisms to have ever posed a threat to domination should be expected in view of the universality of strategic rationality and economistic values in these movements. Contrary to the pronouncements of the scientists of revolution, in all cases the most liberatory revolutionary moments have transpired during the accidental interludes in which a power vacuum occurred. Tremendous outpourings of creativity have filled these brief instants of human history. All organized revolutionary movements have proceeded to structure their revolutions to assure the reconstitution of power—not surprising, given the structure of rationality present in revolutionary organizations and the character structure of the personality-type "revolutionary militant." Failure to reconstitute domination is necessarily perceived as unreason. It is not by chance that the most critical segments of the May '68 French rebellion expressed the principle "Be realistic, demand the impossible," since the "possible"—that contained within the limits of the officially sanctioned discourse—is precisely what was being contested.

It is clear that the problematic of "the seizure of power" has been no less a deception than that of the reform of power from within. Cultural opposition can only create a successful counter-reality by preserving a condition of "marginality" from the standpoint of the dominant institutions. If the temptations of power are not resisted, the vision of the good will quickly degenerate into a new "scenario" with its own "game plan." Consequently, any serious demand for significant social transformation (that is, the demand for the transformation of social significance) must, of necessity, remain self-consciously utopian.

Notes

1. Karl Marx, *The Communist Manifesto*.
2. Arthur Lehning, ed., *Michael Bakunin: Selected Writings* (New York: Grove Press, 1974), p. 175.
3. Michel Foucault, *Discipline and Punish* (New York: Random House, 1979), pp. 130-31.
4. *Ibid.*, p. 176.
5. *Ibid.*, p. 167. Note the entire discussion in Part 3, Chapter 1, for Foucault's often particularistic use of this terminology.
6. *Ibid.*, p. 218.
7. Dario Melossi and Massivo Pavarini, *The Prison and the Factory* (Totowa, N.J.: Barnes and Noble, 1981), p. 194.
8. Foucault, *op. cit.*, p. 217.
9. See "The Concept of Social Ecology" in Bookchin's *The Ecology of Freedom* (Palo Alto: Cheshire Books, 1982). This conception is also present in Aristotelian teleological metaphysics and science, as Jonas points out in *The Phenomenon of Life* (Chicago: University of Chicago Press, 1966).
10. Foucault, *op. cit.*, p. 307.
11. *Ibid.*
12. Michel Foucault, *The History of Sexuality: Introduction* (New York: Random House, 1980), p. 144.
13. *Ibid.*
14. *Ibid.*
15. Thus, when he is, despite himself, most dialectical and Hegelian-Marxist. Note that in "Body/Power" he argues that with "relations of power, one is faced with complex phenomena which don't obey the Hegelian form of the dialectic," after which he presents an eminently dialectical sketch of the development of the phenomena. *Power/Knowledge* (New York: Pantheon Books, 1980), p. 56.
16. Foucault, *Discipline and Punish, op. cit.*, p. 272.
17. *Ibid.*, p. 277.
18. Foucault, *History of Sexuality, op. cit.*, p. 45.
19. Note, for example, the often brilliantly elaborated strategic repertoire of such forms of life as "sexual perversion," "the culture of poverty," and "femininity." These strategies sometimes rise to the level of a tragic art of everyday life, and constitute a devastating immanent critique of Western culture.
20. *Ibid.*, p. 95.
21. As he notes in his rejection of the theory of ideology in *Power/Knowledge*, p. 118.

22. Foucault, *History of Sexuality, op. cit.*, p. 157.
23. *Ibid.*, p. 100.
24. *Ibid.*
25. See Joel Kovel, *The Age of Desire* (New York: Pantheon Books, 1981), for a brilliant analysis of the development of late capitalist culture. The work is one of the few to deal adequately with the coexistence of productivist and consumptionist elements in contemporary society. Several of his composite case studies illustrate well the manner in which the two sets of values can interact in the development of the self.
26. Foucault, *History of Sexuality, op. cit.*, pp. 92-93.
27. Max Horkheimer, *Eclipse of Reason* (New York: Seabury Press, 1974), p. 176.
28. Claude Lévi-Strauss, *Tristes Tropiques* (New York: Pocket Books, 1977), p. 338.
29. Horkheimer, *Eclipse of Reason, op. cit.*, p. 20.
30. *Ibid.*, p. 21.
31. Marx Horkheimer and Theodor Adorno, *The Dialectic of Enlightenment* (New York: Seabury Press, 1972), p. 84.
32. *Ibid.*, p. 6.
33. Herbert Marcuse, *Negations* (Boston: Beacon Press, 1968), p. 203.
34. *Ibid.*, p. 204.
35. *Ibid.*, p. 205.
36. Herbert Marcuse, *One Dimensional Man* (Boston: Beacon Press, 1964), pp. 168-69.
37. Marshall Sahlins, *Culture and Practical Reason* (Chicago: University of Chicago Press, 1976), p. 206.
38. *Ibid.*, p. 211.
39. *Ibid.*, p. 213.
40. Cornelius Castoriadis, *Devant la Guerre* (Paris: Fayard, 1981); published in part in English translation as "Facing the War," in *Telos* 46, pp. 43-61.
41. See Guy Debord, *The Society of the Spectacle* (Detroit: Black and Red, 1970).
42. Erving Goffman, *The Presentation of the Self in Everyday Life* (New York: Doubleday, 1959), p. 252.
43. *Ibid.*
44. Jean Baudrillard, *The Mirror of Production* (St. Louis: Telos Press, 1975), p. 20.
45. Friedrich Nietzsche, *Beyond Good and Evil* (New York: Russell, 1964), p. 261.

46. Friedrich Nietzsche, *The Will to Power* (New York: Random House, 1968), p. 47.
47. Baudrillard, *op. cit.*, pp. 143-44.
48. Herbert Marcuse, *An Essay on Liberation* (Boston: Beacon Press, 1969), pp. 25-28.
49. Bookchin, *Ecology of Freedom*, *op. cit.*, p. 306.
50. Baudrillard, *op. cit.*, p. 139.

more books from **BLACK ROSE BOOKS** — write for a free catalogue

BAKUNIN ON ANARCHISM

edited by Sam Dolgoff

"...by far the best available in English. Bakunin's insights into power and authority, tyranny, the conditions of freedom, the new classes of specialists and technocrats, social tyranny, and many other matters of immediate concern, are refreshing, original, and often still unsurpassed in clarity and vision. This selection provides access to the thinking of one of the most remarkable figures of modern history. I read it with great pleasure and profit."
— Noam Chomsky

"(This book) is the most complete — and interestingly varied — anthology I've seen of this neglected writer. It confirms my suspicion that Bakunin is the most underrated of the classical 19th century theoreticians, definitely including Marx."
— Dwight MacDonald

A new and revised selection of writings, nearly all published for the first time in English, by one of the leading thinkers of anarchism and one of the most important practitioners of social revolution.

453 pages
Paperback ISBN: 0-919619-06-1 $12.95
Hardcover ISBN: 0-919619-05-3 $22.95
Philosophy/Politics

LOUISE MICHEL

by Edith Thomas

translated by Penelope Williams

"Although the Commune remains a controversial phenomenon, one of its best-known figures, Louise Michel, won great sympathy in almost all quarters. ...the woman was **sui generis** *and matches the legend because of her courage, her limitless generosity, and her singleminded devotion to the cause she made hers..."*
— **American Historical Review**

Revolutionary on the barricades of the Paris Commune, tried before the War Council of France, deported to a penal colony, received by enthusiastic crowds upon her return, brillant lecturer throughout Europe, continuously followed by the police, participant in spectacular trials and demonstrations, threatened by assassins, imprisoned time and again, Louise Michel, writer, teacher, poet, feminist, is one of the most extraordinary legends in the literature of freedom.

400 pages
Paperback ISBN: 0-919619-07-4 $12.95
Hardcover ISBN: 0-919619-08-2 $22.95
Women/Sociology/History

TOWARD AN ECOLOGICAL SOCIETY

by Murray Bookchin

"Murray Bookchin may be the orneriest political theorist alive... he's worth arguing with... Bookchin is capable of penetrating finely indignant historical analyses... (This book) is another stimulating, wide-ranging collection... (with) several excellent essays on urban planning, the future of the city, new developments in ecologically sound technology, and the history of utopian thought..."
In These Times

"(This book) is always a provocative work that gives abundant evidence of its author's position at the center of debate... It therefore deserves the careful attention of anyone seriously interested in constructive social thought... It is a work of crucial importance."
Telos

"Bookchin's great virtue — which he shares with some other modern anarchist thinkers like Paul Goodman and Colin Ward — is that he constantly relates his theories to society as it is — not as an abstraction, but a human reality, and to what people can do at the basic social levels."
George Woodcock

In this exciting new collection of essays, which will stand beside Bookchin's well-known classic, *Post-Scarcity Anarchism* (with its seven printings, translated into five languages), the author deals with all dimensions of social ecology.

320 pages
Paperback ISBN: 0-919618-98-7 $12.95
Hardcover ISBN: 0-919618-99-5 $22.95
Ecology/Philosophy

POST-SCARCITY ANARCHISM

by Murray Bookchin

7th Printing

Murray Bookchin's book has by now become a classic. This collection of essays on organisation, technology, Marxism, ecology, the general strike in France, and a wide range of other subjects, continues to be read and debated widely.

Murray Bookchin is the founder of the Institute of Social Ecology at Goddard College and associate professor at Ramapo College. He is author of such far-ranging works as *The Limits of the City*, *The Spanish Anarchists*, and *Our Synthetic Environment*.

250 pages
Hardcover ISBN: 0-919618-47-2 $19.95
Philosophy/Sociology

THE COMING OF WORLD WAR III

by Dimitrios I. Roussopoulos

"In this timely book Dimitrios Roussopoulos faces a fear that is rapidly becoming in all our minds a certainty we dare not admit — the coming of World War III. The only way to defuse the certainty is by mass popular action on a larger scale than ever before so that at least we can add an 'unless' to the phrase, 'The war will happen'."

George Woodcock

"The Coming of World War III is perhaps the most provocative, thoughtful, and important book on the nuclear issue of this decade. It is indispensable reading for all peace activists and thoughtful people generally who are concerned with the future of our planet and our freedom."

Murray Bookchin

"The Coming of World War III by Dimitrios Roussopoulos is the companion volume to the fascinating book this leading Montréal radical activist edited recently under the title **Our Generation Against Nuclear War**. Like C. Wright Mills' prophetic best-seller, **The Causes of World War III**, published 25 years ago, this important new book awarns us of the imminent danger of a nuclear war of world-wide proportions.... For those who feel that the threat of an all-out nuclear war is fast becoming the major issue of the 1980's, this important book will be a useful tool that will help them oppose and reverse the fatal trend towards the total destruction of planet Earth. This is a thought-provoking book that deserves to be read and acted upon by all those who care about the future of the biosphere, and of mankind in particular. It presents an objective and realistic picture of the present situation, and a non-sectarian progressive view of some of the means that should be used to avoid the worst."

Dr. Jean-Guy Vaillancourt
Université de Montréal

It will never happen. It can happen. It will happen.

Politicians and military and scientific personnel working for various nation-states remain firmly convinced that their nuclear weapons policies are both logical and righteous while also believing that there *will never be* a nuclear war.

A large group of scientists, journalists and academics believe that the possibilities of a nuclear 'accident', a computer error, for example, in which missiles are launched by mistake, or the deliberate use of these weapons, can *lead* to a nuclear holocaust.

After working with the disarmament movement for more than 20 years, and having just completed a thorough investigation of the intensified arms race and the emergence of the new disarmament movements in Europe and North America, Dimitrios Roussopoulos believes a third world war *will* happen, because not enough is being done to prevent it. This conclusion has a number of radical implications for activists in the peace movement, sympathizers to its aims and those interested in social change.

This timely volume not only provides a succinct analysis of the various forces worldwide which bring us ever closer to nuclear annihilation, it also takes the reader on a tour of the numerous anti-nuclear and disarmament organizations which are working toward peace and raises a myriad of political issues which contribute to international tension.

The author offers a sympathetic yet critical analysis of the movement — country by country — in a last-ditch attempt to make both activists and the public see the issues clearly and to prevent a third world war.

250 pages
Paperback ISBN: 0-920057-02-0 $14.95
Hardcover ISBN: 0-920057-03-9 $25.95
International Politics/Sociology

RADICAL PRIORITIES

by Noam Chomsky

edited by C.P. Otero

2nd Revised Edition

"...For those who desire a fuller picture of Chomsky's fascinating political scholarship, his *Radical Priorities* is to be recommended... [it] contains a fine essay on Chomsky by Carlos Otero."
— *Harvard International Review*

The world-famous linguist at his best. This collection of Noam Chomsky's political writings — the first since 1973 and ignored by the mainstream reviewing media — brings together some of his most important reflections. Many pieces appear for the first time together in English. A broad range of subjects is covered with a view to alerting people about the problems humanity is facing and possible solutions we can undertake.

In the introduction, C.P. Otero lucidly presents an analysis and overview of Chomsky's social and political philosophy unavailable elsewhere. For the first time, the roots of Chomsky's politics are examined in relation to his theory of linguistics.

This book is invaluable for any general reader who would like to make sense out of the daily press. The second revised edition contains new important essays.

Prof. C.P. Otero teaches linguistics at the University of California, Los Angeles.

481 pages
Paperback ISBN: 0-920057-17-9 $14.95
Hardcover ISBN: 0-920057-16-0 $25.95
Politics/Philosophy/Sociology

DURRUTI: THE PEOPLE ARMED

by Abel Paz

translated by Nancy MacDonald

"...When a column is tired and ready to drop with exhaustion, Durruti goes to talk new courage into the men. When things go bad up Saragossa way, Durruti climbs aboard an aeroplane and drops down in the fields of Aragon to put himself at the head of the Catalonian partisans. Wherever you go it's Durruti and Durruti again, whom you hear spoken of as a wonder-man."
— *Toronto Daily Star*

Forty years of fighting, of exile, of jailings, of living underground, of strikes, and of insurrection, Buenaventura Durruti, the legendary Spanish revolutionary (1896-1936) lived many lives.

Uncompromising anarchist, intransigent revolutionary, he travelled a long road from rebellious young worker to the man who refused all bureaucratic positions, honours, awards, and who at death was mourned by millions of women and men. Durruti believed and lived his belief that revolution and freedom were inseparable.

328, pages, illustrated
Paperback ISBN: 0-919618-74-X $9.95
Hardcover ISBN: 0-919618-73-1 $19.95
History/Labour

THE MODERN STATE

An Anarchist Analysis

by Frank Harrison

"...it is a useful guide to alternatives to the obsession with the all-powerful state in the nuclear age...."
Canadian Journal of Political Science

This important new contribution to theories of the State by political science professor and Bakunin scholar Frank Harrison provides a welcome departure from the straitjacket of orthodox and Marxist approaches.

Starting from the assumption that the theory and practice of State control thus far in history has operated to diminish the freedom of the individual and local groups, Harrison attempts a major re-examination of the history and theories of social change.

The disputes within the First International and the implications of their outcome are related to the historical trajectory of events surrounding the Russian Revolution, the Makhnovist movement and the Kronstadt uprising as well as the recent Polish experience.

Harrison unearths some fascinating original material from the Russian Archives, including the writings and firsthand accounts of little known but important participants in the revolution.

Most of all, this book offers a fresh, much sought after perspective on important historical events, the theories behind them, and where research has to go if a truly liberatory perspective on social control is to be developed.

227 pages
Paperback ISBN: 0-920057-00-4 $12.95
Hardcover ISBN: 0-920057-01-2 $22.95

A PRIMER OF LIBERTARIAN EDUCATION

by Joel Spring

"I find it powerful and liberating... I think this is a very valuable and important book; it has done a great deal to intensify, correct and further radicalize my thoughts."
Jonathan Kozol

"Spring's book is unique. It stands serenely outside the muddy stream of literature spawned by the recent wave of criticism of compulsory schooling. In the midst of paper-mountains 'pro' and 'con', Spring places the radical challenge into its own tradition of libertarian anarchy, and of concern with law and freedom. This is the only readable book I know which does so in simple language and with the clearsightedness of the competent historian. Students of contemporary education cannot avoid this one."
Ivan Illich

157 pages
Paperback ISBN: 0-919618-61-8 $7.95
Hardcover ISBN: 0-919618-62-6 $17.95
Education/Sociology

1984 AND AFTER...

edited by
Marsha Hewitt and
Dimitrios I. Roussopoulos

With the ominous year of 1984 in mind as a social reality more than a calendar year, this collection of essays brings together some of the most distinguished contemporary critics of authoritarian tendencies in our society. The historical, political and intellectual problems that gave rise to Orwell's great book are examined with viewpoints spanning the gamut of serious opinion. The authors offer a fresh and provocative analysis of authoritarianism and its libertarian alternatives.

Contributors include George Woodcock, Murray Bookchin, Noam Chomsky, Frank Harrison, Stephen Schecter, Jean Ellezam, Jean-Pierre Deslauriers, Yolande Cohen, Claire Culhane, John Clark, and Robert Mayo.

200 pages
Paperback ISBN: 0-920057-29-2 $12.95
Hardcover ISBN: 0-920057-28-4 $22.95
Current Affairs/Politics

THE ANARCHIST COLLECTIVES

Workers' Self-Management in Spain 1936-39

edited by Sam Dolgoff

"Although there is a vast literature on the Spanish Civil War, this is the first book in English that is devoted to the experiments in workers' self-management, both urban and rural, which constituted one of the most remarkable social revolutions in modern history."
Prof. Paul Avrich, Princeton University

"The eyewitness reports and commentary presented in this highly important study reveal a very different understanding of the nature of socialism and the means for achieving it."
Prof. Noam Chomsky, M.I.T.

194 pages, illustrated
Paperback ISBN: 0-919618-20-0 $12.95
Hardcover ISBN: 0-919618-21-9 $25.95
History/Labour/Economics

Printed by
the workers of
Editions Marquis, Montmagny, Québec
for
Black Rose Books Ltd.